STRANGE NATION

PUBLISHING

SAVAGE SHADOW

The Search For The Australian Cougar

by David O'Reilly

FOREWORD BY MICHAEL WILLIAMS & REBECCA LANG

STRANGE NATION PUBLISHING

Published by Strange Nation Publishing.
Acknowledgements:
Cover image: "Savage Shadow" images reworked and
            typography by Tim Hartridge.
Book design and production by Deep Hill Fine Art Media
Typeface: Life BT, Birch.

First published by Creative Research, Perth, 1981.

Republished by Strange Nation Publishing,
            PO Box 5, Hazelbrook, NSW, 2779 Australia.
            www.strangenation.com.au

O'Reilly, David, 1951-2006
Savage Shadow : The Search for the Australian Cougar

Dedicated to Den

Contents

Author David O'Reilly.

About the author

When David O'Reilly decided to leave Perth in 1980 in order to travel around Europe and later work as a journalist in London, the unfinished manuscript of *Savage Shadow* accompanied him everywhere on his travels. He finished this, his first book, in a cramped and grotty flat in west London not far from Heathrow Airport. Any environment further away from the huge skies and vast open spaces of Western Australia, with which my future husband had fallen in love, would be hard to imagine. But evening after evening, night after night in that grotty flat in west London, he returned to Cordering in his imagination as he laboured on finishing a book that was very important to him.

David wanted to write *Savage Shadow,* not just to draw together all the fascinating evidence he and others had gathered to that point about the existence of big cats in the WA bush, and not just because it was a great yarn. Even more fundamentally, he wanted to defend the integrity of, and keep faith with, the farmers and many other good, decent people he had met during the course of his investigations, most particularly Dennis and Ross Earnshaw. Like them, David had learnt what it was like to be scoffed at and mocked by others whenever he began talking about the terrifyingly inexplicable screams emanating from the blackness of a WA country night, the many reported sightings of large, stealthy animals roaming the countryside, and the sinister discoveries of dead farm animals and kangaroos with their insides entirely scooped out.

I can remember David saying, over and over again to anyone who would listen (including me): "These witnesses are the most solid, practical, down-to-earth people imaginable. They have lived in the bush their entire lives, and they know the source of every sound, every animal hoof- and pawprint, every tree marking. So if they say there is something strange, mysterious and unidentified out there, then I believe them."

The finished manuscript of *Savage Shadow* was handed over to a small Perth-based publishing company which, soon after the book's first small print run, collapsed and went into liquidation. If David wanted more copies printed, he was informed, he would have to pay several thousand dollars - which he did not have at the time – to buy back the publishing rights. Assuming his book had attracted little more than passing interest, David swallowed his disappointment and moved on with life. After a stint in News Ltd's London Bureau, he worked as a political journalist in Sydney before returning to the Canberra federal parliamentary press gallery, where he rose to be national political editor of the Bulletin Magazine. David and I married in 1984 and went on to have three children, the youngest of whom is severely disabled with cerebral palsy. In 1995, we moved to the UK so our son could access a world-class school for children with this particular disability, and we lived there very happily until 2006, when David collapsed with what turned out to be advanced bowel cancer. He died in November 2006, just a few weeks after his 55th birthday.

David achieved many things in a relatively short lifetime. He was awarded an MA in political science by Sydney University in 1984, and a PhD by Monash University in April 2006, shortly before he fell ill. He wrote a biography of Cheryl Kernot, published in 1997, and at the time of his death was working on two books that were both published posthumously. As a freelance journalist during our years in the UK, David wrote for a number of Australian and British publications, as well as selflessly devoting hundreds upon hundreds of hours to giving our physically disabled son vital therapy and exercise. He was a remarkable and inspirational father whose legacy of love and constant encouragement lives on in his three wonderful children. In 2010, our daughter Laura graduated from the University of Cambridge with a First Class Honours degree in history and is now studying for a post-graduate law degree in Sydney, while our older son Jordan is studying Occupational Therapy at the University of Sydney and intends to work with people with disabilities in his future career.

In David's memory, I decided to establish a small charity called Fighting Chance upon our return to Australia in 2008 to raise money to help people with physical disabilities access therapy and educational services they could not otherwise afford, and to campaign for more innovative employment and accommodation services than are currently available for Australians with disabilities. Our three children are all now very actively involved in helping run Fighting Chance, and our first computer-based employment project for people with severe physical disabilities is due to open very shortly.

For David's children and for me, it is absolutely wonderful to know that 30 years after it was first published, *Savage Shadow* is now being reprinted and re-released, due entirely to the hard work and investigative skills of Rebecca Lang and Mike Williams, who managed to track me down in Sydney and give me the amazing news that far from a long-forgotten 'failure' as David had presumed, his first book is actually something of a cult classic. He would have devoured every word of Mike and Rebecca's brilliant book Australian Big Cats: An Unnatural History of Panthers, and would have been full of admiration for their remarkable research, analysis and writing skills.

We – David's three children and I – will be forever grateful to Rebecca and Mike for honouring and reviving his efforts of three decades ago in this way. Obviously, we all just wish David was here with us to enjoy this moment, although he assured us shortly before he died he would always be with us, and I have my reasons for thinking that in making this statement (as in everything else in his life) he was entirely true to his word. After all, how amazing is it that a book David wrote 30 years ago is now going to be able to help raise funds for a charity specifically established to honour his memory? As I say, I have my reasons for thinking that David is not all that far away.

Sue O'Reilly
Sydney
April 2011

🐾 🐾 🐾

Acknowledgements

My thanks must go to a small band of loved ones. They were all part of the determination that pushed me on, even at times when its worth seemed so indiscernible.

I must thank Bryan and Christina for first making me think it out, the Campbells and Eliot and Jenny for caring and putting up with me.

Also thanks to Jen-girl for all her hard work, Pete for his support and Ikey and Babe for always being there when I needed them.

And last, to Tasha who made it possible.

David O'Reilly

COUGAR COUNTRY RUL...

1. CAR WINDOWS UP AT ALL TIMES.
2. IF BROKEN DOWN STAY PUT AND TOO[T]
   FOR ASSISTANCE - (DO NOT LEAVE CAR).
3. IF ATTACKED TAKE A PHOTO AND
   THEN RUN LIKE **HELL!!**

Local signage warns visitors to tread carefully in Cordering country.

Foreword

More than 30 years have passed since the 'Cordering Cougar' first slipped from the shadows and began terrorising Dennis and Ross Earnshaw, their families and neighbours in south-west Western Australia.

Like something straight out of a horror film, the cat-like creature revealed itself by degrees, leaving in its wake gruesome calling cards that left those touched by the mystery puzzled and afraid. Flashes of yellow fur, wailing screams, bloody corpses - a four-legged killing machine of unknown origin and unfriendly disposition slowly introduced itself to a remote and initially sceptical farming community with devastating results.

Three decades later, we're no wiser as to what these animals are, or where they came from, and today they continue about their business undeterred, protected by the veil of scepticism and disbelief that shrouds this mystery - a mystery with very real teeth and plenty of bite.

People are still seeing these mysterious puma-like animals. And they're still killing livestock.

🐾 🐾 🐾

The Savage Shadow saga kicked off while author David O'Reilly was working as a journalist in the Perth bureau of The Australian newspaper. He chanced upon a news clipping about reports of large cat-like animals terrorising flocks of sheep in the state's south-west.

Intrigued, O'Reilly decided to investigate for himself, unwittingly opening a strange and bizarre can of worms that he could never quite put the lid back on. O'Reilly didn't just end up writing the story, he became a part of it.

O'Reilly approached the subject with all the rigour and impartiality of an old-school journalist and it was while investigating with this air of objectivity that he experienced his own brush with the big cat.

Within these pages you will read of how he came face-to-face with his ghost-like quarry, and was forced to accept that he hadn't simply stumbled into a quirky news story replete with colourful bush characters - a sure antidote for a slow news week - but had in fact become part of a bona fide wildlife mystery. This really was, as newspaper folk like to say, 'a story with legs'!

And it was with this newfound perspective that he rallied behind the farmers grappling with a mystery that threatened their very livelihood, one that put them on a collision course with diabolically narrow-minded public servants and sceptical politicans, and would eventually spark claims of a government cover-up.

The raft of newspaper stories and the resulting publication of Savage Shadow further established the tale of Western Australia's sandy-coloured assassins - cat-like killer creatures that resembled pumas straight out of America's wild west.

With frequent re-telling this story really has become the stuff of legends.

More than 30 years later we would walk in O'Reilly's footsteps as we attempted to make sense of the hundreds of sightings and strange animal deaths taking place in the state of NSW, and later Victoria, before being met with a similar bureaucratic brick wall.

Our own book, Australian Big Cats: An Unnatural History of Panthers, pays homage to O'Reilly's trailblazing reportage, and further explores the big cat mystery, which extends to almost every other state in Australia.

Like O'Reilly, we immersed ourselves 'in the hunt'. We wanted to know for ourselves if this cat-like animal was the 'real deal' or, what seemed more likely, just a mythical moggie, the product of misidentifications, campfire stories, gullible minds and feral folklore.

And like O'Reilly, we were left convinced beyond a shadow of a doubt that 'something' is out there - something with fur, teeth and claws that operates with a speed and stealth alien to this landscape, the reality of which cuts to the bone.

🐾 🐾 🐾

Sadly, David O'Reilly died in the UK before we were able to contact him about re-publishing the long out-of-print Savage Shadow, which has over time become something of a cult classic - partly because of its scarcity but largely because the contemporary WA big cat legend is one hell of a yarn.

Through a series of odd coincidences we were finally able to make contact with Sue O'Reilly, his widow, on her return to Australia, and it is with her kind permission that we have been able to reprint Savage Shadow and make it available to a wider audience.

As we prepared the book for printing, a final twist in the tale led to the discovery of a box of newspaper clippings, early drafts and never-before-published original photographs in a back shed of the family's Sydney home - a goldmine of material, and one that nearly went unnoticed. We would like to extend our sincere thanks to the O'Reilly family for temporarily entrusting us with these precious articles while we prepared the manuscript for publication.

Readers should know that part of the proceeds from this book will be channelled towards a charity set up in David's memory - Fighting Chance - which raises funds for families with disabled children, a cause close to the family's heart and one that helps to partly redress in a small way the inadequate government resources available to these families. Please take a moment to visit www.fightingchancefund.org.

On a final note, we hope you enjoy O'Reilly's book - it reads like a fast-paced suspense novel, yet every word is true.

Mike Williams
Rebecca Lang

Farmer Dennis Earnshaw.

Chapter One

DENNIS EARNSHAW SAT BOLT UPRIGHT in bed, every nerve in his body tingling. All his life in the bush he had never heard anything like it. A towering scream echoed across the country-side, enveloping the perimeters of the farmhouse. The young farmer was suddenly panting. The night's humid, dark silence took grip of his senses and he gently shook his head. Dreaming, he thought. His wife, Henny, lying beside him, hadn't moved, her breathing loud in the darkened room. After a moment, tiredness welled up again, but Dennis still frowned as he slumped back to the pillow. Suddenly, much louder, the noise came again, this time almost familiar, confirming an inexplicable fear. Dennis was cold with perspiration as he swept from the bed into the hallway and the kitchen window's panorama of the country around the farm. His eyes began to adjust to the moonlight, but nothing outside was moving. There was no shuffling or noise in the bush, no scratching against the side of the house. What had he expected, he asked himself?

'Rifle', he whispered, deciding to go outside to investigate. The .243 stood alongside the older .22 on the floor of the small annexe off the kitchen which Dennis used as a study. He instinctively grabbed the more powerful rifle. He didn't quite understand why. Now armed, he swung open the back door and stepped out onto the verandah. It was cooler outside and Dennis realised he had difficulty in swallowing. He stood for a long moment just listening. His stomach was knotting and again he didn't know why. All he could hear was his own breathing. He couldn't make out the sounds of the bush which were as much a part of his night as was the dark. He took a deep breath and peered into the moonlit yard. It offered only shadows. As he stepped off the porch and onto the grass, the night came alive with sounds. Crickets and insects began to buzz again, as if they too had been stunned momentarily by the noise. The world had relaxed and, responding to it, Dennis suddenly felt more comfortable.

He walked away from the house into the jaws of darkness towards the caravan parked at the top of the yard near the wire-meshed chicken pen. He opened the chamber of the .243, its barrel dropping harmlessly to his side. Dennis stood for a long time near the aluminium caravan, glowing under a massive canopy of summer starlight above. A bullock grunted in a nearby paddock and Dennis began to feel a little foolish.

Had he dreamed it? No! It had been too real, he thought. Then what was it? Must have been imagination—a bad dream.

Dennis sighed deeply, then turned and ambled back towards the house. Almost there, he stopped and glanced towards the eastern horizon where a pale blue shaft of light was gradually revealing the black forest outline of red gums and jarrah trees. Spontaneously his mind focussed on the day to come—hectic hours crutching hundreds of sheep with his brother, Ross, and farmhands. Yet somewhere in the sleepy corners of his mind something was nagging him. He realised he was frowning again. What was that? A shiver ran through him as a gathering breeze cut into the receding humidity of the night. Later, it would be a good deal warmer in the crutching shed—and there was much to be done. Dennis walked briskly to the back door, closed it quietly behind him and was soon asleep.

Breakfasts could be chaotic at times in the Earnshaw household. This day, Dennis's father was over from Bunbury, the kids were misbehaving and Dennis was irritable.

'That fence around the eastern pasture needs a bit of work on it, Den,' Ken Earnshaw said. 'Probably have to get at it pretty quickly it's so bad.'

The old man's son didn't raise his head from the account books spread out on the big breakfast table.

'Den?' the old man said. He exchanged glances with Henny standing at the kitchen's pivot—an enamelled solid fuel stove.

'Dennis, your father asked you a question,' she said.

'What? . . . Oh, sorry Dad,' Dennis said, looking up.

'I say that fence in the eastern paddock is a bit weak, lad,' Ken said.

'Oh yeah Dad . . . it will need some work on it pretty soon I think,' Dennis muttered, lost again in the receipt books. The old man looked at Henny again, but didn't speak.

Propped up in her highchair, Monica Earnshaw mischievously eyed her brother sitting alongside her father. Reaching across, she deposited a spoonful of mushy cereal on Dennis junior's head. The little boy let out a wail that brought Henny quickly to the table. Chastised, Monica erupted into tears. With that, Dennis threw his head back and jumped to his feet, gathering the books up into his arms.

'Can't we have any quiet around here?' he snapped, before storming off into the lounge room. Henny looked at Ken, who was staring at his son pacing away.

'Well, what do you reckon has gotten into him?' Ken asked, bewildered.

'I've got no idea, Dad,' Henny replied.

Dropping heavily into his favourite armchair by the fireplace, Dennis scattered the books on the floor around him. His father walked in and sat down. Dennis slumped back in the chair and sighed.

'What's up, mate?' Ken asked.

'Oh, I'm just a bit tired Dad, I guess,' Dennis said and then paused. 'I got a bit of a start last night and couldn't sleep properly—a bit restless.'

Ken frowned. He knew well the pressures Dennis was working under at this time of year. Even the most fertile of the rich wheatbelt land in south Western Australia was a demanding provider. Ken had been born in rural Western Australia in the early days of a pioneering century when a 250-kilometre trek north to Perth was a tough imposition on an isolated, fiercely independent existence. He had given his land at Cordering to his two sons after they had left school. Ross, the younger son, lived in a farmhouse a kilometre north of Dennis. Fifty kilometres inland from the small coal mining town of Collie, their land had made the Earnshaws prosperous and Dennis's instincts as a businessman promised to make them even more secure. A short, stocky man, his large child-like green eyes belied a determined and disciplined independence. His interests had long since expanded past the running of his own spread to the lucrative business of contract harvesting. He pulled together teams of labourers and toured the State for part of each year, working for the big station owners in the north where the rich wheat land extended for hundreds of kilometres before giving way to the tidal wave of desert that is outback Australia. Throughout the Cordering region, the Earnshaw family was highly respected as God-fearing and solid, a family in harmony with the land. Some resented their success but most respected their honesty and business integrity.

'A bad dream,' Ken proffered.

'No, Dad, I've been thinking about it this morning and I don't think it was a dream,' Dennis said. 'It was more. It was loud, almost like a scream.'

'A what?' Ken asked.

'A big noise—loud, like a woman's scream, but much harsher. It woke me up and I went out into the yard.'

'Henny didn't hear it?'

'No, I don't think so.'

'What did you expect to find in the yard?'

'Don't know,' Dennis snorted. 'But I sure didn't find anything.'

'You're a bit overtired from the shearing and now the harvesting, as well as finding time to go over to Bunbury for the flying lessons. You should have a few days off,' the old man counselled.

'Oh, I'll be all right, Dad,' Dennis smiled. 'I may grab Rossy and take him out for a bit of rabbit shooting—that'll clear the cobwebs.'

Dennis went back to his books and the old man returned to the kitchen where Henny was hurriedly readying the two older children for the bus ride to school while the two babies looked on.

❀ ❀ ❀

The old battered table-top utility clunked through a deep pothole as Dennis accelerated and fought the steering wheel to manoeuvre across a rough patch of paddock a kilometre east of Ross's farmhouse. Ross sat in the passenger seat carefully nursing a pair of .22 rifles as the truck bumped along. Dennis braked and it slid to a dusty halt in the corner of the paddock near the fence-line. He leaned forward and with his elbows over the steering wheel rubbed a patch in the cover of dust on the inside of the windscreen. Squinting, he could just make out a flurry of movement low down in the brush some twenty metres away.

'There's a few in there, all right,' he said. 'Grab the rifles Rossy and we'll see how good your eye is these days.'

Both men clambered from the cabin, Ross easing both rifles out and onto an old mat he had slapped on the roof. The younger man looked around and pointed into the brush at the other side of the fence.

'What about through there?' he asked.

Dennis slammed the driver's side door shut. 'As good as any,' he cheerily replied.

The two men hadn't been out rabbit hunting for years. The pressures of running the farms and the harvesting business had been too demanding of their time. But Dennis needed a break.

Work, however, was never far away. Dennis walked over to the fence and wandered down the line poking the posts and trying the tension on the wire between each.

'It's a bit weak here, sure enough,' he yelled back to Ross at the truck. 'Dad was right. Looks like a couple of 'roos went through here as well,' he said, pulling some heavy tufts of hair from the fence barbs. He looked around and saw the mangled and decaying body of a big grey kangaroo disembowelled when it hit the wire in the dark before slamming to the ground in the brush to die a slow death.

'There's a few hours fence-mending for us next week, mate,' Dennis said as he climbed back up the little rise to where Ross was loading the rifles. 'Dad must have been over here in the past few days. He told me about it but I didn't think it was so bad.'

'Bloody 'roos,' Ross grumbled.

Rifles in hand, the two walked to the fence-line, where they eased themselves over by leaning on the nearest post. The bush around them was typical of the heavy timber country of the south-western hump of the State. Massive-trunked jarrah trees climbed imperiously into the sky. Red and white gum trees threw up a green umbrella sheltering the ground from the blistering summer sun. Below, wildflowers and bottle-brush fought a struggle for life with the native grass and mulga shrubs ruling the rock-strewn terrain.

Rabbits scampered through the bush as the men waded in. Ross steadied himself as a doe danced in his sights. He baulked on the trigger as the rabbit disappeared into a burnt-out log. Dennis swung around startled as a ginger fox galloped panic-stricken from a clump of mulga shrubs.

'Scare you?' Ross teased.

'I'll scare him,' Dennis said, training his rifle on the fleeing fox. Dennis' finger gently began to squeeze, his eye steady on the target. Then it too was gone, lost in the undergrowth.

'Ahh!' he grunted, walking on, the rifle slumped to his side. The two men strode on for about ten minutes, carefully watching the wild track, reading it for signs of prey. They pushed deeper into land they owned, but seldom explored. By this time they had reached the western fence-line of Ross's property, without sighting any more game. On the other side of the wire was a big rugged paddock, part of a neighbour's property.

'Let's have a look over there,' Dennis said. 'Charlie won't mind.'

Hopping over the fence, they pushed out into the middle of the field, scouring it for rabbits in the late afternoon twilight.

'Over there,' Ross said quietly, as he spied more bunnies moving in the scrub. Ross cocked his rifle, taking a few steps forward for a better aim. Dennis noticed a big male kangaroo standing on the brush line on the other side of the fence near where they had crossed over. The kangaroo was strangely frozen, alert with its ears pricked and nostrils flared. Dennis took a few steps and gently tapped Ross on the elbow, nodding towards the big 'roo. Then, in a sudden spasm of movement, it lunged away, powering itself with its muscular hind legs and tubular tail. In the same fraction of a moment, a large yellow figure appeared through the trees, moving adjacent to the kangaroo in what looked like an attempt to cut it off. Then, just as suddenly, there was nothing . . .

Dennis blinked hard and looked at his brother. He looked back to the fence-line but could see nothing; sense nothing.

The kangaroo was lost behind a curtain of green and timber.

'Did you see that?' Dennis mumbled.

'What was it?' Ross asked.

'I don't know. What did you see?'

'A . . . tail . . . I think?' Ross stuttered. 'A long tail.'

'Yeah, but what else?'

Ross didn't answer.

'It wasn't a rabbit,' Dennis said with a confused half laugh.

'A "roo. It was a "roo and he was scared and then he just took off . . . and something was in there watching him . . . and he knew it was there and he was terrified . . . and then it just took off after him,' Ross said.

'Yeah, but what?' Dennis said. 'Maybe it's still in there,' he said, breaking into a trot towards the fence-line.

Ross took a breath, grasped his rifle and followed his brother uneasily towards the fence. Both men peered through the trees some ten metres away, searching for any sign of movement.

They stood for a long moment, listening. Nothing came back to them, except the rustling of the breeze in the high jarrahs and the fragile piping calls of their birdlife. Dennis went to the wire and clambered through. He began searching the ground for marks and walked towards where he had first spotted the kangaroo. He could just make out the marks in the dust where it had leapt away panic-stricken. Ross came to the fence and stood by listening intently for any sound as he watched his brother. Dennis began scouting away from the spot.

'What colour do you reckon it was, Ross?' he asked.

'Oh, a sort of yellow, Den, or a light brown, I guess.'

'Yeah,'' Dennis said to himself, suddenly relieved to have his brother with him. Dennis searched the ground for any marks in a series of expanding circles, away from where the kangaroo had stood. On the fourth sweep, he came across deep marks on the ground near where he had lost sight of the kangaroo.

'Here, look at this, Ross. I can't make out tracks but this is where it landed, whatever it was, before it veered off in there after the 'roo,' he said, gesturing into the trees. Dennis began circling away looking for more clues.

'You know, I'm sure it landed there,' he said, pointing to the marks. 'The ground is freshly disturbed and you can see where the 'roo went past and away.' Dennis gestured back through the bush towards Ross's farmhouse. At that, both men became a little uneasy. Dennis looked at Ross but his brother just shook his head gently in exasperation. For a long while, neither spoke.

Finally, Dennis volunteered: 'A big dog—a real big one. And it could move, too,' he added assertively.

'Could move all right, ' Ross muttered, looking around. 'Like nothing I've ever seen before.'

After a moment, he said: 'Do you really think it was a dog? What about that tail? Such a long tail. Have you ever seen a tail that long?'

'Ross, it was a dog. Had to be,' Dennis said, agitated by his brother's persistent questions. 'A big bloke for sure,' he said, suppressing unease in his mind. 'Hungry too, I suppose. We'll have to get the Agriculture Protection Board boys out here to lay some baits. He was big all right.'

'Too bloody big,' Ross said.

'Come on, Ross,' Dennis came back angrily. 'It was a dog—what else could it be?'

The two men just stared at each other.

'Well, it didn't look like any dog I ever saw,' Ross said, 'not with a tail like that—no sir.'

Dennis bit on his lip and glanced away. He walked over to the fence and slowly wandered up the line to the spot roughly adjacent to where he had first caught sight of the yellow movement. Plunging into the bush, he suddenly stopped. There, on a partly exposed area of ground were fresh marks, cutting deeply into the soil.

'There's more here,' he shouted as Ross pushed his way through to where he was kneeling, turning the soil carefully with a short stick.

'Looks like whatever it was sprang from here at the old 'roo and landed over there. We saw it through a break in the trees from out there,' Dennis said, pointing to the open paddock.

'But the other marks are over there, near where the 'roo was standing,' Ross said.

'Yeah. Go over there, Ross, and find those marks and any others that might be around.'

Ross crept over to the original marks, examining the ground.

'Here,' he yelled, as Dennis looked up at him.

'No, it can't be that far, Rossy. Where were those first marks I found?'

'Right here,' Ross insisted, pointing to his feet.

Dennis stood up. 'There's nothing between here and there?'

'None,' Ross said definitely.

'Rossy, that's about 6 metres,' Dennis said. Slowly he began to inch his way over the ground between the two sets of marks.

At the end of it, he straightened his back and looked squarely at his brother. 'Whatever it was, Rossy, it jumped from over there where I was standing to this spot in one go . . . and that *is* a good 6 metres,' he said. Ross looked across the ground stretching away from him and then paused.

A little breathless, he finally whispered: 'Yeah, it is, isn't it?'

Two days later, Ross and a farmhand, Gary Stubbs, were mustering a big flock of sheep. Two yelp-happy kelpie-cross sheep dogs charged around at their heels, propping this way and that to guide stragglers into the flock. The men were moving the sheep up to sheds on Ross's property where a tedious afternoon's work lay in wait. Ross had been putting off the task of treating the sheep but other farms in the district had been suffering big losses through outbreaks of fly-blown infestation. 'Bring 'em round, boys . . . eeeyup,' Ross yelled as the dogs, panting with enthusiasm for the work, directed the sheep instinctively where the men wanted them to go.

Ross watched the flock carefully for any sign of illness or injury. He was concerned at the rising number of sheep found dead in the region, some from no apparent physical cause, others mercilessly torn at and partially eaten by foxes. He was almost certain there had been big lamb losses as well. He was disturbed by the fact that while the lamb numbers were falling away occasionally in some flocks often little evidence of carcasses could be found.

With the mindlessness of their species, the sheep bumped forward in spasmodic bursts, fearfully obliging their canine tormenters. The dogs went after the dawdlers occasionally backing away from the more determined ewes intent on finding their own way.

The afternoon sky was split by a fearsome burst of sunshine after a lunchtime downpour which left parts of the paddocks sodden. There was much to be done. A start had to be made on the drenching before Ross could join Dennis at the other farm for paddock clearing for use as a private airfield. Dennis was determined to have his full pilot's licence before the year was out. He was finding Western Australia's vast distances too great an obstacle to the development of the harvesting business. The licence would allow him to move around the State at will while his crews circulated from station to station in the north. It would also allow him to fly home at weekends to be with Henny and the children once the harvesting was underway.

The job of clearing and preparing the ground for the runway had been time-consuming and Dennis had asked Ross to come over in the afternoon to help with the moving of a stubborn tree trunk. Ross urged Gary on as the flock separated around a big clump of jarrah trees.

The metal walls of the shearing shed came into sight as the two men drove the sheep into a paddock corner. There Gary clambered through the woolly bodies to unlatch a fence gate. As it swung open the sheep burst through and the dogs squeezed past at the fence posts to charge ahead, barking orders at the front runners spraying away in all directions.

The shed sat in an open field 300 metres from Ross's house, the countryside descending gradually on the left to a solid line of trees. At the shed Ross kicked playfully at tailenders as he and Gary worked to pen the older sheep. Then he glanced away across the paddock to the tree line. There was a glimmer of movement in the trees and he peered again to make it out.

'Gary, we've missed one or two by the looks of things,' Ross said. The stockhand turned to his boss but Ross's face suddenly grimaced in a thick frown. 'Wait a minute . . . ,' he said, staring at the tree line.

A big yellow animal was ambling through the bush and Ross could see at once it was not a disoriented sheep or lamb from his batch.

'That's not a damn sheep,' he muttered as Gary too detected its distant progress. '. . . just can't see it properly,' Ross said slowly, awkwardly.

'What in the hell is that?' Gary breathed.

Ross didn't answer; he couldn't think of moving as he gazed across the paddock, entranced.

Suddenly Gary called out: 'Jesus, there's more,' pointing away behind the first animal. Ross could see another, more ginger, figure moving along through the grass, following the first.

'What is that?' Gary suddenly bellowed hysterically.

As though dragged back from a deep sleep Ross gestured faintly to the younger man for silence lest the animals be disturbed. But then he too lost control. He knew his brother and other stockmen would be working on the headers over at his own farmhouse. He looked towards it but could see no-one and then shouted and whistled to attract his brother's attention in the big shed used to house the headers adjacent to the cottage. Dennis clearly couldn't hear him so Ross rushed over to the truck and leapt in. 'Stay here and watch them, Gary . . . I'll get a gun,' he yelled.

In the truck cabin, Ross fought nervously to find the ignition with his key. When the engine turned over he was suddenly reassured and backing onto the track, he looked out the dusty back window to where Gary still stood gazing across the meadow. Along the winding gravel path to the house Ross hauled the truck, then as he burst through the gateway his mind was leapfrogging . . . would Gary be all right? . . . would they still be there? . . . what would he tell Dennis? . . . what were they? . . .

'Dennis,' Ross bellowed as he slammed the truck door and rushed to the back of the house. Simultaneously, his wife, Sue, stepped from inside, her arms full of wet laundry.

'Where's Dennis?' he asked, struggling to contain his excitement.

'Over there,' Sue said, nodding to where Dennis stood bewildered at being disturbed from a difficult repair job on one of the expensive headers.

Ross sprang at his brother.

'What is it, Rossy?' Dennis asked, suddenly alarmed.

'An animal, Den,' Ross blurted. 'An animal . . . a big one . . . with a long tail . . . get your rifle, Den, quickly, before it's gone.'

'Wait a minute, mate. What is it you say? What sort of animal?'

'Just an animal . . . for God's sake, get the rifle and hurry,' Ross implored.

Dennis looked hard at his brother's face, now pale with a glistening trace of perspiration on his forehead.

'I haven't got the rifle with me—it's over at my place,' he said.

'Well, let's get it then,' Ross yelled.

It took many valuable minutes to drive the kilometre to Dennis's farmhouse and back.

'Stay here, Henny, and watch the kids . . .' Dennis said to his own wife, non-plussed at all the commotion. 'Right mate, come on, show me,' he called to his brother as they leapt back into the truck.

As it hammered down the track Dennis gripped the threadbare armrest on the passenger side door. Ross hurled the truck over the gravel and reaching the gate entrance momentarily lost the wheel, the back spinning furiously. Dennis held tight. He had never seen his brother so disturbed.

'Will it still be there?' he asked quietly.

'I don't know . . . I hope so,' Russ muttered.

At the shed, Gary jumped the fence and walked towards them as they leapt from the truck. All three men began babbling in the same instant.

'What's going on, Gary?' Dennis repeated.

Ross walked to the fence, hopped over and started striding across the paddock.

'They've gone now,' Gary said.

'   'What's gone?' Dennis implored.

'The animals. Two of them, I think, one big one by itself and another coming along after it, down there,' Gary said, pointing to where Ross was walking.

'What did they look like?' Dennis asked.

'Big . . . or at least the big one was really big and long with a long tail—really long tail.'

'Hell,' Dennis breathed, 'a long tail.'

'Come on,' he said to the farmhand. 'Tell me more about it.' They headed off after Ross.

At the tree line Dennis loudly demanded: 'Right, where are they now?' Instantly he wished the tone had been different. The other two glanced at one another, looks of frustration touched with anger.

'Look, Den, we both saw it,' Ross said firmly. 'There were two animals and they were walking along from over there. There must be some tracks around somewhere.' He started walking towards a patch of soft ground nearby.

'How big, Ross?' Dennis asked.

'Oh . . . I don't know Den—they were so far away and I just dashed off too soon, to find you.'

'I know exactly how big they were,' Gary interrupted. 'See that log over there? Well, they walked right by it and the big one at the front was about as long as that log.'

Dennis stooped over the log. He could see no marks or signs in the ground that indicated any animal had come by.

'That log's over a metre long so that makes it a pretty big animal, Gary,' he said.

'I remember it clearly, Dennis,' Gary insisted.

'What colour was it?'

'Yellowish, I guess,' Ross said.

'Yeah, but the little one was darker although it was hard to see them properly in the grass,' Gary said.

'Were they running or what?' Dennis asked, pulling a pair of binoculars from their case and sweeping the horizon.

'No, they were just ambling along like no-one could hurt ém. They acted like they had all day,' Gary said. 'The big one was really powerful in the front legs though—seemed really strong.'

The three men then spread out and walked in a straight line past the log in the direction from which the animals had come. They stooped low to the ground searching for any signs of tracks.

They found nothing.

After half an hour, Dennis sat on the log and scratched his chin, glancing at his brother and Gary still busily searching.

'Ross, what do you reckon it was? A big dog or an overgrown mangey old fox? What sort of animal did it look like?'

Ross turned to look at his brother: 'Dennis, I know what I reckon it was,' and turning to Gary he said: 'I reckon Gary will agree with me.' The young farmhand was already nodding.

'It was a mountain lion, just like in the movies,' he said.

Dennis looked at Gary who was still nodding slowly and deliberately.

Then he turned away and gazed over hundreds of acres of trees and shrubs. He suddenly realised he was tired. The day had already been a long one. He was also trembling.

🐾 🐾 🐾

Ross Earnshaw believed that laying baits was the only way to unravel the perplexing mystery beginning to menace his world.

Dennis, too, would privately admit to a tense exhilaration at the thought of the poison explaining the enigma. Ross carefully placed deadly strychnine-laced cubes mixed with conventional pellets of dog food in ordered piles some metres apart. He had chosen a particular spot close to one of the many clay-mound dams sprinkled around the properties for stock watering.

It had not been easy to get the baits. The Agriculture Protection Board officers worked under strict rules governing to whom and for what purposes they could distribute one of their most effective weapons in the fight to hold down the numbers of pestilent wild dogs, feral cats and dingoes in the state's pastoral areas. Ross had asked a local APB officer to help him obtain the poison because of his concern over what appeared to be a new problem in the South West agricultural areas. Each meat extract cube contained enough strychnine to kill a wild dog up to 30 kg in weight within minutes. And Ross had enough, in fact, to kill many times over. The speed of death was the poison's only redeeming feature—the rest was a gut-searing agony as pungent poisonous juices vomited into the back of the animal's throat. Carefully disguising the cubes with the pellets, Ross realised he was not really sure what he was chasing. He chose a clear evening well after sunset to lay the baits near the dam on his own property. His plan was to lay them in the dark and then return well before daylight the next morning to check them, so avoiding the possibility of them being taken by scavenging crows or eagles. He also knew that the properties' dogs would be chained during the night and would not be released until after he had gathered in all the baits the following morning.

'That'll fix it,' Ross said, carefully washing his hands in the dam to remove any trace of poison.

Early next morning, Ross and Dennis were talking excitedly again about shadows in the bush, the prospect of what they might find tantalising them as they drove out to where the bait had been laid. Ross stopped the truck a good distance from the dam and the men walked quickly across the paddock. There was no sign of a body at the bait site. On closer inspection they also realised there was no bait—all the pellets and cubes had disappeared.

'It's all gone,' Ross said in disbelief—'the whole lot.'

'Whatever took it won't have gone far,' Dennis added firmly, looking around.

There was no sign of anything resembling tracks in the hard clay. The men set about searching the area close to the dam. They found nothing until Ross noticed in the soft clay at the water's edge what could have been the faint outline of tracks. But they were badly blurred.

Then moments later Dennis found what appeared to be a deep distinct footprint etched into the side of the clay wall around the murky dam water. It was a quite well defined animal's paw print.

He carefully cut out a big lump of the wall and gently set it down as the rising sun cast it's warming rays over the search area around the dam. The men could find no body and Ross was downcast.

'I can't understand it,' he said ruefully after two hours of searching through the paddocks to a radius of 1 km from the dam. 'If something ate those baits it would stop dead in its tracks within minutes. It doesn't make sense. It looks like something ate it all, wandered over and had a quiet drink and then just took off. It doesn't make bloody sense.' Ross stood pensively, learning against the front guard of the truck.

'There's only one thing to do Ross,' Dennis said after a long moment. 'We'll prepare some more baits and do it again.'

The next day they did just that—repeating the precautions of the previous night. And after spreading a larger amount of loaded cubes around the dam they returned the following day. Again, every trace was gone. Another long search produced no explanation, no tracks—nothing apart from yet another carcass—a dead ewe, lying within 200 metres of the dam's edge, it's neck broken.

By now the brothers' patience was strained. They resolved to repeat the procedure yet again and on the third morning they drove back to the paddock to examine a still larger lure. Nearing it, they realised that this time only part of it had been removed. At the dam they soon realised that every toxic cube had been left untouched. But virtually all of the small meat pellets had been selectively taken.

As the two walked back to the truck talking wildly, miles afield a pair of large unblinking eyes perused a flock of decidedly nervous sheep. Confident of anonymity in the undergrowth the eyes focussed coldly on the sheep, interrogating the scene for any sign of danger. Supremely confident, but ever wary, they contemptuously skipped over the sheep, now desperately circling into a tighter and tighter island of agitated bodies. Then, answering some primeval call, the eyes were suddenly gone.

Far away, a phantom cruised silently and effortlessly through the bush, ever unseen and hidden behind the walls of a timber fortress.

🐾 🐾 🐾

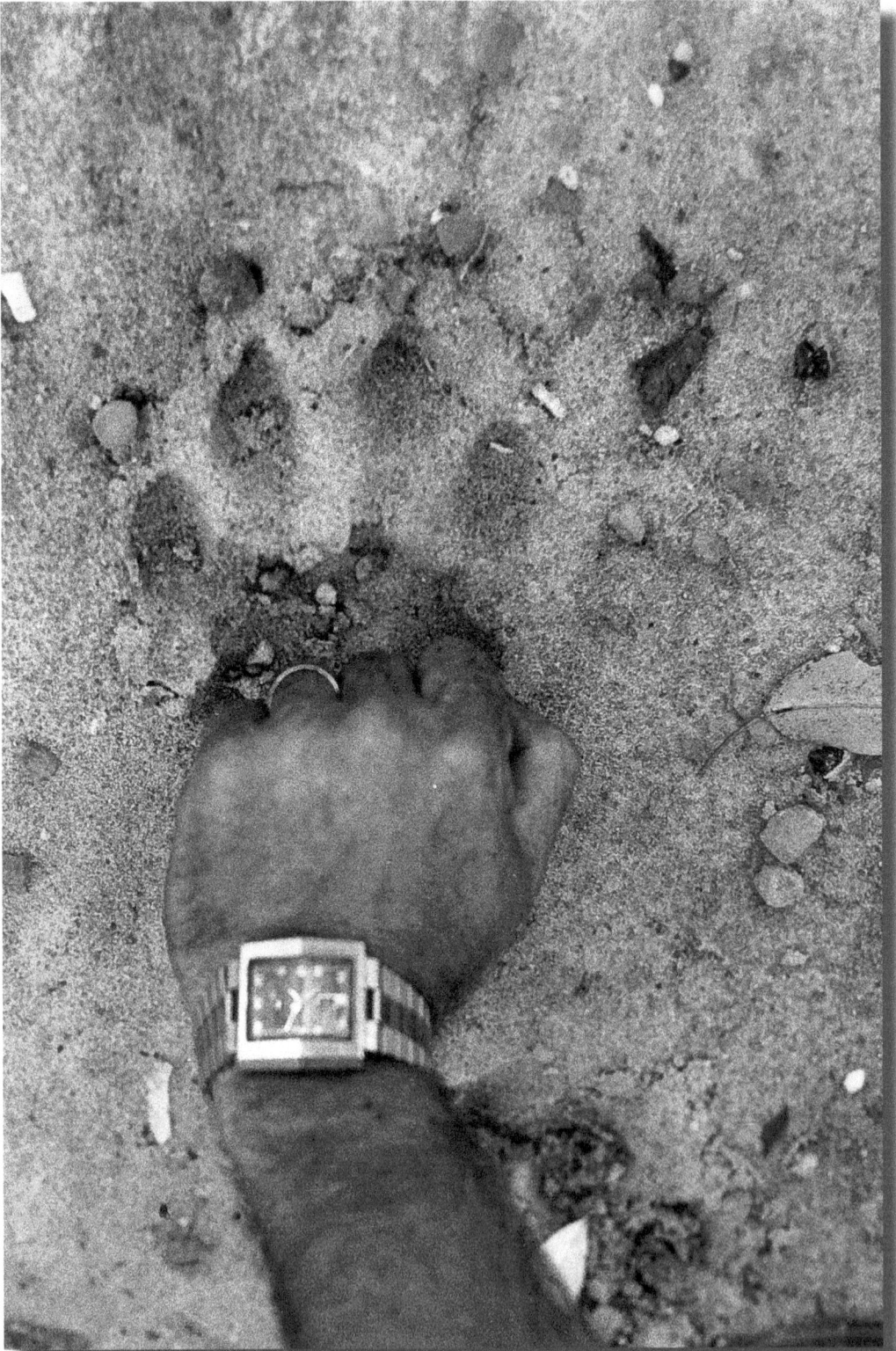
A lion print photographed at a Perth lion park for comparison.

Chapter Two

IMPATIENT NEWS EDITORS CAN BE TERRIBLE BORES. This day, mine was giving me a particularly difficult time. The fact that I was 4000 kms away had nothing to do with it, of course. His point was that he had a national newspaper to put out and I was running the Western Australian bureau of that paper, *The Australian*. I was therefore obliged to provide him with something to put in it. My point was that there was very little *news* that day in Perth or anywhere else for that matter throughout the state. It was an uncommonly quiet day.

'Well, we're desperately short of copy from just about everywhere around the country so see what you can get for us by the time I call again after lunch,' he said, crankily. Ringing off I tried all members of the bureau staff for interesting story ideas we could develop for the next day's paper but a recent busy period had left them all a little jaded. The week before we had worked very hard covering a major political row inside the Western Australian state government, and with big announcements in the state's mining and offshore oil exploration industries the pages had been relatively easy to fill. In fact Western Australia had been featuring prominently in the paper for some months. I had gone to Perth from *The Australian's* central office in Sydney in April 1978 to expand and develop the paper's operation there. With the introduction of sophisticated facsimile equipment, we could transmit the paper directly across the heart of the continent within minutes from the eastern to western coasts for the first time. This obviated the need to fly plates over each day—a time-consuming process which meant *The Australian* was not on the streets until the afternoon. With the new facsimile link, early morning print runs allowed us to markct *The Australian* as a genuine morning newspaper in Western Australia for the first time. To sell the paper there, our expanded staff had to get the important local stories.

I picked up a back copy of the only other morning newspaper in Perth, *The West Australian,* a long established parochial daily, which sold some 250,000 copies throughout the state. Only on the major stories were we ever competing with *The West Australian.* It was the local publication with detailed interest in every event taking place around Western Australia. Our small bureau staff, on the other hand, was really only interested in writing larger stories with national implications. We had to fight for the limited space each day in *The Australian* against news stories coming in from bureaux in all other states.

As I browsed through the week-old copy of *The West Australian,* I was scouting for hints of potential stories that could be developed. A short article run on one of the paper's inside pages captured my attention under the headline "Traps Go Out for Mystery killer". The story referred to an alleged large catlike animal which had been killing lambs and sheep in a small area of the bush-covered south west of Western Australia, centering on the Cordering region. Doggers employed by the Agriculture Protection Board, a section of the state Department of Agriculture, had apparently gone to the area to investigate. The story made mention of a local farmer, Dennis Earnshaw, who was claiming the animal had been killing his stock. The small item fascinated me. I re-read it more carefully. I glanced around the big desk littered reporting room and realised most of my staff as well as that of *The Sunday Times,* the Perth-based Sunday paper in our parent group with which we shared facilities, were out to lunch. Alone in a corner across the room sat one of *The Sunday Times'* senior reporters, 60-year-old Brian Pash, a well known Perth journalist who had worked with the paper for about 12 years.

'Brian,' I said walking to his desk and sitting down nearby, 'Have you seen this?' He took the copy of *The West Australian* and examined the story.

'Ah,' the old man snorted through one of the grimy roll-your-own cigarettes that perpetually hung from his lips. 'It's the cat,' he said, looking at me with more than a glint in two piercing brown eyes camouflaged behind bushy eyebrows that overhung his face.

'What cat?' I asked.

'It's true,' he said simply, waving a hand and taking the cigarette butt from his mouth, realising it had gone out.

'Whatever they tell you, it's true,' he said standing, absent-mindedly looking around for his perennially lost packet of matches.

'I've written about it but nobody believes me either,' he said, extracting a match from the box discovered under a pile of old press releases. Sitting down he lay the box on its side and with one hand flicked a match across its surface. It leapt into flame and as he took a huge breath he re-lit the crumbling cigarette. Staring across the room and savouring the breath in his lungs, a distant smile spread across Pash's face.

Eccentric in a crumpled-suit way he had long been regarded as the writer on *The Sunday Times* to whom "mystery" stories were handed when they occasionally arose. He had developed a reputation as being something of a "phenomenon" roundsman.

Pash stood up again and began clearing dozens of chaotically strewn papers on what must have rated as the most untidy desk in the 80-year history of *The Sunday Times*. Gathering some up into a worn brown satchel, he glanced at me as he reached down his coat from a nearby peg.

'I did lots of stories on it but nobody takes it seriously. It's out there though—there's too many of them that say they've seen it. The problem is proving it,' he said, shuffling across the office towards the door. 'And then there was that incident some years ago over at Nannup where a bunch of university students painted a sheep and spread stories about it being a "tiger". All that did was make it more difficult to convince people about the real cats'.

'Hang on Brian, tell me more,' I yelled after him.

'Sorry, dear boy, I've got a luncheon appointment, he said with a flamboyant gesture of the hand. He smiled back at me—a boyish, infectious grin—as he began to leave the office. 'Later, later,' he called in the corridor, an opaque figure descending the office stairs beyond a glass partition wall.

I looked at the newspaper article and realised my phone had been ringing for some minutes.

Later in the day I had completed much of the week's administrative work. I snipped the article from *The West Australian* and decided to make a few enquiries about it. From the telephone directory I located the address and phone number of the farmer mentioned, Dennis Earnshaw. When I dialled the numbered a softly-spoken male voice answered.

'I'd like to speak to Dennis Earnshaw,' I said.

'Speaking,' the voice replied.

'Mr Earnshaw, it's David O'Reilly, bureau chief of *The Australian* newspaper based in Perth,' I began.

'Oh,' Earnshaw said, a note of reticence instantly alerting the self preservatory instinct that develops in most journalists. This one has no love of newspapers, I thought, but continued, 'Yes, and I'm interested in a small article I noticed in an edition of last week's *West Australian.*'

'Don't talk to me about *The West Australian,*' Earnshaw interrupted. 'The reporters on that paper wouldn't know what time of day it was and they sure wouldn't know a good story if they fell over one'.

'Be that as it may,' I persevered, 'I'd like to talk to you about this strange rumour of an animal running around in the bush down your way'.

'It's not a rumour,' he said, 'it's just a fact'.

'What is?' I asked, taken aback by the disjointed direction of the conversation.

'The cat,' Earnshaw said decisively.

I shook my head. 'Can we start at the beginning, Mr Earnshaw? Exactly what kind of animal are we talking about? And who has seen it—have you?'

'Of course I've seen it,' he said, sharply.

'You have?' I asked.

'Yep'.

'Ah . . . you say you've actually seen it yourself?'

'Yep,' he said again.

'And what is it?'

'I reckon it's a mountain lion.'

'Oh,' I said. 'But we don't have mountain lions in the Australian bush, do we?'

'Well, that's what all the wildlife books say,' Earnshaw replied.

'But you say we do have mountain lions?'

'I know we do,' the farmer said emphatically. 'And I know a lot of other people who know so too.'

My immediate reaction was to ease myself out of the conversation. For the moment it occurred to me that I had encountered another of those creatures that are the bane of the profession—scatter-brained lunatics with weird schemes and stories or publicity-hunting opportunists. But I persisted. There was something in his voice—a steady moderation. Earnshaw's initial resentment at being bothered by a pressman had subsided and I sensed he wanted to talk. There was also honesty in the soft pitch of his words.

Dennis Earnshaw's story began to unfold—the story of a 32 year old family man running a quietly successful farming enterprise who was struggling to explain a phenomenon which puzzled him and which he increasingly suspected was undermining his livelihood.

'Lot's of people around here claim they have seen something but they all basically describe the same animal,' he challenged.

'And we reckon it's a mountain lion. I know it doesn't make sense but I've got tracks that nobody can explain and I've got professional hunters here working on it and they can't explain it either so you tell me what it is.'

'How long has it been going on?' I asked.

'Well, my brother and I saw it last year but we've been suffering stock losses for a few years now and really haven't thought anything of it. We've always put it down to natural causes or foxes,' he said.

'The problem is,' Earnshaw went on, 'I cut the cup bone from the neck of a nine-month-old steer that I found dead in one of my paddocks. The bone was fractured clean through. I reckon it was killed by a blow from the back which broke its neck. There's not a lot of foxes or wild dogs that could manage that.'

Within a short space of time the conversation had gripped my imagination. I suddenly had an urge to investigate what this man was saying. I was basically sceptical . . . and yet, if it were true then it could be the most important wildlife story in Australia. Earnshaw said he was positive that a large, scientifically unidentified feline animal was loose in the West Australian wilds. If what he was saying was true, it had the potential to rewrite a chapter in the nation's bush ecology.

I wanted to know more. Soon I was spitting out questions as fast as I could think of them. I was looking for a flaw, not so much in what he was saying as in how and why he was saying it—ulterior motives, contradictions or faint indications that something was wrong. How many people had seen it, I asked. What did they believe it was? What did it look like? How did it kill? Who was losing stock and in what numbers? A patchwork of mystery began falling together. After an hour on the phone I left the farmer to get back to the more mundane tasks of the office but the story continued to fascinate me.

Later I contacted the office of the W.A. Minister for Fisheries and Wildlife, Mr Graham MacKinnon. In response to my enquiries his press liaison staff acknowledged there had been some interest in the claims of farmers like Earnshaw in the south-west. They relayed to my office, via telex, the text of a press release Mr MacKinnon had issued on the matter.

The release read:

The Minister for Fisheries and Wildlife, Mr MacKinnon, has asked his department to investigate claims that a cat-like animal is killing lambs and sheep in southern farming areas.

He was told more than a week ago that at least four farmers were convinced that a cougar or cougars were responsible for killing stock in southern parts of the state. It has been claimed that some cougars escaped from a circus more than 15 years ago and have since bred, ' Mr MacKinnon said.

'Personally I am sceptical about this theory. If there were any cougars prowling about I feel certain that there would have been more concrete evidence by now. After all, there are expert doggers and naturalists in this state, yet no cougar has ever been caught, nor have the remains of such an animal ever been found. However, I can understand the concern of farmers when they find stock destroyed in a mysterious way.

Mr MacKinnon said from the description of the way stock had been killed it would have been an abnormally large cat responsible. He said that feral cats could grow to a very formidable size and were a serious problem to native animals in the south west.

'Despite their size I doubt that a feral cat could crush a sheep skull. To my mind it is more likely that dogs are responsible for the killings. A large cat would not have small feet'.

Mr MacKinnon said that foxes with the mange were often mistaken for cat-like animals.

'If they get mange and their hair falls out they look quite different. In fact mange patches can even be mistaken for stripes or spots.'

Mr MacKinnon said that he could understand the concern of the farmers. Quite obviously from reports he had received there was a "phantom" animal plaguing stock in the southern farming areas.

It was important that the mystery be cleared up as soon as possible and that was why he had asked his department to investigate the matter.

The belief that big cats had been stalking around the south west is not new.

At various times over the past 30 years there have been reported sighting of a "tiger-like" animal.

Some believe this is the Nannup Tiger. However the most persistent story is that there are cougars in the south west. It has been claimed that some cougars escaped from a circus just after the war.

I have been told that at least four farmers are convinced that a cougar or cougars are responsible for killing calves recently. Even though I don't think there are any cougars in this state I have still sought such information from the Department of Fisheries and Wildlife as a result of these recent incidents. The Conservator of Wildlife, Mr Harry Shugg, has informed me that many instances of strange animal sightings are in fact foxes. If they get mange and their hair falls out they look quite different. This would account for some of the strange, tiger-like animals claim.

It could also account for the belief that there is a Nannup Tiger. It needs to be remembered that feral cats can grow to a very formidable size. In fact feral cats are a very serious problem in the south west.

'To my mind it's more likely that dogs are responsible for the latest killings. Often domestic dogs form into killer packs,' Mr MacKinnon said. 'Some people would be surprised to know that their docile pet dog can become vicious when in a pack. It is quite frightening the amount of damage that dogs do to stock each year. Losses run into thousands of dollars. It needs to be remembered there are dogs such as the Rhodesian Ridgeback and the Afghan Hound that were essentially trained to hunt lions and are kept domestically.

'So it is quite possible that there are strains of dogs that are efficient killers of stock in this state. I am not one to scoff at people. Quite obviously from the reports I have received there is a "phantom" animal or animals of some kind plaguing stock in the south west.

'If detailed information is presented to me by farmers who have lost stock in a mysterious way then I will have the matters investigated by my department,' the minister's press release concluded.

Some days later I contacted Earnshaw again by phone and informed him I was interested in meeting him and investigating the matter. We then made arrangements to meet at his farm during the next week. But that meant reference to a map of the state, which as a recently arrived New South Welshman, I was only just beginning to explore. Western Australia covers a third of the area of the Australian continent—a massive on-going landscape of parched northern desert and flint hard iron ore country with a population of 1.2 million people. It was however at that time the fastest growing state in the nation. People were moving west from the urban eastern seaboard in growing numbers courted by the magnificent climate, outdoor lifestyle and exploding business potential of the place—the rapidly growing industry and mining developments which promised to make Western Australia one of the richest states of any nation in the world.

Collie, a town of 17,000 inhabitants, sat on the direct southern rail link from the state capital in the heart of Western Australia's rich wheat and sheep country. It was the only place in Western Australia where coal was found and the town had been built on one of the richest deposits in the world. Coal was first found at the edge of a pool in the Collie river in 1883 and the first commercial shaft was sunk in 1889. The state government began developing the coal fields at the turn of the century and production on a commercial scale was well in progress by the early 1900's. Today more than 1 million tonnes of coal is produced in the fields surrounding the town, extracted from two open cut and one deep mine. With reserves expected to extend well into the next century Collie coal will help fire the development of the State's vast mineral resources.

Prior to my departure from the office I asked Brian Pash about the town and the farming areas surrounding it. He thrust a pile of photocopied newspaper cuttings into my already cluttered arms as I was leaving. I stuffed the notes into a folder, intending to read them in the south west.

A 250 km car journey south from Perth took me down the Albany Highway until I reached the quiet town of Arthur River. From there I swung off the main highway west towards the ocean and through the West Arthur River Shire. The journey slowed when I attempted to decipher the rough directions Earnshaw had given me to help find his farm. Reaching a gravel road east of Collie I travelled through thick timber country until I reached a remote railway siding and farm gate which I realised would lead to the Earnshaw farmhouse.

At the rear of a blue roofed farmhouse I pulled up near a parked caravan, and a short chunky man in denim jeans, and khaki jungle shirt came to greet me.

Earnshaw struck me initially as reserved and essentially his own man. The latter impression was to grow in coming days as I got to know him. At first he was wary. He had been misquoted in the local country press and in the Perth papers and despite his initial politeness he was clearly in no mood to be over-friendly to inquisitive reporters invading his home. When it became clear that I was genuinely interested in what he had to say he began to open up. The impression I had gained on the phone strengthened—he wanted to talk. And he wanted answers. He wouldn't admit it but I quickly formed the impression that he was becoming known to the more sceptical residents of the South West as some kind of troublemaker. Some of his acquaintances were perplexed about the publicity that seemed to be increasingly generated around him. And that was a worry to him.

'The last thing I want in all this is publicity,' he said earnestly after he had introduced me to his wife and children and we settled down to talk in the fibro room attached to the back of the farmhouse and used as a study and storage room for everything from rifles to the farm's VHF two-way radio telephone. Earnshaw installed the radio to keep in touch with his wife at the farm whenever he travelled the property's perimeter or when flying back from Perth or the wheat harvesting in the north.

'I don't want my name in the paper, if only because it is starting to give the wrong impression. I've been trying to encourage other people to speak up about it but a lot are shy or afraid of being ridiculed. Even people around this area think we're nuts and after a while the ridicule makes you angry. So I guess it's fallen to me to become some type of spokesman about what's happening. I'm not happy with the West Australian newspaper group because they just don't seem to believe what we're saying. They have run stories at times but nobody has been enthusiastic enough to get involved. We've talked to reporters on the phone but the impression we get is that they think we're strange. Until now there's only been Brian Pash at *The Sunday Times* who's been sympathetic. Oh, and a young television fellow was down here some months back talking to us. He didn't stay long but he said he wants to cover it for television if we can come up with a dead animal.

'So I'll talk to the Press if they quote me properly,' Earnshaw went on. 'A few stupid things have been written and it is making it harder for us to keep it in perspective.'

He then went into elaborate detail describing the incidents that had occurred on either his own or his brother's property. In the recent season alone he claimed to have lost $3000 worth of lambs to unexplained predation. He produced the parched lump of clay dug from the dam wall on Ross's property. Embedded in it was a graphic footprint—four clearly marked toe prints and a triangular rear pad pushed into the clay when it was soft with moisture. Earnshaw put the clay mould on a little tin tray on the table and I examined it. He sighed. My initial reaction was that the print was small, perhaps 5 cm across. I asked him whether it was not a dog or fox print.

'It's feline from the shape of the back pad and the toes and because you can't see any toenails. I have never seen a fox or dog track like that in my life. And it would hardly be a bush cat because they just don't grow big enough to have the body weight to make such an imprint, he said.

Earnshaw produced a caramel coloured bone taken from the neck of the dead steer. The "cup" bone had what appeared to be a distinct fracture mark extending across its upper area.

'People throughout the Cordering region have been losing stock and some claim they have seen a big feline animal in the bush—there are also reports from further afield but I can't vouch for them.' Had the authorities been alerted, I wondered. Earnshaw sniggered.

'Yeah . . . well. We've asked the Agriculture Protection Board for help but we got the distinct impression they're just scared. Some of the local boys concede something is wrong with all the stock losses but publicly they won't say anything. Different officers just say it's dogs or foxes and have sent out professional doggers to lay baits around the area.'

'Any luck?'

'A few foxes but try as they may they still haven't come up with any wild dogs that could kill a steer,' Earnshaw said quickly. 'My sister-in-law Sue telephoned around enquiring whether there had been any circus accidents that might explain some kind of wild animal running loose. She talked to an officer at the Fisheries and Wildlife Department in Busselton who told her of a reported circus accident in the south west where at least one pair of cougars was among a number of animals that got away. One of the two Agriculture Protection Board officers later verified this saying he was briefed by his superiors about the accident and that he thought they had all just died out in the bush,' Earnshaw said.

'A circus accident' I said eagerly.

'Mmm . . .' he said pensively. 'I can't see it myself because the movement of animals is pretty tightly controlled and it would be very hard to hush up an accident where a couple got away and started breeding up in the bush. Still, it's a theory you hear a lot of and if it is right there could be hundreds of them out there by now,' Earnshaw said glancing through the study window to the forest beyond. 'Basically though, the Agriculture Protection Board doesn't seem to want to know anything about it. A few of us have been saying that someone will be accountable for our losses if it's discovered there's an introduced animal out there. I reckon they're worried that if it is right they might be in trouble for not doing their job properly.'

During out chat, Dennis Earnshaw took me around the farm showing me the back sheds full of expensive, newly acquired harvesting equipment. He introduced me to his father, a gentle old man with soft eyes and the same squat build as his son. He was staying at the farm for a few days. With his wife, he lived in a comfortable bungalow at the sea in Bunbury but he came to the boys' farms regularly to help out with the work and visit local friends. Because of the pressure on bedrooms in Dennis Earnshaw's rapidly expanding family, Ken and the children's grandmother stayed in the fully equipped caravan parked at the rear of the farmhouse during their visits. The 6 metre Millard mobile home contained all the luxuries—spacious, with sleeping room for four.

Dennis Earnshaw's property sat alongside his brother's—3,800 ha, half of which was cultivated sheep and crop land, the rest virgin bush, undulating over ironstone outcrops in a thick jarrah belt on the edge of the dense forest that extended west over the Darling Range to the coastal plain and north to Perth. On a quick tour of the region with the farmer in one of his property vehicles I was introduced to a number of spots where his brother, himself or farm employees had sighted the animal. We detonated a cloud of billowing dust down the old gravel road past the gateway to Ross's farm as we chatted about the region's most mysterious inhabitant. Earnshaw punched the car horn as we hurtled past a young woman clambering from her stationwagon to unlatch a gate. He braked fiercely and reversed back to where the woman stood smiling, hands on hips.

Kerry Hughes came to Cordering 12 years earlier after her marriage to a local man, Terry. The daughter of a headmaster who spent his life travelling from one country school to another. Kerry's childhood was spent in a variety of W.A. rural towns. Her husband was a close friend of Dennis Earnshaw from childhood and had lived in the region all his life. He periodically worked with the Earnshaws in the cropping side of their business. The Hughes farm stood on a treeless ridge surrounded by paddocks in which a substantial herd of horses grazed.

Eighteen months earlier Terry Hughes had sighted a small black animal moving fast through scrub near his farmhouse. He disregarded the incident though he was quite puzzled by it, feeling sure he had seen some kind of small black panther. So briefly had he sighted it pursuing a small group of paunchy wethers out of the brush that he thought nothing more of it.

And then late one afternoon in 1978 his wife was driving the children back from Collie after an afternoon's shopping in the town. It was 6.15pm and in drizzling rain the evening twilight was descending. Kerry switched on her headlights.

'I was concentrating pretty hard because of the drizzle—it was hard to see and I was worried because there were a few nasty potholes on that part of the road,' she said. 'Well, I slowed down as I came to a little rise with the windscreen wipers going. As the headlights lit the flattening rise in front of me, I saw this animal. I think it was walking away from me because I didn't notice its flanks—just its tail and I couldn't see its head. Suddenly it moved side on and disappeared off the side of the road.'

'What colour was it?' I asked.

The girl shuffled her feet in the gravel and stared at the road's edge. 'It's hard to say because of the rain. It looked sort of wet and seemed to vary in colour shades but I think it was a light brown generally.'

'How far away was it when you sighted it?'

'About 25 metres.'

'And what first struck you about it?'

'I guess the major thing was how powerful it looked in the back legs—like a lioness you see on television. But it had this long tail and loped along when it was running away from me—like you see greyhound dogs only it wasn't a dog, it was a cat . . .'

'What happened then?'

'Well I didn't know what to think but I suddenly got scared, planted my foot and rushed home to tell Terry. I described where it was and he went over to get Den and work out what it was,' she said looking at Earnshaw.

'We found some marks on the road all right but you couldn't tell what had made them. It could have been a dog or a cat but they were pad marks and they showed something had definitely gone over the road there,' he said.

'What do you think it was, Kerry?' I asked.

'Well, it had this long tail which didn't stick up and didn't stick down; it just stuck out behind it but it was very long. I didn't really see its head properly so I can't really say what it was but it looked powerful.'

The girl paused before continuing with a slightly embarrassed laugh. 'It gets to the stage where you think afterwards, hell, what exactly was it? After Terry rushed over to get Den to look for the tracks I was sitting at home worrying that I might have sent them out on a wild goose chase. But then they found the marks. The whole thing happened so fast I couldn't see the head and I just didn't see it for long enough but I know for sure that what I did see wasn't normal. If it's the same animal the others say they've seen then I would be very concerned—not just because I've got children who I can't watch every minute of the day on the farm but also because however it got out there it should never have been allowed to develop without us knowing what it was.'

Kerry Hughes also related an incident that had occurred a few months earlier on the farm. She and her husband discovered a foal— eight months old, suffering a massive chest wound. 'Its chest was ripped open about ten centimetres across in a shredded wound—all the skin was just hanging down,' she explained. 'The Agriculture Protection Board said it had probably got caught on a wire fence but that's rubbish—all the wire on our horses' paddock is soft—plain wire. We searched the paddock looking for barbs or some old wire that may have been thrown in there but we couldn't find any. It took the horse a long time to recover. Terry had to treat it for days and days and we still nearly lost it. We keep the foal's mother in the same paddock and she's always been extremely protective. Now we think the foal could have been attacked by something which was chased off by her. It was badly knocked around and Terry was sure it had taken a battering in a scuffle. It looked like something had slashed downwards at its chest and left the flesh just hanging. We've never been able to work out what happened.'

Leaving Mrs Hughes, Earnshaw drove us through a nearby gate and out onto a paddock where a small flock of sheep was grazing. Driving a wedge between scattering groups of them he came to where one lay motionless on the soggy ground. The wether had been killed by the marauding predator, Earnshaw alleged. There was no sign of a struggle. The sheep was simply lying on top of its own legs as if it had collapsed suddenly down onto them.

'We've been finding them like this for a while now and never really worked it out. I guess I've lost about 200 sheep apart from about 27 lambs that have just completely disappeared. It's just not right – but until

Ross and I saw it we hadn't put two and two together,' he said seriously. 'Now, that sheep hasn't been attacked by dogs or foxes because there would be fleece all over the paddock. And if it had died of natural causes it would have lain on its side there kicking until it expired—there's usually marks on the soft ground when they die naturally. They kick little grooves with their feet but you can see there is nothing there with this one,' he said pointing. 'Some of them we've found with their bellies cut open and internal organs eaten out but others are just like this, left without a mark on them. It doesn't make sense. And look at this,' he said, lifting the sheep's head onto his lap by gripping the ears. The skull swivelled sickeningly in a loose circle. 'I reckon this animal was killed by a blow which broke its neck,' the farmer said, staring up at me.

Earnshaw also outlined to me a number of unusual features about the footprints that Cordering farmers had found in the district. He said that once they began to realise something was strange about the stock deaths, the farmers noticed the strange appearance of often quite large feline footprints. And he claimed that many of the scuff marks appeared to have been made by a five-toed animal.

'From what we can see, the only animal that ever puts the fifth toe onto the ground is a feline type,' he said.

Later in the afternoon Earnshaw led me on a guided tour of red and white gum trees hidden in a remote stretch of bush adjoining his brother's farm. There he pointed out sharp, pencil like scratch marks, some up to 15 cm in length and spaced up to 2.5 cm apart, torn jaggedly into the bark of the tree trunks at various heights from the ground. Invariably the marked trees seemed to be of the same style. Angled up to 45 degrees away from the ground, they all had high overhead boughs which flattened out parallel to the ground.

'This animal is scratching the trees and then using the high limbs to either bask in the sun or to keep an eye on things.' Earnshaw said with unapologetic directness in the face of my bewildered frown and cynical questioning.

On our return to the farm I realised I needed to drive to the coast to find accommodation for the next few nights at Bunbury. Dennis Earnshaw mentioned that a couple of hunters would be going out that night on a spotlighting expedition to try to sight the cat. 'They're staying in another caravan over at the back of Ross's house,' he said. 'They've been going out in a flat-topped utility the last few nights but haven't had any luck so far. One is an experienced kangaroo hunter from the north called Bert Pinker who reckons chasing them with lights will be the only way to shoot one. He reckons they'll pick up the reflection from its eyes in the dark.'

'They haven't seen anything so far?'

"No. Ross and I went out with them a few times and we occasionally saw big eyes in the dark, far off. They seemed to be too big for foxes or stock but we couldn't get close enough to make out exactly what they were. It was getting too hard for Ross and me to go out every night till 3 or 4:00 am and then work the full day so we're having a break tonight while the hunters go out themselves.'

'Do you think they'd let me go out with them?' I asked.

'I don't know—they're pretty wary of strangers,' Earnshaw said.

'If you come back this afternoon I'll go over and ask them. It's no good now, they're probably still sleeping. I'll try later—but no promises.'

'Fine,' I said, 'but listen, I must get away now. I want to talk to a few people around the district and get over to Bunbury.'

'Yeah,' Earnshaw said a trifle preoccupied. 'Listen . . .' he said after a moment, 'I've got a friend coming down here later this afternoon and I'm not sure what time. He's Dick Old, the Minister for Agriculture and Leader of the National Country Party. He's the member down Katanning way and his family has known Dad for years. He's agreed to come down to talk to me about this. The trouble is, it's basically a private chat while he's down here on other business, you know? He won't want any press around. Umm . . .'Earnshaw said uncomfortably.

'That's alright mate,' I said quickly, 'I'll keep a low profile if I get back while he's still here. Don't worry. What time do the hunters go out?'

'They usually leave about 8 at night and stay out till the early hours. Have you got plenty of warm clothes? It gets very cold.'

'Yeah, I've got a big duffle coat. Anyway, I should get going so I can be back to find out if they will take me,' I said, climbing into my car.

Nearly two hours later I drove into the beachfront tourist town of Bunbury. Once booked into a local motel I had in mind finding the local regional headquarters of the Agriculture Protection Board and asking a few questions. I plonked down on the bed in my room and pondered the events of the day. As I made a few rough notes it occurred to me I hadn't looked at the paper cuttings Brian Pash had given me. I took them from my attaché case and began to read.

On November 12, 1972 Pash had written a story published in *The Sunday Times*. It read:

Two strange creatures which looked like black panthers are terrorising a farming area north of Koorda in the central wheatbelt. The animals, jet black from head to tail tip have killed piglets, herded terrified sheep into groups and eaten carcasses.

I paused as the words sank in. Glancing back to the date of the newspaper cutting, I read on:

The wives of some farmers refused to be left alone at night and have ordered their children not to venture far from the homesteads.

At least eight people have seen the animals in the past two months. One farmer fired five shots from a .22 calibre rifle at one of the animals and missed. He also chased the animals in a utility for more than three miles at speeds of up to 45 mph.

The animals have been tracked by a warden of the Fisheries and Fauna Department. No one can say what they are. Departmental experts are baffled. Nearly all the sightings have been made on properties at Kulja in the Koorda shire, about 50 miles north-east of Wongan Hills.

Kulja farmer George Moir said the two creatures appeared about two months ago. They were rounding up sheep which were panic-stricken. At first he thought they were dogs but when they were near he saw they were completely strange. He got into his utility and gave chase.

'They did not run like dogs,' he said. 'They were nothing like dogs or dingoes. They loped along with the front feet coming down alternatively about eight inches apart. It was like a canter.

'They were black all over, at least 2 ft high with a long slender body and a tail the same length as the body and curling at the end.

'My fastest speed was 45 mph and I couldn't catch them up. When we came to a fence one took it in his stride and the other, which was lagging, crashed into the wire. It recovered quickly and climbed over like a cat. At the next fence they both went over with no trouble.'

Mr Moir lost them when he had to stop and open a gate.

He informed the fauna warden at Wongan Hills, Mr Don Nobel, who came to the farm and followed their tracks. Mr Noble followed the tracks for another five miles and said the animals had not eased up in their flight.

Mr Moir had found several of his piglets dead with their throats gashed and their hearts torn out.

Late one evening the pigs were making a commotion so he went out of the house with his .22 rifle. He saw one of the black creatures by the pig sties and fired five quick shots which missed. He believed the creatures have mauled dead sheep which may or may not have been killed by them.

Their system of eating was to strip all the head until all that was left was the jawbone.

Mr Albert Orchard, of Melbille, Mr Moir's brother-in-law, saw one of the creatures crossing the road while on a visit to the farm. Local farmer

Frank Orchard also saw a black animal in the scrub. The two creatures have also been seen on the farms of Alan and Ron Johnson, adjoining the Moir farm. The brothers have seen the creatures several times and heard what they describe as blood curdling howls at night.

The Johnsons have lost 14 pigs, each killed by the two black creatures.

Women refuse to be left alone at night and none of the Johnson children are allowed to stray beyond the farms. Whenever the farmers go to the paddocks, they take guns. Fresh tracks are often found near the houses in the mornings. Recently, small pug marks have been found near those of the adults indicating the two creatures have had a little of cubs.

'There is no doubt these things have a few people worried,' said Mr Moir. 'I always take a gun with me when I go out.'

The Johnsons and Mr Moir have compared notes on their sightings. They have studied the illustrations in a book of the world's animals. The one creature they agree is identical to the two that are inhabiting their farm is the black panther.

The Director of South Perth Zoo, Mr Tom Spence, said yesterday that the noise panthers made was a barking cough. He said that the description of the creatures also fitted the jaguarundi, a South American animal of the cat tribe. The jaguarundi had the reputation of being untamable, vicious and bad tempered.

The story concluded.

Shuffling through the remaining papers I came up with another Pash article published by *The Sunday Times* on November 18, 1972. It read:

Two strange cat-like creatures which have been terrorising properties north of Koorda struck again this week. They rounded up a flock of sheep, stampeding them through fences and killed two lambs.

The creatures, not unlike black panthers in shape and size, then backtracked and followed a farmer's wife who was riding a motor bike.

Mrs Lilian Moir of Kulja said: 'At first light I heard a commotion in the paddock. I drove the motor bike into the paddock and found the sheep had panicked, broken down a fence and got into the barley. It took some time to get them back to their paddock where I found two dead lambs. One had its neck broken and its tongue was eaten out.

'On the way back to the farm I noticed pug marks over my motor cycle wheel tracks. The creatures had backtracked and must have followed me for a while.'

The creatures were first seen around the Kulja farms two months ago. Mr George Moir chased the two creatures in his utility for more than three miles at speeds up to 45 mph. They have been sighted by at least eight people.

The descriptions have tallied—cat-like, bigger than an Alsatian dog, jet black from head to tail, long slim body, a narrow head, a long tail that curls at the end.

Fauna warden Don Noble of Wongan Hills, tracked the animals but has been unable to identify the tracks.

Another Kulja farmer, Ron Johnson, and Mr Moir say that the nearest wild animal they resemble is the black panther. Mr Johnson set a trap 8 ft high and baited it with a sheep carcass. The trap was sprung and the carcass partly eaten but because he did not cover the top, the creature got out.

This week plaster casts of the tracks were sent to Perth for identification. The casts were regarded as not good enough to be read because they were taken from a sand print. However, they appeared to be un-dog like and made by a creature much larger than a dingo.

Mrs Moir was contacted this week by Mr W. Adams of Cunderdin, who said that 10 years ago he was in the district with a black creature similar to those seen today. He had not reported it at the time because of possible disbelief and ridicule, The story read.

I took careful note of the last reference in the story. It was obvious than an important part of the explanation for this increasingly mysterious problem would be the question of timing. Earnshaw had mentioned Agriculture Protection Board officials talking about a circus accident in the early 1960s and now here was a man quoted in 1972 saying he had first seen a big cat 10 years earlier. In February 1973 Pash wrote another article on what had become known as the Kulja or Koorda panther. Kulja, a tiny town, is located 248 kilometres north-east of Perth in the shire of Koorda.

Pash's story said:

The Agriculture Protection Board does not intend to do anything about the Kulja "panthers" which have been terrorising farming areas for six months. The Board believes that the panther-like creatures are black kangaroo dogs gone wild.

This is denied by Kulja farmers who have sighted, chased and shot at the creatures and have suffered stock losses. But a senior A.P.B. control officer who investigated the sightings at Kulja, in the Koorda shire about 50 miles north-east of Wongan Hills, reported there were two kangaroo dogs left from a nearby native camp. A spokesman for the Department said: 'The dogs were probably abandoned from this camp which was only a mile or two away. In any case, vermin control is the farmer's responsibility on his own property. If there are stock losses then it is up to him to do something about it.'

Kulja farmer Ron Johnson said the creatures were still in his area because he has found tracks near his shed and piggeries. He said one set of tracks would be bigger in circumference than the bottom of a large cool drink bottle. He estimates the weight of the animal to be about 140 lbs. Another similar set of tracks indicated a female and a third set showed the pair has a young one. 'The size of these tracks unnerved me a little,' he said.

He has had two separate sightings, the first when he chased them at speeds up to 50 mph in his vehicle and second with his wife. Each time they vanished into the bush. He said at least 11 people had made separate sightings.

Mr Johnson trapped them twice in home-made cages with rabbit and each time the animal escaped leaving massive tracks. 'The nearest we can compare this animal to is the panther,' he said.

62

The Johnson family has also heard the creatures howling in the bush at night and he said 'the sound made our blood run cold.'

Then again on June 8, 1975 *The Sunday Times* published yet another Pash story which read:

A black feline-looking creature as large as a panther and muscled like a lion has been sighted by visitors and residents in the South West.

The creature is unlike any other animal ever seen in the bush. Its face has been described as fearsome, its body squat and strong and ebony all over. As it runs it lopes along with a cat-like grace.

One theory is that the thylacoleo, or marsupial lion has returned to the Australian bush after a time lapse of 6,000 years.

One recent sighting occurred at the north-west side of Stirling Dam where the creature walked into the cat's headlights. The four occupants of the car agreed it resembled no other creature they had seen in the bush or zoo. It blinked at the car lights and walked diagonally across the road with a rolling motion.

Mrs Freda Shalders, Harvey, said: 'We could not believe our eyes. I'd never seen any creature quite like it. It was solidly built, pitch black, and cat-like in the way it moved. It had an almost stumpy tail. The face was like a cat's but large and thick. After a minute it loped away into the bush.'

Mrs Shalders said that her husband and two friends, Mr and Mrs Jensen of Harvey all agreed they had seen 'something out of this world.'

A similar animal has been sighted by a Bunbury veterinary surgeon, a former resident of East Africa, and three farmers.

Its territory appears to have been the Harvey-Brunswick-Australind area and sometimes in the Darling Range, The story read.

The story concluded by referring to a naturalist and zoo owner Mr Ian Offer, who ran a sanctuary at Benger, a few kilometres north of Bunbury. I dropped the newspaper cutting to my lap. The more engrossing it all became the more surprised I was—it seemed inconceivable that nothing of this had been reported at any length in the Eastern States. This I ascribed to the fact that in many ways, the communities of the major population centres in the east had remained largely ignorant of Western Australia and what went on there over the years. Certainly the Australian bush abounded with tales of mysterious animals in some form or other but I was impressed by some of the details in Pash's reporting. There was a strong consistency in the events outlined by his witnesses involving the physical dimensions and colour of the alleged animals. Why was it, I asked myself, that there seemed to be two colours involved—black and a variation of light brown? If some kind of community hysteria was gripping a large area of the state, why was there not a greater assortment of observations—bear-like, dog-like, spotted, striped, or multi coloured animals? I was perplexed and determined to press on. I asked at the hotel reception where I could find Ian Offer's Wildlife park, and then made for the outskirts of town.

Thirty kilometres north from Bunbury along the South Western Highway I turned off at a sign reading *To Wellesley Road Wildlife Park* and drove across a grassy flat coastal plain until I reached the sanctuary. Stepping out in the car park was like being thrust into a tropical jungle. All manner of exotic animal calls chorused through the trees from the sanctuary, a thickly wooded menagerie of cages beyond an imposing iron fence.

At the small office I asked for Offer. A rotund man in military style jungle dress and a pair of rubber boots strode towards me. 'Who wants him?' he asked in a direct but friendly tone.

'I do,' I retorted.

'And who may I ask are you?' he said, dropping a furry animal into a small wire cage and snapping its door shut.

Half way through my introductions Offer's friendly demeanour deserted him, as it had done Earnshaw. The old story, I thought. The Ranger had been misquoted about the animal on a number of occasions and his patience with the media was wearing thin. I explained to him that I had nothing to quote yet.

Reluctantly agreeing to talk 'off the record' he beckoned me to a nearby corner of the park where he was erecting a wooden enclosure which would later become a walk-through aviary.

Offer spent much of his spare time exploring the bush and swamp land surrounding the 13 ha park. He had stocked it virtually alone and developed a considerable reputation as a bushman and animal expert in his eight years of running it. Among the animals in the park were varieties of kangaroos and wallabies including the Brush Tail Rat Kangaroo, rarely seen by the public and in dwindling numbers in the wilds. Offer had caught three in the forest of the Darling Range and had also recently imported two Tasmanian Devils from which he was breeding for the first time in Western Australia. The one hundred species of mammals and birds lived in carefully maintained pens and cages sprinkled around the landscaped park. At its heart were 3 ½ ha of natural peat swamp on which Black Ducks and swans lived. The everglade-like swamp in its natural state had proved a major attraction for the 25,000 tourists who passed through the park each year.

'So you've seen this cat thing too?' I said.

'Of course I've seen it,' Offer said, biting a twig and scratching the ground with his boot. For a moment it seemed I had threatened his professionalism. 'I've seen quite a few things in this bush that I can't explain but I can't beat that fella,' he said. 'Some of the people over Cordering way say they've seen a yellow coloured one. I don't know about that—the fella I saw was black—jet-black, and there are a lot of other people that have seen a black one too. I was driving up towards Harvey one night when this thing walked across the road. When I saw it I accelerated to it and then stopped. It just pulled up at the road edge and looked at me through the windscreen, sizing me up. It was black and big and well muscled. Like a panther or a sort of bear.'

'Did you get out and chase it?'

'Did I what? You must be joking—and besides it just disappeared into the bush before I could do anything.'

After a moment, Offer said: 'Anyway, what are you interested in this for? If you're going to write a story for your newspaper then don't start quoting me. I've had a gutful of you blokes getting it all wrong. I told one reporter about some prints I found out back here and he quoted me as saying they were as big as my hand,' he said, lifting a pudgy outstretched hand into the air. 'Jesus, that upset me. What I said to him was I'd found prints that I couldn't cover with my clenched fist. Now that's a different sized footprint.'

'Well, if I quote you at all I'll say you found prints you couldn't cover with your clenched fist, right?' I said seriously.

'Alright,' he said, breaking into a smile.

'What do you reckon it is, Ian?' I asked. 'Where did it come from?'

'I've got no idea—just theories' he said. 'It's possible that some animals got off a boat and bred in the wild—maybe a couple of mascots from a visiting naval vessel in the war. The real question is whether it was introduced here by man or whether it has existed in the wilds all the time.'

'But how could that be?' I protested. 'If it's been here all the time why wasn't it recognised long ago?'

'Look, Western Australia is not like the East. There's so much bush here that's never been touched by man. You know I can take you places within a few miles of this park that no man except me and the Aboriginals have ever seen. In the East you have much less area and so many people. Here the population has only recently started to grow yet there are millions of hectares of bushland. Australia is the only major land mass in the world without a species of big cat—or is it? It could be the animal is the descendant of the marsupial lion that is known to have lived several thousand years ago in the days of the giant wombat and giant kangaroo. Who knows, it could be that a cat animal was introduced into the bush somehow and has managed to breed up with a native cat. In any case, one thing's for certain—phantoms don't leave footprints'.

Offer claimed that during the 1930s Western Australia's marsupial population was hit by a mysterious disease which decimated large number of animal species. 'It's only now that we're beginning to see some species, like the quokkas, coming back. It could be that it's only in recent years that the populations of a lot of different animals are expanding as a result. The cats could be breeding up—that's why people are seeing more of them.'

As we talked a brilliantly-coloured peacock wandered past in among the tourists, picking at the grass for food.

'This whole thing has got me flabbergasted,' I said.

'Don't worry mate, you're not the only one,' the park owner replied.

Offer's major wildlife breakthrough has been his discovery in 1972 of the existence of a wombat in Western Australia. He claimed he had caught one in a cage north of his sanctuary; the last common wombat was previously thought to have existed in Western Australia 30,000 years ago. Foresters had told Offer a wombat was sighted some weeks earlier. He set a trap near a group of burrows and a small female later took a bait of currant bun. Despite his elation at the find, a minor furore soon exploded. Some wildlife authorities claimed the animal had been introduced from the east where it was prolific, an allegation Offer angrily denounced. He claimed his wombat differed from the variety in the east—it had smaller ears, the body was lower to the ground, the roman nose profile was flatter, it was more dish-faced and its eyes were closer to its nose. Offer believed his animal resembled a smaller species once found on South Australia's Eyre Peninsula but now presumed extinct. He claimed his discovery indicated the wombat existed in Western Australia despite scientific indications from fossils found in caves at Yallingup that it was long extinct. A storm erupted a week after the capture when the chief fauna warden at the Department of Fisheries and Wildlife , Mr Harry Shugg, said the wombat was brought from the eastern states, but Offer was adamant.

'I challenge anyone to tell me where in the eastern states wombats like this can be found,' he said.

And after inspecting the animal at Offer's park, the Director of the South Perth Zoo, Mr Tom Spence, said he was sure it was 'something different' but stressed he was not qualified to verify sub-species.

The wombat which Offer called Honey settled easily into captivity as a major drawcard in a large earth covered cage complete with simulated bush conditions in the park.

The sun was quickening in its descent overhead as Offer and I spoke. I left the park for Cordering assuring him I would surely see him again before my enquiries were through. As I began the long drive back to the farm over the Darling scarp, the range of hills that split the coastal plains and the timber country of the hinterland, I was lost in thought. What impressed me was how the validity of this absurd proposition depended on the integrity of the people I had met. All I really had to go on at this stage were a few first-hand accounts of encounters with something which left no real calling card. I needed hard evidence. Ian Offer, at least, had reason to promote the story, there being no doubt that it would generate customs at his park, but I suspected that was being too hard on him.

I reached the Earnshaw road nearing dark. A pair of distant lights and a rising cloud of grey dust told me a car was approaching ahead and then on a wave of clinking stones a big limousine charged by. Dick Old, I thought.

Dennis Earnshaw greeted me at the back door. 'Was that Dick Old I saw just leaving?' I asked.

'Yes,' Earnshaw said. 'He's been here most of the afternoon talking about the cat. He sounds sympathetic but it's clear there's nothing he can do. Says he'll ask the people in his department to move their enquiries along, though.'

'I wonder if he'll talk to me about it?' I said.

'You can try him when you get back to Perth but I doubt if he'll commit himself. He agrees something's going on but he obviously won't go out on a limb about it.'

'Amazing people these politicians,' I said to encourage the young farmer who seemed disconcerted.

'I suppose you want to talk to the hunters now,' he said. 'I haven't had a chance to go over today but we can now. They should be well awake and getting ready for tonight's hunt.'

Ross Earnshaw's farmhouse loomed ahead in the darkness. Built in 1953 it was for some years the family's main residence. Earnshaw wheeled the stationwagon past it to the left and the headlights pitched across its red brickwork onto a caravan parked at the rear near an enormous open storage shed. As he jerked the handbrake up and dimmed the lights and the fluorescent green dashboard, there was only darkness, the silent echo inside the car cabin and a dim light flickering through the caravan window.

'Listen, I'm not sure how these blokes are going to react to this so why don't you just stay here for the moment?' Earnshaw said. 'I'll find out if they'll let you go along.' Throwing the car door open he trooped off towards the van and when I wound the passenger side window down a deepening evening chill stung my face. Earnshaw unlatched the van door and climbed in to a friendly chorus of greetings from two men. After ten minutes of muffled conversation, he leaned out in a column of light and gestured me over with a broad wave of his arm. In the doorway he made room for me to climb aboard, snapped the door closed behind me and introduced me to Bert Pinker who sat on a cramped bench seat around a table at one end. At the other, Mick Simpson sat hunched on one of the four van bunks.

Pinker looked up but said nothing beyond a barely intelligible grunt of greeting. He continued concentrating on the assemblage of a cigarette from a hide pouch of tobacco strewn on the table. He put the cigarette in his mouth and pulled the throw-away lighter from his pocket as Earnshaw briefly backgrounded my interest.

'So you wanna write the big story,' Pinker scowled through the cigarette now glued to a protruding lower lip.

'Well, I'd like to find out what it all means before I write anything,' I said a little flustered.

'Well mister, you've come to the right place,' he said rudely, adding sharply: 'Sit down.'

Pinker's face was thrown into sharp relief by the unapologetic light hanging over the table. He was a big man, barrel-chested and barely able to sit comfortably behind the small table. He wore a black woollen sweater drilled with ragged holes at one shoulder and across the midriff, and peered out from under a grubby towelling cricket hat pushed forward onto the huge, jagged nose dominating his face. At one and the same time he sucked on the cigarette and gnawed ponderously on what I presumed was a lump of chewing gum. It was obvious neither man put much priority on hygiene. The caravan itself which had been their home for nearly two weeks, although an older model than that at Dennis Earnshaw's farm, was still in good condition.

Pinker burped rudely and pulled an ashtray, already piled high with tobacco debris, across the table between dirty plates and spilled food. He looked tired in the harsh light—deep lines etched into a gravel face. Motley hair hung dankly around his ears from under the floppy hat.'

'Dennis tells us you want to come out with us tonight,' he said rigidly as if setting a tightly sprung trap.

'Yes, I do,' I said, already tiring of the unnecessary antagonism that struck me as somewhat theatrical.

'Well, as I said to Dennis, he's the boss. This is Dennis's caper and if he says you go, you go,' Pinker said, dropping ash onto a china saucer. He pushed his cap forward over his eyes and leaned back as if to sleep. 'So I guess you go,' he said stiffly.

'Listen mate, if I'm going to be in your way then we'll forget it,' I said quickly. 'I don't want to push in if I am not welcome.'

'Eh, China,' he said, appearing again from under the hat.

'Dennis said you go, so you go, right?'

'Okay,' I said, 'thanks.'

'You never know—you might be the lucky charm we need,' Mick said from the warmth of a bundle of blankets under which he had quietly taken sanctuary. 'We've got to get it soon,' he continued, 'Bert's getting too bloody hard to live with'. Everyone laughed and the tension was eased.

Shortly after Earnshaw left for home and bed. He looked ragged and tired as I thanked him for his hospitality at the car. He was sincere in his reciprocal expression of thanks for my interest.

I returned to the caravan uneasy about the night ahead with my strange new bedfellows, but buoyed by the rapid progress of the day's events. For an hour I made my way gingerly through a disjointed conversation with Pinker. Mick said very little, only stirring from the bunk once to make us a pot of tea, poured into chipped old cups. Yet another smouldering cigarette sent a thin tracer of smoke up past an eternally squinting eye as he poured the brew. Then he climbed back onto the bed, a cup in one hand, the cigarette still fixed to his face.

Finally I touched the soft underbelly of Pinker's enmity when conversation stumbled onto the question of kangaroo hunting in the north. Thereafter, Pinker enthusiastically told me the story of the two men's long partnership—one, a crack shot and the other a life-long friend who rarely left his side. I listened intently as Pinker began to unwind, my interest only marginally requiring embroidery to continue disarming his suspicion. Pinker had been a hunter all his life, the son of a hunter and of a family of hunters, an experienced bushman who lived near Geraldton. When the talk got around to rifles, Pinker pulled from its cover the .243 that was obviously the most important thing in his life. His eyes were shining from the moment he lifted it respectfully onto the bench to clean and oil it. When Mick stirred from his slumber and mumbled something about making a move to the outside, Pinker was more relaxed and I had overcome an obstacle I would rather have done without. Mick left the caravan to prepare the flat topped utility for the night's outing.

'Bert, tell me, why did you come here?" I asked as he slipped the oiled rifle carefully back into its cover.

'I heard Dennis was having a bit of trouble over here so I rang him and asked if he'd let me come down for a couple of weeks to see what I could do' he said, awkwardly pulling on a mud speckled wind cheater in the confined space behind the table.

'Yes, but why are you here? What's the interest for you? You aren't being paid for this, are you?' Pinker looked at me across the table and stabbed his smoke out. Staring into the improvised ashtray he said soft: 'There's things you've just got to do, you know. My Pa is the best shot I ever saw and I've seen a bit. My older brother is the same. Maybe now we're both better than Pa, but we never have him on because he's Pa.' Pinker began rolling another cigarette.

'A couple of years ago me and me younger brother were out hunting, doing some target shooting in the bush. We were staring down the sights of our rifles to see who could hit a spot in a tree the closest, when we saw something move in the scrub. He seen it and I seen it . . . we both had it in our sights but neither of us fired. And then it was gone.'

'What was it Bert?' I asked. The hunter grunted.

'If it had been a fox or a dog it would have been dead with two big holes in its guts but neither of us fired. I never seen anything like it.' Pinker ran an immense hand over the week-old stubble on his face and snorted.

'I don't know what it was,' he said slowly. 'I just dunno.' There was a long silence and then he looked hard at me, a deliberate cold face. 'I just don't know what it was but I do know it's out there,' he said shifting his stare to the open doorway. There was bewilderment in his eyes.

I sat without speaking as he slid out from the table, and stooping under the low doorway, went down the stairs into the night air.

'Where are you Mick, you old bastard?' he yelled.

I remained at the table for a long while as the two began preparing the truck. It occurred to me to pull out a pad and make some notes. I decided I didn't need it.

🐾 🐾 🐾

A kangaroo carcass with a possible broken neck.

Chapter Three

OUTSIDE BERT WAS BURIED TO THE WAIST under the bonnet of the utility, struggling to find the right battery terminal connection in the dark. When Mick brought a torch, Bert ran the lead cable for the big 100 watt spotlight out from under the secured bonnet along the truck on the passenger side. Pulling on a pair of wooly gloves over the sleeves of an old army great coat Mick heaved his portly frame with some difficulty onto the flat top and took the light from Bert.

'Come on mate, grab your coat and get off your ass,' Bert said in the caravan, gently lifting the oiled .243 from the corner where he had been cleaning it. He grabbed six ragged cushions from the bunks and outside pushed three up against the window in the ute behind the driver's seat. He carefully snuggled two .22 calibre rifles on the cushions and then wedged the other three in on top for stability.

I slipped under the cable on to the passenger seat. Bert hauled the .243 from its cover and pushed it across the front seat onto my lap.

'Ever used a rifle?' he asked.

'Ah . . . no,' I mumbled, startled to see the barrel laying across my legs. 'Is it loaded?' I queried.

'It sure is, baby,' he reassured. 'It's loaded but its safety catch is on—that doesn't mean it can't go off, though. You've got to nurse it if you want to stay in here—otherwise you ride up top. If we see anything I'll throw my door open and do the job from out the window or leaning on the door frame. Got it?'

'Yeah, 'I gulped.

'So what you've got to do apart from watching for anything in the dark is make sure the rifle doesn't bump around too much when we hit potholes—otherwise you might come home with only one foot'. Inexplicably, my left leg had developed a spontaneous bout of pins and needles.

Bert started the truck up and behind us on the table top Mick grabbed the rail with one hand, the big arc lamp firmly clamped in the other.

'All set?' Bert yelled.

'Let her go,' his compatriot called back.

The spotlight cut a pillar of brightness for hundreds of metres into the bush and far across the hillsides. As Bert reversed across the gravel driveway the light sheared onto Ross's farmhouse, illuminating its entire length. I was amazed at its power but Bert was typically nonchalant at the fierce funnel of light piercing the meadows.

'As Mick sweeps the light around just watch out for any bright lights,' Bert said. As we slowly clunked past Ross's farmhouse, high in the air invisible beads of moisture were slowly gathering in their millions.

By now Bert and Mick had a fine understanding of the local terrain—the bushman's instincts coupled with Earnshaw's outline of exactly where on the two properties sightings had been concentrated. Bert followed a number of set piece manoeuvres around the farms each night but increasingly this worried him.

'From what I can see this thing is smart—too bloody smart, he said as we motored past the railway siding and gate that led to Dennis's house.' I've just got the strong feeling that it doesn't think like a dog or a cat, or any other animal we know of, for that matter. It's almost as if it can stay one step ahead of us all the time. I just want to get close enough for the one shot, that's all. All we've seen since we've going out is the eyes a long way off, but these strange tracks are around. It's a question of outthinking it. We usually go out two or three times a night, depending on the weather. We break at around midnight the first time for a cup of coffee. But I reckon it might be on to us by now. It just sits back out there and watches us. It knows our habits by now so I think it might be time to break it up a bit—go out at different times, maybe start earlier. It's smart, all right,' Bert intoned to the darkness, his head swivelling, following the gentle sweep of the arc of light.

Occasionally the beam fell on startled stock which turned eyes onto it, reflecting back flickering diamond-like beads of multicoloured light. Cattle revealed slightly larger blue-white eyes, well spaced apart. The eyes of even tiny insects and spiders low in the grass sparkled as the light cruised past.

'The light we want is even bigger than those cattle eyes,' Bert said as we followed the light's monotonous transit around the ute.

'They're about as well spaced but much brighter and white. One thing's for sure—it'll only be one shot when the time comes. That's all I'll have—one go. If I miss I reckon no one will be able to have a second go at him. This bloke just learns too quickly.'

I looked at the bulbous face in the dark. 'Only one shot?'

The big hunter looked at me. 'I had him once and didn't even pull the trigger. He'll only give me one more chance like that and I won't shoot till I know I've got him. I could have had him before when this goes off,' he said patting the rifle our laps shared, 'I'll stop him.'

Ten minutes after leaving the farm Bert pulled off the main road at a gate. Mick jumped off the back and unlatched it so the truck could ease through into the first of many vast open paddocks in coming nights. The ute jerked its way across the ground, Bert occasionally dropping a hand to the rifle on instinct when we struck a particularly deep hole.

After hours of cruising the area Bert was beginning to become irritated by the lack of action. Apart from the usual signs of stock grazing or 'roos moving off anxiously when we approached, the light uncovered nothing out of the ordinary. Three times though we came upon dead sheep lying on their sides in the paddocks. By outward appearances it was impossible to determine how they had died. Bert and Mick rolled them over and examined their heavy woollen necks closely. The big hunter suspected they had been attacked.

'Shit, it's getting cold up here,' Mick yelled after some time. I realised the warmth of the cabin was beginning to make me feel sleepy.

'Should I give him a break?' I asked Bert.

'He wouldn't get down from up there if it was pissing down with rain,' he laughed, adding, 'but you might just hold the torch for a while so the old bloke can reload his smokes,' as he eased the truck to a standstill so I could jump out. Extricating myself from under the muzzle I climbed onto the flat top. When the ute jolted back into motion I gripped the cabin railing with the under-side of my left forearm and held the torch while Mick removed his gloves to light yet another cigarette with a pair of trembling grease-stained hands. A fat little man of about forty five, his thick thatch of black hair hung around a plump unshaven face, fashioned in ochre. His heavy-lunged wheeze was even more pronounced in the open air. Stumpy fingers, blemished by clutching thousands of cigarettes, quickly pulled the warm gloves back on.

Mick never spoke much. I suspected he was more suspicious of my interference with his work than the now talkative Bert. On the tabletop without the problem of a dust-smudged windscreen, the light seemed to give a limitless insight into the nightlife of the scrub. Foxes danced for a few steps, then turned transfixed by the light, easy targets. Bush cats— domestic tabbies gone wild—made the same fatal error. Increasingly I noticed a build up of cascading white specks clouding the view in the hall of light.

The night's journey took us to the perimeters of paddocks strewn around the farms. We searched for any erratic movement until our eyes ached. The searchlight occasionally leapt into the sky, cutting through clouds of fog before petering out, high in the dark emptiness. Back scanning the ground, the busy fragments of moisture in the air were thickening, gradually blocking our view.

'Fog,' Mick muttered with a grunt of displeasure. 'We may be getting to the end of it tonight, he yelled down to Bert. There was no reaction for some minutes. Then: 'Right boys—let's have a cup of coffee and wait till it clears,' Bert called out.

The utility picked up speed. On the tabletop the cold drilled into the marrow as we burst back towards the caravan. I ducked down behind the cabin and Mick chuckled grimly with the smouldering torch in his hand, his face pressed hard up against the onrushing squall.

The fog wasted no time in setting in once the coffee was poured and after a short drive around a nearby paddock at 5 a.m., Bert called the expedition off for the night. Visibility was no more than about twenty metres.

I curled up on one bunk in the caravan under a pile of stale smelling blankets and slept through till early morning to the sonorous background of a snoring duet.

When light crept over the tree-tops I quietly slipped out of the caravan and joined Dennis's family at the farm house for breakfast. Then it was time to head to Bunbury.

At the motel I settled down to a morning of phone calls to the Perth office, note-taking and analysis of events to date. I was somewhat disappointed by the previous night's search. Obviously I had no idea of what to expect and Bert had chastised my haste in hoping for dramatic developments. He wearily pointed out that he and Mick had spent many nights patiently cruising the bush to no avail.

'But when you see this bloke's eyes you'll know it,' he had promised. I was in two minds though about the whole affair. A preposterous time-wasting fabrication? Possibly, I thought. But then, just if . . .

Later in the afternoon I decided to grab a few hours sleep. It would be much needed in coming nights I surmised. Much later I awoke with a start. It was near dark. I had overslept and a long car trip back to the farm awaited. Showering and dressing I was quickly on the road. It was well after dark when I pulled into Ross Earnshaw's driveway. There was no light at the caravan at the back of the house and when I got there, there was no utility either.

'The buggers didn't wait,' I said.

Back on the main road I swung left, trying to anticipate where Bert would have started the night's hunt. Two miles further on I detected a trace of lamplight flashing through the trees. Soon I was adjacent to where the ebbing motion of the beam probed the blackness in sharp bursts. I pulled up and could see the utility moving fast across a field a hundred metres away. I doused the car lights and got out. Instantly I recognised Bert's and Mick's voices, near hysteria, roaring over the truck's revving engine. It was bursting around the field, pivoting here and there and changing direction at frantic speed. Both men were yelling uncontrollably.

Bert stopped the truck momentarily. All was silent but then he screamed hoarsely again 'There!', and the truck lunged forward. Nonplussed, I climbed back into my car, turned it around and across the road, pointing headlights into the paddock as a signal. The commotion died down and the ute sat quietly in the field with only the motor running. Then gradually it eased its way towards me.

'Well, you just missed some fun,' Bert yelled when he recognised my frantic waving. 'Pick you up at the farm.'

At the caravan Bert pulled up, jumped from the truck and thumped his dusty cap on the ground in a war-dance of frustration. Mick spat out obscenities and walked behind the shed to urinate.

'What happened?' I pleaded.

'What do you think happened—we saw one!' Mick yelled.

'You what?' I said in disbelief.

'We saw one and not a hundred feet away,' Mick called out.

'I grabbed the rifle,' Bert interrupted, 'but it dashed to a pile of burned tree stumps. I had to wheel around and chase it—you should have seen it move across the fucking field,' he was yelling.

'Couldn't you get a shot?' I said.

'Get a shot?' He said, exasperated. 'You should have seen it moving!'

Mick was nervously lighting a cigarette, striding around and puffing with excitement.

'What did it look like?' I said.

'Just like Den said. He's got them here all right. It was a little yellow one with the same tail they all talk about,' Bert said furiously. 'That'll be as close as anyone will need to be to bag him. Wait till Den hears about this!' The big man strode into the caravan and came back with a box of rattling bullets. 'Come on, let's go,' he said as we climbed aboard.

'Jesus,' I thought, 'why did I sleep?' Mick and I clutched the truck as Bert plunged into the inky cold.

Much later I was beginning to feel the effects of so little sleep the previous night. But there was a new tension in the hunt, an air of expectancy as the light probed on.

It was becoming hard to keep my body buoyed against the jolting for hour after hour while peering into a hypnotic darkness. It occurred to me that it would be easy for the mind to play games under such duress. The bush's shadows took on an eerie purple lustre in the starlight. Bert and Mick prattled on all night about the animal they had chased. There was a new and breathless tempo about it all.

It was nearing our midnight coffee break when I jumped off the truck to unlatch a gate. Bert drove into the paddock and as I closed the gate he drove off. I stood with my mouth ajar. He just kept going. I realised for the first time just how much a part of me the truck had become. The thought of finding my way back to the farm through a dark bush, the home of a mysterious predator, chilled my spine. Thankfully, the prankster stopped, reversed back and shoved his chuckling head out of the window to ask me if I wanted a lift to the local coffee shop. He needn't have bothered.

In a paddock later we came upon a big herd of kangaroos grazing 300 metres away. Bert could resist no longer. He stopped and carefully lifted the .243 onto the window frame of the open driver's door. In the light I could just see the vague outline of a group of "roos moving jerkily over the paddock.

'Stop, you bastard,' Bert mumbled, staring down the barrel of the primed rifle. One big buck reared up and peered into the light, mesmerised. I stopped breathing as Bert gentle squeezed. A thunder clap hammered my ears and a patch of dust exploded on the kangaroo's shoulder, hurling it backwards, whip-cracking end over end to a trembling death. Bert took to the quivering body with knife. He was also a trained butcher as the sureness of the blade demonstrated. He cut the beast virtually in half. The legs he threw onto the tabletop to be boned out later for the farms' dogs but the forequarters he carefully left attached to most of the internal organs. Sometime later he carefully planted the steamy upper body, the intestines hanging out in dull purple sacks, onto a big patch of sandy ground in the middle of a field.

'Tomorrow we'll come over this way to see what's had a feed. Should be a few tracks left on this soft stuff,' Bert said, digging his boot heel in the sand.

After a short coffee break we were out again. For the first time, even Bert complained about the cold but I could see how the past few weeks' hunting had become a narcotic for the two men. We left the public road and slipped through yet another gate in a back paddock on Ross Earnshaw's property. Bert manoeuvred through a thick patch of trees down a slope. At a break in the jarrahs I scanned the light across a paddock extending away up a distant, undulating hill. As the beam moved on the rise it picked up a sharp light.

'Stop!' I yelled, but Bert had seen it too.

'That's him,' he said starkly. The light flickered almost like a dreamy blink and was gone.

'Christ,' I yelled, 'where is it?'

'Back to the right,' Bert screamed, his control again abandoned.

'Slowly . . . . scan more to the right . . . now faster, faster,' he bellowed.

Bert jumped from the truck, priming the rifle in the air and jerking the safety catch off, ready to discharge. I made three or four broad, slow sweeps of the hill, a grey, formless horizon. Suddenly higher on the ridge the light appeared again, slightly dimmer but just as large—a stunning beacon. Then it disappeared again, like a trap snapping shut.

'He's gone over that ridge,' Bert yelled, clambering back into the truck. 'We'll get around the other side and maybe pick him up when he comes through'.

In a moment we were hurtling across the pasture towards the ridge. Then we circled to the left around and over it. I estimated the ridge's top was about 600 metres from where the light had detected the eyes. Despite surging adrenalin, I sensed it had taken us far too long to reach the ridge. Bert and Mick knew it too but we still stopped to scour the fields with the search light. A teasing, ghost like apparition had done just enough to ignite semi-hysteria in us. Bert tried to plot its movements from the direction it appeared to be travelling but it was clear that it was long gone from close proximity. After cruising the hill for about an hour we stopped for a parley.

'So that was it,' I said, eagerly accepting for the first time one of Mick's roughly-hewn cigarettes to explore its fascination.

'That was him all right,' Bert said pensively.

'It was bright, as you said it would be, but if that was the animal's eyes, why did it appear there was only the one light?' I asked.

'I reckon that's what happens when you catch the eyes in the light and the head is partially turned—that's why the colour of the eyes seems to vary a bit. The giveaway that time though was the second sighting. I reckon it snuck a look at us, ducked its head and got going. It headed for the top of the rise and then it just glanced around on the run to check us out before going over the hill. It was him for sure.'

'Knew you'd bring us luck,' Mick piped in, for once drawn from his citadel of stony silence.

'Jesus, it's starting to bug me,' Bert then said. 'We go out night after night and don't get near a thing. Then within a couple of hours we chase a baby around a paddock and then mumma comes out of the woodwork to check us over.'

'You think the one you chased in the truck was a young one then?'
I asked.

'Yeah,' Bert said. 'It was small, and dumb too. It shouldn't have let us get as close as we did like that. We just stumbled over it. Had to be a young one. And I bet that was the old lady just come to make sure we weren't causing any trouble,' he added punching the dark over his right shoulder with a thumb.

The rest of the night fell into the pattern of the previous. A heavy fog settled in and we lurched back to the caravan at about 5 a.m. Despite the fact that we were all very tired I slept for only two hours and walked again to Dennis's farm for breakfast. I had to make a decision about how long I could stay away from the mounting duties in the Perth office. I decided I could not afford to leave the story for at least two more days, and issued instructions for the running of the office by phone from the farmhouse. I then rang the central office of *The Australian*, located in Sydney, and explained the background to events as they were unfolding. My superiors expressed great interest in running a story on the phenomenon, so shortly after lunch I filed a lengthy news story by telephone direct to Sydney, for use in the following day's paper.

Later that afternoon Bert, Mick and I drove Dennis to the scenes of the action. Bert found what he claimed were feline footprints at the base of a charcoaled tree stump where the panic-stricken animal had taken cover during the wild chase in the paddock. The marks were distorted but the hunter was adamant they resembled nothing he had ever found in his years in the bush. When we found the spot where the light had detected the eyes, the great distance across the paddock up the slope made nonsense of the suggestion that we had detected the smaller eyes of foxes or sheep.

Dennis Earnshaw had been talking to local Agriculture Protection Board Officers who had informed him that Department doggers would be sent out to camp over near Darkan, the tiny town sited on the railway line a few kilometres from the Earnshaw farms. He had also been told that the well-known wildlife expert and television celebrity, Harry Butler, had been invited to come into the area and examine the matter of the mysterious stock deaths.

During the afternoon, Dennis also informed me his father was heading back to Bunbury after staying a few days in the luxurious caravan at the rear of the farmhouse. He suggested that I might move into the caravan, obviating the need to travel back and forward from the coast. I accepted the offer but decided that as I had to go back to the Bunbury motel to pick up my effects, I would spend the night there and miss that evening's hunt. I wanted to write a feature article for the paper on the background of the phenomenon and I had so little sleep in the last few days that I doubted whether I could get back for the night's exercise. I headed for Bunbury, intent on getting a solid night's rest and returning the next morning.

And on that morning *The Australian* published my story on the front page. Under the headline: "Is the Killer Cat a Feral Puma?" the story read:

> *Farmers in the south of Western Australia are convinced they are on the verge of overturning one of the basic laws of Australian ecology—that the bush has no big cats.*
>
> *More and more experts are now questioning that hypothesis in the face of evidence coming in from thousands of square kilometres stretching from Koorda, 240 km north-east of Perth down as far as Esperance on the coast near the Great Australian Blight.*
>
> *Regular all-night hunting expeditions are threading their way through thousands of hectares of bush looking for signs of big cats, said to resemble the American puma, whose existence has yet to be established as scientific fact. The hunters, however, many of whom claim to have seen the cats at one time or another, are adamant that it is now only a question of time.*
>
> *Professional dingo hunters from the State Department of Fisheries and Wildlife have also set up camps and this week it is believed wildlife expert Harry Butler will join the search.*
>
> *Other state departments will make enquiries to determine what the mystery animals may be and how they got into the bush.*

I have just spent four days travelling an area inland from Perth to Darkan, then west to Bunbury on the coast, talking to property owners, hunters, slaughtermen, zoo keepers and local authorities about the cats.

Everywhere the story was the same.

Details of contacts with large wild felines were identical and there have been so many sightings claimed that even the most cynical locals agree there must be something out there.

Property owners are losing hundreds of head of sheep, costing them thousands of dollars and dozens of lambs have disappeared without trace.

According to locals, all the lost stock died of broken necks and trackers showed me varying sized paw prints which they claimed were those of large feline animals standing up to a metre high at the shoulder.

I saw many of these pug marks around dozens of sites of sheep kills in the region.

The State Minister for Fisheries and Wildlife, Mr MacKinnon, said last week: 'Quite obviously from reports I have received there is a phantom animal or animals of some kind plaguing stock in the south west.'

However his Department stands by claims that feral cats, domestic cats gone wild, or bush dogs are killing the sheep. I spent three nights on a utility truck with armed hunters searching the scrub and gum tree forests regions in the Shire of West Arthur.

Twice the hunter's spotlights detected the large yellow eyes of indeterminate animals moving fast through the bush some distance away.

And on one occasion the hunters chased what they described as a catlike yellow animal at close range through an open paddock while I watched from a vantage point 100 metres away.

The story concluded.

As I drove into Dennis Earnshaw's property that morning I was startled to see a news car from Perth's Channel 7 television station parked at the house. Inside chatting to Dennis were John Collis, one of the station's leading reporters, and his cameraman, Brian Dunn. My story had created great interest in Perth that morning.

Some months earlier Collis had worked on the cat story without much result and had come to a verbal arrangement with Dennis Earnshaw that if any inexplicable felines were killed on the property, Channel 7 would have exclusive rights to film it. The sum involved was so small as to be virtually meaningless—so much so that it completely undermined the possible argument that the Earnshaws were promoting a fabrication for their own financial reward. Collis informed me that the article had created a certain amount of interest in Perth including a great deal of speculation on various radio programmes. The fact that *The Australian* had given prominence to the farmers' claims had started a reassessment in Western Australia of their significance.

Collis, a likeable reporter whom I'd met on previous local assignments, said he believed more media people would be in the area in coming days to follow up the article. He had rushed down because of his previous interest in the story. After a short trip to Cordering a year or so earlier when he had met the Earnshaws Channel 7 had run a brief television interview with the young farmers. I was initially pleased by the response to my story but alarmed at the thought that newspaper reporters from our competition could soon be arriving. When it became clear that Channel 7 had tied up the film rights, I privately spoke to Dennis Earnshaw about the still photographic rights. We came to an arrangement that in the event of a kill on his property, *The Australian* should have exclusive world rights to the still photographs for a week, after which other media groups could have access. The deal was authorised by my editor after we had agreed on a price, which again, amounted to a virtual token gesture.

Earnshaw had lost over $3000 in lambs that season alone and his concern at the growing losses was very real. Overwhelmingly though, my interest, demonstrated in our agreement, was an article of faith indicating I was genuinely concerned about what the farmers were saying. I still privately harboured massive doubts about the claim that big cats were rampaging through the bush but I could come to no definite conclusion. Professionally I was determined to maintain interest until it became clear that the story was definitely flawed. I was frankly pleased that the money was not important to Earnshaw who certainly could have negotiated a much larger sum particularly from the prosperous Perth television organisation. Our agreement meant more to Earnshaw than financial reward but he was probably also grateful to have a few hundred dollars towards meeting his costs if and when the story broke with a kill. A strong question of pride seemed to be involved for Dennis Earnshaw, who increasingly struck me as a man of considerable moral principle.

John Collis shared my fascination with the story. He was even further captivated when the events of the previous evening were outlined. It was his intention to join us on that night's hunt if it could be arranged. And I was frankly happy to have more media people involved as long as they weren't reporters from the opposition papers. I needed to bounce ideas off Collis and watch his reactions to the myriad questions that needed answers.

Earnshaw was again concerned about whether Bert Pinker would tolerate two more intruding hitchhikers, this time complete with camera and sound equipment. After lunch we drove to Ross's farm to awaken the hunters. They had apparently been out all night and had not spoken to Earnshaw since their return in the early hours to their caravan. Heavy black rainclouds were clumped high in the sky in the east as we approached the caravan where Pinker was standing bootless despite the moist ground underfoot.

He was furious. The previous night he had taken his gamble and lost. Mick had sighted what appeared to be a large feline animal in a spotlight 200 metres from the truck. Bert had squeezed off that one shot. And he had no body to show for it.

'Did you hit it, though? Earnshaw asked, his voice instantly disappointed.

'Of course I hit it,' Bert said, unconvincingly. 'It stood there looking at us—we could see the eyes and I could detect the shape of its body in the brush. I got it in the sights and dropped the barrel just under the eyes to get the chest, then fired. I hit it—I'm sure I hit it. I could see it tumble backwards through the smoke with that big tail going everywhere,' Bert said, now apologetically pursuing Earnshaw's approval. 'I'm sure I saw it get up, then stagger sideways and then go again. But if I hit it where I thought I did, it should be dead by now. It was the .243 and that rifle would kill an elephant'.

Bert was clearly in no mood to be introduced to the TV crew but later we all climbed onto the tabletop and he took us to where he had made the shot. It was raining gently as we circled the 200 metres from the gully where he had pulled the trigger to the timberline where the spotlight had found the shadow. Bert and Dennis searched the brush for a sign while apprehensive members of the fourth estate looked on. Although it had drizzled steadily through the night Bert was insistent there should be blood. A high velocity projectile at such short range would cause an ugly wound and almost certainly be fatal within hours. Then on a small piece of bark Dennis found one quite distinct large spot of blood. Bert was certain it was from the cat but the lack of more stains worried me.

'The only thing I can think of is that I hit him in the shoulder instead of the chest and it went through the heavy muscle then without striking bone,' Bert said.

'So why didn't the shock of it stop him?' Dennis asked, his agitation veiling a deep frustration. 'If the bullet went through him though, then maybe it's lodged in a tree or something,' he added, looking around. His uncle, Ron, was already at work with a pen-knife in a jarrah tree another 50 metres into the brush, directly on line from where Bert said he had fired.

Sometime later he dug from the tree the projectile, turned inside out and flattened, indicating it had, in fact, hit a solid object before it crashed into the bark. Dennis sat in the truck and over the two-way, radioed his wife at the farm. Within minutes Henny was making phone calls and soon dozens of locals began appearing in a snaking trail of vehicles, converging from farms all over the district. Most of them were armed and after an hour 30 men spread out at wide intervals to begin a one-line procession search through the bush, seeking a dead or wounded animal.

In principle, the search idea had appeared a good one, but once we began plodding into the thick timber country many of us became a little uneasy. The prospect of being suddenly confronted by a wounded animal of some size enthused no one. Few of the men spoke as we stepped out the march. And the further we walked, the more we became separated from our neighbours, splaying outwards in the denseness. It was becoming increasingly difficult to see one another through the forest. John Collis and his cameraman walked along behind, filming the exercise, but I decided early to stay close to Bert, or, at least, Bert's .243. Walking about three metres behind him as silently as possible I stooped to arm myself with a hefty lump of timber. Once he stopped and looked around with a nervous grin on his face as another twig cracked under my clumsy feet.

'Never spent much time in the bush, have you?' he said, putting a stiff index finger to pouting lips.

A little further along he half stumbled when a log moved under his foot. In a furious flurry a fat red fox dashed out of the log, just feet from our path. Pinker swung around, his rifle hip-high. He looked momentarily shaken, then expelled a chest-full of air loudly through his mouth as the fox galloped off. For the first time I was genuinely alarmed whether we were doing the right thing. I also felt like an absolute fool with a big chunk of wood in my hand. Nevertheless I kept a firm grasp on it.

Dennis Earnshaw was now unsteadily making his way through the bush a few metres to the right of Bert. We began moving over towards him. After a short chat they decided to call the search off as no one had reported anything even vaguely resembling a track, let alone a bloodied animal's body. After nearly an hour the word was passed along to head back. The terrain was becoming heavily impregnated with ragged granite outcrops and one of the farmers was talking about a group of cave structures built into a hill further into the bush. No one ever went there, he said. It occurred to me that sort of rocky land fitted the common image of the mountainous home of the American cougar.

Back at the vehicles, the farmers began dispersing. Collis and I had diplomatically resisted the temptation to press some of them on their feelings about the animal. They were stiff-faced country folk, warm when they warmed up and obviously wary of the media. We had no desire to offend people who had given up their time on a busy working day to join a fruitless hunt at a moment's notice. It was interesting, however, to realise just how effectively the bush telegraph of the region worked.

Dennis took me back to his farm where I filed a follow-up story to that morning's front page article and a lengthy feature piece backgrounding the whole issue. Collis, Dunn and I were guests of the Earnshaw's for dinner during which conversation rarely left one fascinating subject.

Later in the caravan at Ross's farm we were busily pulling on as many clothes as we had with us prior to the evening's frosty outing. John Collis was mesmerised.

'I've only just realised the ramifications of this story—God only knows what will happen if these jokers shoot something,' he marvelled.

In the end the best thing Collis and Dunn had going for them was their sophisticated film and sound equipment. Bert looked put out at the suggestion that more media people were along for the ride but Dunn cheekily pointed out that there would be more light when film was being shot. The big hunter reluctantly agreed.

Unfortunately, the night proved to be uneventful. Only once did we sight any large eyes in the underbrush, although we found numerous dead and mangled sheep. Many of the bodies were virtually unmarked but obviously had been killed by blows which broke their necks. There was always very little sign of any struggle.

At around 3 a.m. we returned to the hunter's caravan and thence to bed. Dunn won the comfortable double bed in Dennis's caravan in a three-way toss of the coin. Collis and I made do with improvised single bunks in the section of the caravan compartment which doubled by day as a mini loungeroom. Despite our exhaustion Collis and I lay awake for hours talking out every aspect of the mystery. We struggled to remain as objective as possible but we could come to no more solid conclusion than that the story offered one of the most perplexing and fascinating episodes either of us had encountered in our careers.

As we slept through the early morning, thousands of copies of *The Australian* were being distributed in Perth and elsewhere around the nation. On page 3 the paper carried a story under the headline: 'Big Cat Hunter Claims a Hit,' which read:

Hunters were scouring a small area of south-western Australia last night after apparently having shot and wounded a mysterious catlike animal which has been stalking stock in the area.

Local property owners and marksmen intensified their search after the near kill early yesterday.

A West Australian hunter, Mr Bert Pinker, who has been heading the hunt for about 12 days, wounded an animal from a range of 200 m with a high-powered rifle.

But although traces of blood were found the animal, which the hunters say resembles an American puma, could not be tracked.

Late last night teams of hunters were combing two properties in the Cordering region about 230 km from Perth.

Hunters have been using powerful searchlights for more than a week in an effort to locate the mysterious animal in the dense bush.

Sightings of unusually large white eyes, believed to belong to the cat, have been made almost nightly.

But Mr Pinker's shot was the first attempt by any of the hunters to kill the animal.

He said yesterday the hunt was being made difficult because Australians had no experience of hunting big cats.

'I've been in the bush all my life and I've never seen anything like this,' he said.

Reports of big cat sightings are commonplace in this vast area of south-western Australia.

The hunters believe that Mr Pinker's shot may have struck the animal in the shoulder without killing it.

They think it is one of the five which inhabit the area where the shot was fired. Rain showers during the afternoon made tracking difficult.

Wildlife expert Harry Butler is expected to be in the Cordering area tomorrow to investigate the reported cat sightings.

Elsewhere in the paper *The Australian* also ran a detailed fifty paragraph feature story on the Cordering stock losses, the farmer's claims and the controversial explanation. Within hours the impact in television, radio and newspaper newsrooms around the nation, and especially in Perth, was dramatic.

🐾 🐾 🐾

A kangaroo shooter takes aim on Dennis Earnshaw's property.

Chapter Four

I WAS SITTING IN HENNY'S SUNLIT KITCHEN trying to work out my next move. Her husband was working busily around the farm and Collis and Dunn were out shooting some background film in the bush. I needed another angle to sustain interest in the story. Thankfully, my superiors in Sydney were enthusiastic about keeping it running but they kept asking me why one of the animals could not be shot or caught. To that I had no answer.

Then something Earnshaw had mentioned to me and which Graham MacKinnon has referred to in his press release jumped into my mind—the question of a circus accident in the south-west. I decided to make enquiries from the farm about when and where such an accident was alleged to have occurred. I contacted my office in Perth to check that all was in order and took down a number of telephone numbers of Government departments and agencies that conceivably could know about such an incident.

When I had rung off the phone began buzzing. Over the next few hours Dennis Earnshaw talked to radio stations and newspaper reporters calling from around the country. He was jubilant. *The Australian's* story had created nationwide interest and the farmer was well pleased that people were listening to what he had to say rather than just scoffing.

I decided the best place to start would be at the top—with the man responsible for the Agriculture Protection Board, the State Minister for Agriculture, Mr Dick Old. I rang his office and talked to his press liaison man, John Lawson. An affable friendly man, Lawson gently ribbed me about stirring up nonsense in the bush, but when I put to him the question of a possible circus accident, he suggested I contact the Agriculture Protection Board direct. He recommended the Board's Executive Director, Mr Dick Tomlinson, and gave me his office number.

Tomlinson was equally approachable though similarly sceptical about the cat story. He said he had no personal recollection of any reported accident at the time suggested, in a career with the Agriculture Protection Board which extended back to the Board's establishment in the 1950s. Tomlinson assured me he would make enquiries of his people and come back to me at the farm as quickly as possible. Within an hour the phone rang.

'I've checked with officers in my department,' he said, ' and there is some indication that a circus accident could have occurred in the south-west in the early sixties.'

I was stunned. ' Could you say that again?' I spluttered.

Tomlinson hesitated at my obvious astonishment. ' Yes, one of our former regional officers down there, John McSwain, believes there could have been some kind of accident around the time you suggested,' he said.

I asked him about McSwain's recollection.

'The problem is that it's so long ago,' Tomlinson said, 'but he has a vague recollection of some talk in the area about an accident. He didn't investigate it himself—as I say he just had a vague recollection about it. He said the rumour involved a circus vehicle that was supposed to have collided with a car.'

'Where's McSwain now?' I asked.

'He's now based in the Department in Perth but he can't remember any of the details, as I said.'

I asked Tomlinson whether official documents were in existence which referred to such an event. Had McSwain filed a report? There had apparently been no need because it was not his responsibility.

'As I said, it was only a rumour that he had some vague recollection about,' Tomlinson said.

'What about Agriculture Protection Board documents on the movements of circus animals around the state?'

He replied that all such documents had been culled from the records prior to 1965. ' We just can't go on keeping all sorts of minor records for ever, you know.'

'Then what of Federal Government documents presumably covering the movement of animals between states or on entry to the country—quarantine papers, for example?' Tomlinson replied that these too had been culled prior to 1965.

'So in effect, you're telling me that there are no documents in existence relating to the movements of animals in the early sixties?' I said. He replied, somewhat pensively, in the affirmative, and insisted he could find no one else in his Department who had any information on the reported accident. I was flabbergasted by the development. It appeared that I was suddenly on the verge of a major story. Not only were regional Agriculture Protection Board officials not informed of an accident involving the possible escape of dangerous animals, but all records that could conceivably throw light on the incident appeared to have been destroyed.

On the basis of the Tomlinson conversation I immediately filed a news story to the paper for use on the following day. It was potentially the most significant development thus far.

Collis and Dunn returned later to prepare for the night's hunt. They brought with them the disturbing news that, according to some of the locals, there were other reporters snooping around the region. I realised my newspaper competition was closing in.

After dinner, Dennis Earnshaw had to drive to Collie on business and Collis, Dunn and I drove to Ross Earnshaw's farm. On arrival at the caravan we were disturbed to find the shed surrounded by a battery of news cars. Reporters from two newspapers—*The West Australian* and its stablemate, *The Daily News*—a full camera and sound crew as well as a reporter from Collis's opposition, television station Channel 9, and sundry other regional press people were awaiting us. Collis began mumbling expletives as we climbed from the car.

Poor Bert Pinker was under siege from two of the reporters who were insisting they should accompany the hunting vehicle that night. He was making the point that it was not his responsibility to say who could go and who couldn't but his truck obviously couldn't accommodate the swelling crowd. One of the reporters was being decidedly insistent and his demeanour quickly degenerated into offensiveness when we arrived. Collis was in no mood to be polite when he saw the opposition camera crew standing by, ready to shoot film. He had that contract with Earnshaw for the film of any kill made on the property and he bluntly made the fact known. I pointed out to the newspapermen that I, likewise, had an agreement with the property owner covering still photographs.

The argument that ensued became quite heated. One individual claimed the media had a right to any breaking story—it could not be confined to any one group. That, of course, would have been the argument I would have used had the circumstances been reversed. However, I calmly pointed out it would not be safe to overload one vehicle with so many people, complete with cameras and sound gear, while loaded rifles were in use. And if it was their intention to use their own vehicles to tag along I suggested they see the property owner about getting permission.

Our whole stand, of course, was extremely tenuous, but all's fair in love and the newspaper business. By this time I had put in so many sleepless nights I was becoming defensive about a story which had only exploded into life through my efforts. The "intruders" then stormed off up the drive to Ross Earnshaw's farmhouse and dragged the unfortunate young man from his evening meal into a nasty argument. In his brother's absence it fell to him to authorise any more enquiries on their land.

' I came down here to get a story and I'm going to get one,' one of the press men asserted with charming directness.

' And I want some news film of the hunt,' a television crewman added.

While amicable, Ross Earnshaw was much more reserved than his brother. He was clearly out of his depth with a cadre of hostile journalists trained in foot-in-the-door techniques of extracting information, explanation or authorisation. He insisted however he could make no decision about permitting new people on the Earnshaw properties until his brother returned later that night. And that was when Bert Pinker stood up from one of the heavy grain sacks on which he had been seated, puffing away quietly in the shed near the caravan.

'Listen,' he said, addressing one of the more pugnacious of the rabble. 'You blokes get all your gear on the back of that truck. We're going hunting.'

Pinker walked along the side of the truck to hook up the lights to the car battery, past where Collis and I stood, stunned. As he walked back again, a wink flashed from under that ever-present towelling hat.

'We'll go out and get you some terrific pictures of the hunters in action and you can write some words,' he said loudly, prompting the interlopers to clutter hurriedly aboard the utility with their tripods, camera gear, film boxes and sound equipment. Collis began to object as they made themselves comfortable on the truck, but Pinker slammed the driver's door shut and smiled cheerily through the window as he threw the vehicle into gear and the scrambling batch of newcomers nearly off the back. Collis was livid but I calmed him, urging him to leave it to Bert. Mick threw the light switch on the hand-held spotlight and they drove off. I had been concerned at the direction the confrontation was taking. We were on very shaky ground, openly objecting to other media groups' right to a story.

A short time later the truck came to a standstill by the caravan and Pinker politely ordered a gaggle of wind-blown reporters off the back. On it lay yet another dead sheep found in a nearby paddock. As the newsmen disembarked he attacked the body with a knife, slashing through its heavy woollen neck, skinning it carefully to expose the throat. The entire neck region was blackened and bruised from the jaw to the shoulder.

'Another one with a broken neck,' Pinker said quietly as the photographers snapped away. He pulled the bloodied body from the truck and dumped it under cover in the shed before climbing into the caravan to clean up. Then he walked past Collis and myself and out of the corner of his mouth said simply, 'Get on.'

Within moments the old firm was back in action wheeling up the driveway for the night's hunt to the dismay of a furious group of news-hounds at the caravan, watching us depart. Bert had taken them for a short burst around the farm, stopping occasionally to allow them to take pictures and "can" some live action film.

'No way was I going to let them rude bastards come with us tonight,' he said. 'You blokes have been putting all this time into it night after night and when things start to hot up they butt in, demanding to be in on it. All they wanted to do was push us around and tell us what to do. Anyway, I needed Dennis's permission to authorise it,' Pinker said, giggling. 'Left ém floundering, didn't we?'

I was concerned with the ethics of such a confrontation and whether there could result a backlash against my employer. But in the end my primary aim was to get exclusive stories and I believed we were on the verge of a breakthrough. Unfortunately, though, it didn't come that night.

After many hours of slowly coursing through the bush we could find no eyes blinking back at us from the glare of the spotlight. Tired and very jaded, we trooped to our makeshift beds and in the warmth of the caravan I again pulled off the old pair of football socks that provided just enough defence against the blistering cold while we jousted with a shadow.

The next morning we had more visitors—this time Bert Pinker's younger brother, Brett, and a few of his friends.

I was concerned, as was Collis, with the lack of developments. My bosses, like his, were worried that the story was fading; that unless we could produce some hard evidence it could appear we were doing nothing more than chasing myths with a bunch of crazy farmers. I was also very tired after the night hunts which required a great deal of concentration and little sleep, as well as the pressure of meeting the paper's deadlines during the day. Collis and I decided that night would be the last we could afford to spend in the region if nothing eventuated. Much as we hated to admit it, the story was flagging and there was much to be attended to in Perth.

That night showed signs of becoming a shooting gallery contest between Bert, who was himself very tired, and his brother, a brash, smaller version of the older man, with a similarly fervent love of rifles. Brett was staying with friends at a nearby property for a few days. They practised popping stones off fence posts in the evening, ostensibly to adjust their sights but, in fact, as something of a lark.

A pair of obviously close brothers, testing their skills against rocks and trees, however, was doing nothing in the cause of explaining the phenomenon. I was beginning to have serious doubts about the whole mechanism of these nightly excursions. It occurred to me as the brothers blazed away that there wouldn't be a fox, kangaroo, mountain lion, or any other animal for that matter, within miles of the racket. And the beam of light seemed to me to be something of a mistake. Pinker often mumbled fearfully about the intelligence he perceived in the predator's behaviour through its tracks and the occasional glimpses of eyes.

After the shoot-out was resolved to Bert's delight, we were noisily travelling along the main road atop the ute when the driver suddenly yelled out and hit the brakes. Reversing the truck, he leaned out the window, looking hard over the yellow gravel by the roadside. He jumped out and, circling around a piece of the wash, knelt in the light. There, etched into the ground were distinct animal footprints up to 5 cm across. Something had gone across the road in front of the oncoming vehicle and after close inspection Pinker pronounced that the tracks were minutes old. An animal passed in front of the light literally moments before we had cruised by and the explanation was obvious. On the right hand side of the roadway from where the animal had come extended an open field over many hundred metres in all directions. On the left was a labyrinthine forest of jarrah tree denseness.

'The bloody thing could see us coming and realised it would be safer in there than on that open ground when we drove by,' Pinker said, pointing into the black tangle.

During a slow night, in which fatigue and the cold were becoming increasingly difficult adversaries to ward off, I left the warm cabin for a spell on watch on the flat-top with the others. With six people aboard at any one time it was very cramped, the priority being to find a place of cabin frame to hold on. At one stage I was leaning over the side of the truck over the passenger seat. My legs were very tired and I occasionally dropped my left leg over the door to generate circulation. Every now and then I noticed I was bumping something with my foot. I glanced down and realised I had been kicking the barrel of Brett Pinker's loaded .22 Hornet rifle, complete with heavy duty barrel. He was snoozing in the darkened cabin with Bert, the rifle rearing from between his legs and its barrel protruding from the window. It was, of course, loaded and powerful enough to blow my foot off. It occurred to me that there was enough fire-power on the truck to set up a lucrative small armaments business.

Once during the night we detected the big give-away eyes in the dark. Far away on another fence line there was suddenly that distinct, slow blinking motion. After a mad dash across the paddock Bert and Brett gingerly approached the fence, slipped over it and crept tentatively into heavy woods on the other side as far as the funnel of light overhead from the table top could extend. After an hour's search they returned, walking forlornly out of the scrub, the rifles hanging at their sides as limp as our spirits.

The next morning another story appeared in *The Australian*. It read:

> *The West Australian Government has conceded that a travelling circus was involved in a traffic accident in the south-west of the State in the early 1960s, strengthening theories that escaped cougars may have bred in the area. The admission came yesterday from the State's Agriculture Protection Board as the hunt for a mysterious cat-like animal was continuing about 80 km from the reported accident site. Property owners are searching large areas of bushland in the Cordering region, 230 km south-west of Perth, after a hunter reportedly shot and wounded a large cat-like animal early on Monday morning. The Director of the A.P.B., Mr. Dick Tomlinson, said that a former regional officer in the*

*Bridgetown area north-east of Cordering remembers a
circus accident sometime early in the 1960s. The Officer,
Mr John McSwain, reported that he recollected a circus
vehicle colliding with a private car. One of the circus's
elephants had to be used to pull a vehicle out of a ditch. Mr
Tomlinson said Mr McSwain had had a 'vague recollection'
about the accident, but said no official documents relating
to it existed.*

Despite the excellent coverage *The Australian* had been giving my
material, it became clear I had to give up the chase for the moment and
return to Perth where my office duties were beckoning. Collis and Dunn
also decided to leave, sharing with me a rankling sense of frustration.
On a slow car trip back to town I was bedevilled by a feeling that I could
have been wasting my time pursuing something which had only grown
out of a confounding community hysteria. After all I had not seen any
real, incontrovertible evidence of a mountain lion's existence. All I had
were people's words for what they believed they had seen - ambiguous
footprints and the deaths of stock and kangaroos. The evidence was
entirely circumstantial. But I was haunted by what I perceived as the
integrity of the people I'd met and their apparent sincerity. For the
moment a host of questions remained unanswered.

Some days later in Perth I decided to pursue the matter with the
various authorities involved. I again called the Agriculture Minister's
office and arranged with pressman, John Lawson, to talk with Mr Old.
A lean and greying, somewhat dapper man, Dick Old had been leader of
his party since 1974. The member for the Katanning electorate, he had
been a farmer and successful businessman since leaving the R.A.A.F. after
service in the war. As party leader he was suffering a major constitutional
crisis inside the National Party which in later months split it wide open
in Western Australia and led to the defection of the lay president and
three leading M.P.'s who formed a separate, rural-based political group.
The reason for the party split, which was of great concern to the Party's
federal leaders including Deputy Prime Minister Doug Anthony, was Mr
Old's alleged subservience to his coalition partner, Liberal party leader,

Sir Charles Court. The charge against Old was that he and his lieutenants in the parliamentary party had failed to pursue the interest of country people if it contravened the expressed will of the senior coalition partner on certain issues. The rebel political group later called itself the National Country Party platform in the bush. Its three MPs held their seats in the '80 election, so setting the scene for a period of instability for Dick Old in country areas and for Sir Charles Court in Government. The Government's majority was reduced in that election and the National Party MPs showed themselves willing to vote against the Government in parliament on key issues. Old, of course, bitterly rejected the criticism of him from the first, and on my return to Perth from the country I decided to use the question of the growing political split to set up an interview in which I could also ask him about the cat mystery.

We sat informally on a luxurious lounge in his spacious downtown Perth office suite overlooking the city and the river. Clothes hung elegantly on Old's slim frame but there was something fragile about him. He was clearly a politician under great strain and he stonewalled on most of the political questions during the interview. Once that discussion was out of the way I said I wanted to talk about a matter in which I knew he had taken a personal interest. I briefly outlined my involvement of recent weeks. Old confirmed his interest in the matter, and said that following his recent visit to Earnshaw's farm he believed that there was a strong element of substance in the farmers' claims. It was clear that a predator was killing stock, but as far as offering an explanation, he had no comment.

'Look, I appreciate that these people are farmers who know everything there is to know about their own environment. When they say something is wrong you have to listen to them. But unless they come up with some substantial evidence we can't do anything. Now if they shoot one . . . well that's a different story,' he said, more animated. The Minister was clearly being very cautious. I asked him about the attitudes of other members of the Government, in particular, the Minister for Fisheries and Wildlife, Mr MacKinnon. I had been informed by various Government officials that Mr MacKinnon had been privately scathing in his criticism of the theory. Old carefully responded by saying that there were 'some members' of the Government who were brave enough to openly scoff at the story.

'But I prefer to keep an open mind,' he said. Like most shrewd politicians, it was more his options than his mind he was keeping open. As I began to make my departure Old's attitude curiously seemed to mellow.

'Look, you've asked me to be frank about this and I think I have been,' he said in a more familiar tone. 'I know you've been looking into it but I'd appreciate if you would keep me informed personally of any new developments.' The request struck me as unusual but I assured him that I would keep in touch. With all the facilities available for him the Minister for Agriculture was asking me to keep him informed? Perhaps it amounted to a professional compliment. Or was there an element of politicking involved?

Outside Old's office I asked John Lawson what he thought of the cat theory. 'A lot of rubbish,' he said, his face smothered in a broad smile. 'If there are all these things running around, how come no-one has shot one? It's not as if that area of the state is empty, like desert. Why haven't people seen these things all the time? Somebody down there is just making up whoppers,' Lawson said.

Some days later I rang Dennis Earnshaw and he informed me there had been more sightings in the region. There was also a report circulating that a circus vehicle had spent time at an engineering works in Bridgetown in the early 1960s while welding repairs were made to a cage door. As well, A.P.B. officers had been visiting the area regularly, requesting the locals to pass on any sample of hair or droppings found in the bush which they believed were from the predator. Earnshaw also informed me that he had ordered from the United States a sophisticated piece of military hardware in the form of a night scope which, when attached to a rifle or camera, would allow the user to virtually see in the dark. He said he had been in touch with Dick Old about the matter and that the Minister had told him there was a possibility that the government would later purchase the expensive scope once the cat matter had been resolved.

That week Mr Old's office released to the media a press statement which read:

Western Australia's "cougar hunters" will be aided by modern military technology in the near future, when a sophisticated military telescopic sight arrives from the U.S.A.

The sight, which utilises starlight, has been ordered by Cordering farmer, Mr Dennis Earnshaw, who has suffered heavy stock losses through the nocturnal visits of a savage predator.

The Minister for Agriculture Mr Dick Old, who visited the Earnshaw property recently, said this week the Agriculture Protection Board was most interested in the sight, and had discussed with Mr Earnshaw the possibility of negotiating to buy from him when the hunt was over.

'These sights cost thousands of dollars,' Mr Old said. 'They are sensitised to absorb tiny traces of light, as do cat's eyes, and electronically magnify them.'

The Board has ordered from the U.K. some binoculars which work on a similar principle, and have an infra-red attachment as well, but they are unobtainable until next year because the British Army has ordered the whole of the next nine months' production.

This sort of equipment will be most valuable to the Agriculture Protection Board's research section, particularly in their studies of nocturnal predators.

Mr Old said the Board was closely involved in the Cordering investigations through its field and research staff.

'There are certainly some unusual features about the Cordering story,' Mr Old said. 'And I certainly do not discount the possibility that animals other than dogs might be involved.'

Earnshaw also informed me that a senior A.P.B. officer, Des Gooding, who seemed to be handling the Board's inquiries, had been in the region talking to farmers and had even gone out one night on the truck with Bert Pinker.

Next day I contacted Gooding by telephone at the South Perth headquarters of the Department. He was abrupt and guarded, aware of my close involvement in the story and hesitant about making any definitive statements about something which he nonetheless conceded was baffling. He admitted that there was enough circumstantial evidence to warrant the Agriculture Protection Board investigating 'to try to pinpoint what sort of animal we are dealing with.'

'As far as I'm concerned, I can't say if it's a cougar or not. There is something killing sheep and kangaroos and it's not the sort of predator you would normally expect to find in the region. But there are highly qualified people saying it's nothing more than a big dog or pigs, or maybe a dingo. From the evidence I saw it could have been a cougar but I can't say conclusively what it is.'

Gooding revealed that laboratory tests were being run on samples of hair and faeces. 'In a week or so we might have the results and we could know by then. If there is a cougar out there and these samples are from it then I would hope the tests will tell us what we want to know.'

Unfortunately it wasn't to be that simple. A week later I rang him again and the test results were in. They had shown the hair to be from a cat but Gooding said it was impossible, according to his technicians, to tell one type of cat's hair from another. Officers had obtained cuttings from cougars in the Perth Zoo and also the prints of their footmarks and were comparing them with the farmers' evidence. But it appeared all cat's hair was so similar as to be impossible to identify one type from another. 'So the hair we've got could as easily be that of a bush cat or a feral cat as any mountain lion. It's proved nothing.' Gooding said.

The reaction of the Perth media after I had returned to the city from Cordering was interesting. The nasty confrontation at Ross Earnshaw's farm had become something of a talking point at West Australian newspapers. Both *The Daily* News and *The West Australian* chose to take no further interest in the story, for the moment, apart from one brief reference in the back page *Daily News* column, *Bill Lang's Look*, of June 14, 1978.

Cheque book journalism has finally come to the old west. Some of the loudest screams at Cordering came not from the legendary cougar but the media. That is, the media who got down there to find the principal characters around the countryside tied up in contracts. The sharp shooting Earnshaw brothers for example have been signed up by Channel 7 for exclusive television rights if the creature is shot. The Australian *has them in a deal for exclusive picture rights. A reporter and photographer I know were without their cheque books and got the story only after much arguing, yelling and arm waving.*

I found the reference somewhat unfair to the Earnshaws, they being the kind of ordinary country folk who took this kind of jibe hard. It had not been easy for them to bear the brunt of continual community ridicule and their determination to prove their case had indeed cost them dearly, financially. Yet I knew that recouping some of their big financial losses was the last thing in either Dennis or Ross Earnshaw's mind.

The Perth papers had chosen to give only cursory attention to the story until I provoked national interest in it at that time. While both the other papers had carried minor stories, very occasionally, over the years, it had mainly been publicised by Brian Pash. There had been no serious attempt on the *West Australian's* part to send reporters to the region to investigate in any full way as I had done. For a newspaper group with a virtual monopoly on the daily news-gathering business in the State, and a group which proclaimed itself to be the bastion of printed news record, its failure to give the story adequate attention was surprising. Though the claims of the farmers were not new, and they were extraordinary, this only meant the story was that much more potentially explosive.

The business of journalism is based on, and fostered by, the challenge of securing scoops - front page stories sell newspapers. It is well accepted commercial practice to contract for exclusive picture rights on important stories.

🐾 🐾 🐾

The U.S. army developed what is conveniently referred to as a "star-scope" for its military activity in Vietnam. Basically, its purpose was to allow soldiers to see at night and it proved to be one of the most effective and feared weapons of that war. Attached to a rifle in the same manner as any conventional sighting scope, it intensified incoming starlight or moonlight in a three-stage process. Incoming light passed through a refracted lens, and as it did, the photons were amplified and projected onto a phosphorus screen. Looking through the scope, the darkness became a blurred world of dull green light, but in that dullness moving shapes could easily be detected - a man's shape and size would, for example, stand out against the blurred green background of jungle. The weapon had a real psychological value in Vietnam. With it, the shield of darkness was lifted in the knife-edge world of jungle warfare.

Dennis Earnshaw learned of the scope and hoped it would help him on his own battleground. He contacted the scope's manufacturers in Pennsylvania, U.S.A. but a number of problems arose when he attempted to import it. Tight regulations long covered its use in the U.S.A. and Earnshaw had to give the State Department specific details of his requirements so great was the fear that such an effective weapon could fall into hands of terrorists. When the bulky five pound military scope finally arrived in Western Australia Earnshaw had to give assurances to the local authorities that its use would be specifically limited to hunting stock predators.

It cost Dennis Earnshaw over $6000 to import the star-scope an immense outlay for the farmer to sustain, and a clear indication of how fierce was his determination to prove the farmers' case. On top of the landed cost, the sales tax on it amounted to over $1000.

Earnshaw asked Dick Old whether he could apply to have the tax waived - the scope was being imported specifically for the extermination of vermin and the Agriculture Department had expressed interest in purchasing it once the farmer's job was done. Dick Old took the case to the Federal Government the Minister assisting the Treasurer, Michael MacKellar, the Minister for Primary Industry, Ian Sinclair, and the Deputy Taxation Commissioner, Mr M.T. Healey.

The Taxation Department ruled that although the Agriculture Protection Board might take the scope later, this would not affect the requirements on Earnshaw, as the purchaser, to pay the tax.

Dennis Earnshaw's bill for the importation of the scope soared to $7,122.13.

When I contacted him next by phone, he informed me that the scope had arrived and he was busy affixing it to various rifles. With that, I began making preparations for my second and most significant visit to Cordering.

❈ ❈ ❈

Cat-like scratch marks and dirt kicked over a kangaroo carcass found on one of th farms.

Chapter Five

IN MY OPINION, NEIL ELIOT was one of the best photographers in Western Australia. That was not a judgement based conveniently on the fact that he worked for my newspaper group. I daresay there would be those at our opposition papers who would not agree with my evaluation. But apart from my instinctive liking for him, Eliot had a good eye for a picture and a hunger for creating news that seemed noticeably absent from some newsrooms in Perth. Some six months earlier he had been hired by *The Sunday Times*, and with the *Australian's* expansion, I was using him with the other *Times'* photographers for our work. Despite his often boyish bravado, Eliot seemed to me to be potentially a top class photographer. So I decided to take him to Cordering with me.

The possibility of photographing the predator, given the massive advantage the starscope would apparently provide, enthralled me and it had a similar impact on the photographer from the moment I explained the background to the week-long trip I was planning. There had been considerable good-humoured banter in the office at my expense over the stories. Even in our organisation there were those who were certain I had been duped. And in fact this was symptomatic of many opinions about the cat claims throughout the State. It was so stunningly bizarre that few would believe it. This was its 'Catch-22'. The suggestion was so outrageous that many people couldn't even think seriously about it. But if they weren't willing to examine the mass of circumstantial evidence, they couldn't really understand what was a feasible proposition. To my mind it was important to examine the proposition *because* it was so outrageous.

Eliot and I left Perth intending to spend a full week in the south-west. While he expressed enthusiasm about the job, I realised during the drive down that he harboured the same basic scepticism as so many others. But now he was working on it as a story and was obliged to approach it with an open mind. *The Australian's* expansion into a fully-fledged daily operation had created a new sense of co-operation with The *Sunday Times* staff. But even among my work mates I constantly encountered this good-natured disbelief. Most people seemed, in the end, betrayed by that shadow of doubt, occasionally uncovered behind the best-intentioned, patient and sympathetic hearings.

I said very little to Eliot about the job during the journey. I needed to use him as another barometer as I had Collins and Dunn. I was anxious to observe his reactions as the days stretching before us unfolded. If we came away again without a dead or captured animal or even photographic evidence of its existence, then I could take a lead from his reactions to details I feared could have been obscured for me by my growing friendship with the farmers.

Later that day I relaxed as Dennis Earnshaw and the gregarious Eliot came immersed in a friendly world of conversation about camera lenses, light settings and shutter speeds. Eliot was fascinated with the starscope and anxious that it might fit his cameras. Earnshaw, for his part, was grateful for the professional advice as the two set about fitting the scope to Eliot's cameras. Within an hour they had successfully used an adaptor to attach the starscope to the front section of Eliot's 50mm standard lens on a Nikormatt FT3 camera. The two secured the scope to the camera on a tripod standing in the middle of the kitchen floor.

As I chatted to Henny Earnshaw, a delightful, somewhat shy lass, there was a knock on the door. A gnarled middle-aged farmer appeared in the kitchen in baggy trousers and work shirt, its sleeves rolled up over heavily veined arms, fibrous and strong from a lifetime of farm work. Charlie Sumner was one of Dennis Earnshaw's neighbours, known in the region for years as something of a loner but a man who had grown friendly with the Earnshaw family, as increasing concern about the predator gave them common ground for communication. Dennis Earnshaw admitted that, prior to the sightings he himself experienced, he had put Charlie Sumner's claims down to the excesses of an eccentric.

Earnshaw introduced the new arrival around, barely breaking his concentration from what was a tricky job securing the equipment.

'Well, Dennis,' Sumner began slowly, 'I've got a 'roo out back in the truck I think you should look at.'

'A dead one?' Earnshaw asked, still absorbed by his tinkering.

'Very dead, and you know who killed him,' the farmer said in a steady, unhurried voice.

'The cat?' Earnshaw asked, swinging around.

'Yep,' Sumner said, smacking his lips, a trace satisfied he had finally grabbed the room's avid attention.

Moments later Sumner dropped the tailgate of his utility with a thud. Under a bloodstained and worn hessian cover lay a partially-skinned twenty kilo kangaroo. Sumner grabbed it roughly and swing it over the truck. He grabbed at its furry underbelly, yanking at it until he exposed a gaping wound thirty centimetres long on its underside.

'It went in through there and had a feed,' Sumner said. "All the good bits! And look at this,' he said, pulling the dead animal by its tail and lifting the fur from its back where he had partially skinned. it. On the underneath surface of the fur there were three distinct scratch marks about one centimetre apart and two centimetres long.

'Well, if you want to stop a 'roo running away from you the best idea is to grab him,' Earnshaw said, in intensive examination of the area where the scratch marks had cut through the hide to mark the flesh below.

'Neck's broken too,' Sumner mumbled as Eliot, encased in a deep frown, grabbed the 'roo's expressionless face and swivelled its small skull from side to side.

Back in the farmhouse Sumner was fascinated by the starscope and was also keen to divulge his theories about the mystery.

'Well, this ain't for printing in the paper,' he said, a little unnecessarily, in an indolent drone.

'I haven't seen one, mind you - not for sure - but I know they're there all right. They've been killing stock and lots of 'roos, like that fella out back, for some time. There's lots of folks here about who say they're dogs, but not me,' he said, sipping a cup of tea at the kitchen table. 'Nope, not dogs. You know,' he continued, 'I reckon they're having a big effect on the 'roos too - killing all the little ones.'

I glanced at Earnshaw as the implications of that sank in. 'How big an impact?' I asked.

'It's smart, this critter, whatever it is,' Sumner went on without taking a breath. 'It gives the does a fright and when they take off to lead the cat away from the joeys it just pulls up, trots over to the young one and has a free lunch. Easy.'

It hadn't previously occurred to me what the implications would be if the cats were in fact interfering with the natural balance of the bush. All the textbooks claimed that Australia's unique wildlife had developed in 'splendid isolation' since the separation of the great continental land masses eons ago. If a new and efficient predator had been recently introduced, what would be the long term effect on the nation's wilds, I wondered.

'The way this fella operates, he would clean up a lot of the wildlife in this bush, I reckon,' Sumner observed.

Eliot whispered: 'Shit,' without taking his eyes off the assembly job. 'That's one side of it you didn't tell me about,' he said, momentarily shifting a glance at me.

'No,' I replied.

🐾 🐾 🐾

One advantage of the briskly cold nights at that time of year was that they were usually quite clear. The scope gratefully sucked in all the light available from the stars and moon overhead. On the face of it, Earnshaw's expensive new toy now gave us a massive advantage. Weeks earlier Pinker and his offsider had left Cordering for home and a deserved rest. Both were virtually exhausted from their frustrating endeavours and I suspected that much of Pinker's enthusiasm had evaporated after that missed first shot. I also suspected they had realised long after the rest of us that spotlighting was a virtual waste of time against such a shrewd adversary. We all now hoped the starscope would make the big difference. With it we could cruise the farms within the vicinity with the vehicles' lights off, and only the gentle rumbling of an idling engine to give our position away. With the scope pointed out the car window, mounted on a camera or a rifle, we could delve into the darkness in near-anonymity. As well, inside the car was distinctly warmer than standing on the back of a bumpy truck.

Nevertheless, Eliot and I dressed for a chilly outing. Entranced by the prospects offered by the starscope, Charlie Sumner politely enquired if he could go along for the ride. Earnshaw had no option but to agree although four of us inside a station-wagon, managing an unwieldy rifle with a cumbersome scope on top, would put a premium on space. I shared the backseat with Sumner as Earnshaw's car coughed into life. We couldn't have wished for a clearer night - stars above sparkled against a vast blanket of darkness.

Stock grazed silently, blurred shadows in a hazy green window to the night. As we began to cruise the gravel side lanes of the properties I wondered whether the cat would sense the introduction of the farmer's new weapon, or whether it would merely provide another simple test to be overcome by a startling capacity for unchallenged survival. Eliot had taken a series of test photographs through the starscope, but now it rested on the .243, the entire structure proving difficult to manoeuvre inside the full cabin. Sumner had first watch and our conversation became subdued when he rested the barrel of the rifle on his door window frame and eagerly pushed his face against the rubber eye piece. Over coming hours we toured the properties, taking 20 minute spells of duty with the starscope.

Gazing into the eye socket, the sensation was quite unusual. After about 20 minutes, one eye became totally accustomed to the green haze, the other wincing to concentrate all attention on the shadowy outlines moving in the fields. At the end of each session we suffered the most peculiar confusion as one eye struggled to adjust to the darkness again, both temporarily blinded as they sought a compromise.

After an uneventful night we were all heavily fatigued, due mainly to the physical demands of holding the heavy rifle in cramped conditions, but also from the mental pressure. Charlie Sumner made his way home in the early hours, after we had made arrangements to visit his farmhouse in coming days to examine some of the 'evidence' he had assembled. Eliot and I went to our beds but sleep again proved as elusive as the marauder. As I had done with Collis, we sat up till dawn discussing the phenomenon. Eliot's early traces of detachment were showing distinct signs of defrosting. The photographer was impressed by the direct honesty of the people he'd met. Try as he may, he was having real problems ascribing to them ulterior motives that would prompt them to concoct their claims. For me, it was like a familiar refrain.

That evening Earnshaw suggested we visit a nearby farm to talk about the owner's encounter with the cat. More than any of his neighbours', Jim Putland's property was punctuated with the often rounded, moss-covered granite boulders that were a feature of the higher ground of the south western region of Western Australia. A formation of these rocks, heaped one upon another, sat, in fact, within a few hundred metres of the backdoor to Putland's farmhouse, beneath a canopy of jarrah trees and grape vine greenery. It was at this battery of stone that Jim Putland's attitude to rumours of the marauding cat animal so suddenly and so completely changed.

Earnshaw, Eliot and I sat in the comfortable ranch-style living room at Putland's farmhouse before an enormous, crackling fireplace. Outside a stiffening mid-evening breeze rattled at the windows as the farmer, an athletic, greying man of about fifty, tentatively outlined his staggering confrontation with the cat. Prior to 1978 Putland had disregarded the claims of his neighbours with no more interest than the sweep of a hand. He'd heard of the statements being made by people like Earnshaw, Sumner, Wheeler and Hughes, but he'd scoffed at them, often with uncharacteristic derision. Jim Putland was one of the most highly respected farmers in the south west, having settled in W.A. in 1964 after moving from rural Victoria.

Around 7.30 one night in July 1978, he was clearing up in a back shed after a day's shearing. Only one chore remained before his evening meal - the feeding of the farm's dogs. In the darkened yard he made his way with a hand torch to where the dogs were tethered and poured the animals' feed into trays. One of the neighbour's dogs was trying to join the meal, so Putland firmly waved the intruder away.

'Go home, you bugger,' Putland called, as the dog trotted off in the direction of the neighbour's farm.

The farmer then noticed his own dogs were becoming restless and not as keen as usual to take their feed. He shone the torch around the yard and suddenly the breath caught in his throat. There behind the pile of moss stained rocks he saw the sharp but lazy reflection of two brilliant eyes. He knew at once some kind of animal was lurking beyond the cluster of rocks.

Putland stood frozen as he moved the torchlight over the rock face. His dogs had disappeared.

Then, almost unbelievably, an enormous cat-like animal appeared atop the tallest of the outcrops. It had sprung up to four metres from the ground in one effortless, silent burst.

The farmer was terrified. A few metres away sat the strangest animal he had ever seen. It sat upright staring down at him, its pug-face expressionless, its tail playing around its body like an enormous snake. Then a hot surge of fear rocked Putland's stomach and chest. The animal was on the ground, walking towards him. It had eased itself down the sheer rock face as if in slow motion - one smooth jolt. As panic surged into the farmer's brain, he realised he couldn't run. It wasn't until the animal veered away in an almost ponderous, sway-back stride, that Putland realised he was moving, charging towards the back door of the house on legs tense with fear.

With a spotlight and rifle he rushed out again into the dark yard but the animal had vanished.

This confrontation proved to be perhaps the most crucial as the mystery deepened after 1978. Later that evening the usually unflappable farmer was on the phone to Earnshaw, his voice wavered with shock. Putland had seen one of the animals at closer range than anyone else in the south west up until at that time. His sobriety and level-headed honesty made him an important first-hand witness as the Cordering farmers sought to compile the evidence.

But other important incidents followed soon after on Putland's farm. The next evening his son thought he saw a large, unidentified animal moving near the house, on his return from a rural youth meeting. And some days later a stock marketing agent from the Elders organisation drove a car full of visitors from Perth along the gravel driveway leading to Putland's farmhouse. The Putlands weren't home at the time, but as the visitor's car rolled up to the backyard one noticed a large grey animal moving through a paddock several hundred metres away. The car stopped and its occupants then watched for a full ten minutes as the cat meandered, slow and untroubled, across the paddock.

Putland said the animal he had seen in the torchlight appeared to be a light brown colour. He said it would have stood as tall as a large dog and had what appeared to be a large dark tuft at the end of its tail.

'And I reckon, at a guess, it would have weighed near two hundred pounds,' he said.

So dumbstruck had he been by the sighting that Putland made a special trip to Perth to talk to the zoo. During feeding periods at the South Perth animal sanctuary, the attendants separated some animals caged together when food was introduced. This practice was followed in the cage containing the two female cougars.

One animal was enticed into the small concrete "house" in the cage and locked from outside while food was given to the other animal. Then the cage door was unlatched and the first animal freed and thrown its feed of meat.

When Jim Putland arrived at the cougar cage only one animal, the much smaller, was visible. He was sure it resembled the animal he had seen at his farm but he believed it was too small. He walked away to find a zoo attendant to discuss his sighting, and on his return to the cage some time later, both animals were visible, gnawing on their food.

'That's it,' Putland said, gazing wide-eyed at the significantly larger cat. To the farmer's mind the larger cat closely resembled the animal he had seen in physical features, colour - and size.

🐾 🐾 🐾

Following our talk with Putland, Neil Eliot and I readied ourselves for our second night in the hunt at Earnshaw's farm. Earnshaw had been having trouble securing the scope to his .243. The rifle's recoil was throwing the scope sight out of alignment, making accurate aim extremely dubious. He had laboured over the rifle for hours that day, struggling to cut deeper grooves into the grain of the mounting so it wouldn't slip when the rifle was fired. Frustrated by his efforts, Earnshaw said the only way a truly accurate shot could be guaranteed would be with a recoilless rifle - perhaps an armalite. I climbed onto the back seat of the stationwagon, Earnshaw driving and Eliot alongside him, taking first spell with the scope. The photographer leaned back against his door, the rifle's barrel passing in front of Earnshaw's chest, leaning on the door frame and poking out the window. When my turn came I leaned it out of the door behind Earnshaw, resting it on my knees. It was the only comfortable manner in which the operation could be conducted.

Towards the end of the night, the strain of constantly staring into the dull glow of starlight was beginning to tell. I developed a mild headache and every session with the rifle seemed to become progressively longer, there being no shortage of protestations when each other's sessions came to an end. What had begun as a fascinating novelty the previous night had quickly become a demanding chore. Earnshaw then began taking turns with the rifle and scope while Eliot drove. But despite the difficulty of managing the weighty equipment, and the tiring mental effects, there was that ever-present promise that one of us might distinguish a strange shape moving among the flocks. After hours with the scope, it was easy to distinguish the individual shape of the bush animals - kangaroos, foxes and rabbits. It had always seemed to me that the night was a time of complete stillness, a dead void when the bush somehow just stopped living. The starscope showed just how much the night was a time when the bush literally breathed with life. But it was not the familiar shape of bush cats or brush wallabies we sought - it was something else, something hypnotically inexplicable. And it was about 2.00 a.m. when I believe I finally saw it.

Eliot was sleeping and Earnshaw was at the wheel. As we cruised down a back lane adjacent to Terry Hughes' property, I had the rifle barrel balanced on the door, my right eye pressing the rubber eye piece far back to expose the lens. Slender, heavily leaved marri trees bordered the roadway and momentarily blocked my view of an open paddock beyond the road verge. I whispered to Earnshaw to accelerate until we came to a break in the trees. At once he eased the car back down to its dawdling pace. The paddock stretched up a rise to the right in the direction we had come from. I lifted the rifle in the air, and adjusting my eyes firmly to the socket, swept in a slow arc to the left, as the breadth of the paddock opened before me. When I bumped the centre columns of the car doors with the rifle barrel I slowly scanned back to the right, perusing the open field for the slightest sign of unusual movement. At the right angles to the back door it happened. Just for one instant I saw something. Either my brain or my eye registered its fleeting presence twice, in distinct split moments. Then it was gone. But in that microscopic double-take I recognised its shape. I had seen a robust cat-like figure moving at startling speed, in huge bounds, into the scope's view and then just as quickly out of it again. In that second instant, my mind's eye captured its shape roughly centre of the green haze. Had it not been for that second crystalisation, I would not only have been unable to determine its shape, but I doubt I would ever have believed I'd seen anything at all.

But for all that, it was not the shape of the blinding movement that told me I had witnessed something significant - it was my own reaction. So great was the shock of it that I virtually lost control. I screamed at Earnshaw, exploding with unabashed and uncontrolled hysteria. My head snapped back from the eyepiece with shock. Then I peered again into the scope. There was nothing there and I started yelling again, struggling awkwardly with the rifle to get out of the car even as Earnshaw, startled by the outburst, was still pulling up. Eliot was abruptly awake as I gathered myself on my feet on the road way, struggling to peer through the scope in the direction the shape had moved. I blurted uncontrollably to my companions, now stirred into action. I was stunned by an image that had not yet fully moulded itself in my mind but which was at the same time burned into my memory. I stood there prattling uncontrollably. For the moment, with a million galaxies sending me the star light to pierce the darkness, I had seen *something*. What I believed it was left me spellbound.

"What did you notice first?' Earnshaw asked, taking the rifle from me and resting it on a fence post to sweep the starscope's gaze higher up the field.

'Its tail Den, its tail,' I said, excitedly realising as I spoke how often I had heard others talk of it. 'Such a long tail - it was going like a train . . . a really big animal with this tail stretching behind it as it went.' Eliot was looking on, still half asleep but wide-eyed, his camera draped around his neck, the flash unit hissing gently in the dark as its battery charged up, ready for action.

I fell speechless.

Earnshaw walked back to the car and, carefully laying his rifle and scope on the back seat, made himself comfortable up on the upholstery's edge, his legs dangling onto the road.

'Well, one thing's for sure,' he said in the sharp, silver moonlight, ' it's gone now. But,' he added, taking a long tired breath, 'I reckon you saw it, mate. By the sound of things, you saw one. It's unbelievable. Across that paddock is Terry Hughes' house and eighteen months ago he thought he saw this small black panther in one of his paddocks. We may have just stumbled on to the same animal, only a bit older, a bit bigger, and a hell of a lot faster on its feet,' he said.

After the encounter, sleep was impossible to come by. After breakfast at daybreak, Earnshaw accompanied Eliot and myself on a tour of the district, meeting more neighbours. They were all aware that I was in the area again and wanted to talk to more of them as they began to have more trust in me. We drove over to Charlie Sumner's simple brick and fibro bungalow hidden behind a wall of jarrah trees, twenty-two kilometres from Earnshaw's.

Sumner produced a group of white chalk footprint casts of various sizes - two of them quite large but with protuberances which resembled thick sharpened toenails. It struck me that in variably cats' toenails were retracted unless they were striking with the paw or moving quickly from standstill. The larger casts looked like the footmarks of large dogs, but Sumner insisted they were not. He claimed that what appeared to be nails were in fact bumps that had occurred with the pouring of the plaster. They were copies taken from the original footprint which was cast with hot bee's wax by a Donnybrook farmer, Arthur Williams.

I was uneasy about the apparent toenails but Sumner also produced photographs of various stock animals found dead in the fields. Significantly, he produced a series of photographs he had taken of the kangaroo he had previously brought to the Earnshaw farm. He had found it lying on its side, partially covered with a blanket of dead leaves, twigs and dry soil. The old farmer said this appeared to be part of the killing habits of the large feline predator. He also produced a number of photographs of kangaroo skulls, and two dried skulls themselves, which he had found in the bush. All had splintered holes driven through them on the forehead on either side of the bridge of the snout. The holes pierced the skulls, splintering them on the upper forehead. The farmers claimed these animals had been grabbed by the heads in the attacks that killed them, their skulls pierced by teeth snapped shut by immensely powerful jaws. Summer agreed to allow me to take all this evidence to Perth for a week. I wanted to ask Des Gooding what he could offer by way of an explanation.

'That won't do you much good but there's no harm trying. I've shown it to them but they don't want to play ball,' Sumner said dryly. His patience with some of the regional A.P.B. officers was wearing thin.

George Wheeler was in many ways the most important man in the early evolution of the cat mystery. For over forty years he had lived on and around two big properties, 20 kilometres from the Earnshaw farms. Everyone in the district knew George. Not everyone liked him, not everyone understood his quiet independence. They'd see him driving his trucks, mustering sheep or working the fields—standing well over two metres, his bulky arms tanned darkly from years in the sunshine, hanging from inevitable denim shirts, sleeves habitually cut away at the shoulders.

To some, seventy-year-old Wheeler had developed a reputation as one of the most authoritative bushmen in the area. Time and again over the years he had been approached by the authorities or other farmers for advice on many aspects of the local rural life. Probably more than any other he was regarded as the man who knew more about the region's bush. Over the years, apart from his farming interests, he had learned and practiced, to a refined stage, the work of the bush dogger. And it was George Wheeler who probably first came to realise that all was not well in the timber forests. There was little he didn't know about the baiting and trapping of vermin - wild dogs, feral pigs, dingoes, foxes and bush cats.

He talked more deliberately, slowly and apprehensively about the cat phenomenon than other farmers I'd met. But he was more insistent, more determined and more immovable in his belief that a new kind of large feline was dominating tracts of the landscape.

In his farmhouse, he sat slowly recounting his developing awakening to the truth. As early as 1973 Wheeler was puzzled by signs that something was amiss. He initially believed that some kind of new wild dog was roaming the district. He prepared his time proved baits - his version of the secret formula prepared by individual doggers to attract vermin canines to their traps. Wheeler's recipe was a boiled-down combination of parts of dead dogs - the aroma from the foul, bottled concoction was a fail-safe means of attracting wild dogs to the traps, but the exact ingredients of his own formula Wheeler kept to himself.

The problem was that after 1973 the formula wasn't working. He was troubled by strange tracks and occasional inexplicable stock kills. But increasingly, his trapping and poisoning programme wasn't working and for him this was almost unconscionable.

'Early on, it got to the stage where I said to a few friends like Charlie Summer that this was not a dog,' he said.

'It went on for periods of three or four months over the years. All the signs would appear that something was getting into the bush but I just couldn't track him. Then it dawned on me that it wasn't making the mistakes dogs make because it wasn't a dog at all. I didn't know it was a big cat in the early years but I was sure it was a strange animal. It just didn't have any of the habits of dogs.'

'Then in 1977, I was driving through the district one night, when I noticed in the headlights this black dog running along-side the road by the truck. At least I thought it was a black dog and I thought it may have been my old pooch. I thought he might have jumped off the back of the truck, so I pulled up and got out but he was still sitting there on the back, wagging his tail at me. I had seen the rear end and tail of this animal in the light, but because I couldn't see its head I wasn't sure what it was.'

Wheeler found large track marks on the road verge, from which he made a plaster cast.

'It had me beat - you just don't see dog prints like that.'

Later that year George was coming back after dark from top dressing at his brother's nearby farm. He could see strange bright eyes ahead, in the lights of the tractor he was driving. Twenty metres off he slowed down as he approached the lights. He saw the dull outline of an animal easing itself into the bush.

'Its head and shoulders were partially hidden behind a Blackboy. It didn't move away quickly. I saw the rest of it and it was fuller in body than a dog, its legs were thicker, it had this tail and was black as soot. He was as black as the wings of a crow.' Wheeler estimated the animal's body weight to be at least 60 kilograms.

'When you think big dingoes go up to about 40 kilos, it gives you some idea how big this thing was. It was quite full in the underbelly, and when it went off into the bush I could just hear this *pat, pat, pat.*'

Wheeler was insistent that one aspect of its body stood out - its long whipped tail.

As the 1970s drew to a close, Wheeler grew deeply concerned about the increasing signs of the predator. In one season alone, he and his brother lost a total of 600 lambs on two properties. A farmer who traditionally achieved around a 95 per cent lambing each year, by 1978 his lambing was barely 50 per cent. By the end of the '78 season he knew something serious was happening. Yet everything he tried - every trapping and baiting technique he developed over the years - came to nothing, time and time again. He saw the signs of the animal's presence, intensifying his frustration as time went on, and his trapping and baiting methods failed repeatedly.

'The signs are all around all right: like the 'roos - they won't go into some sections of the bush like they used to - they prefer to camp in the clearing and avoid some scrub areas.'

Although a modest, reticent man, Wheeler expressed anger at some of the efforts of the authorities - particularly their claims that dingoes or wild dogs were killing stock.

'If there is a dingo going through a district like this, then you'll know it,' he said. 'There just aren't any dingoes in this piece of bush, and I should know because I killed the last one, and that was twenty years ago. Since the escalation of killings started some seasons back, I should say that not one of them could be attributable to a dingo - and there just aren't any wild dogs or feral pigs in this bush either. Definitely not. In mid 1978 there was one pig which went through an area near here. He came down through the gullies and wallowed in some mud, and then disappeared. It could have been a domestic pig gone wild, which then decided to go off home, but apart from that fellow there haven't been any feral pigs in this district for years.'

Wheeler's great fear was the possible effect of the predator on the local environment. He said he could see a catastrophe coming. 'These things are very damaging. They're going to eat out all the joeys and then we had better look out for our sheep, lambs and other stock.

For example, we were getting a few colonies of possums building up a few years ago but now they seem to be gone - they are a thing of the past. And there was a time when there would be maybe 500 'roos roaming through a big area of land nearby - maybe a thousand acres. Now, though, you can go up there night after night and never see a 'roo.'

Wheeler admitted he was particularly exasperated by a couple of incidents when kangaroos were found drowned in water courses on his properties. The animals were known to be shy of water yet some had been found floating in a dam.

'There's no 'roo dog that will terrify a boomer enough to make it back into a dam so far that it gets out of its depth and drowns. If it was a dog, there would be tracks all over the place where it tried to get at the 'roo. And if anything, it's the 'roos that drown the silly old dogs when they get too excited and come too close - the old boomer will grab the dog and hold it under with its back feet until it drowns.

'We've found places where this animal has gone down for a drink and leaned right over without putting its feet in the water. The kangaroo numbers are definitely dwindling - they breed once a year, and that one joey is being grabbed each year,' Wheeler said.

After many years of patient hard work, Wheeler gave up hopes of trapping the cat.

'I'm quite convinced now it can't be trapped - once I laid 18 traps through some scrub, and next day I found its tracks in and out of the area, where it had skirted each trap without setting it off - if you tell me that animal is not clever I'll go quietly,' the farmer said.

Wheeler had one other unusual experience in his long battle to catch a ghost. He filled a natural rock formation, a hollow ironstone, with strychnine-based poison. The rock, found in areas of W.A., is of high iron concentration, hollowed out inside with an iron crystalline surface. Wheeler filled the rock with fat, laced with poison. It weighed over 2.5 kilos and was smothered with fat.

'It would have killed 50 foxes if they'd all had a lick, but after I'd planted it near where I thought the cat was operating, I went out to check it, and it was just gone. Now I defy anybody to find that stone. It weighed a good five pounds, but something picked it up and just carted it off. There's no way in the world any human would have found where I left it,' Wheeler said.

That night Earnshaw, Eliot and I decided to change our strategy. Rather than cruise the paddocks in the car, we would try to entice the prey to us. With Henny's blankets and generous supplies of insulating tape we blacked out all the windows of the stationwagon, save one. Earnshaw picked out a weakening sheep from his flocks, and in the late afternoon threw it on the utility and drove to the paddock where I had seen the shape in the scope the previous night. There, he stood on the sheep's head and slashed its throat, holding it down while its life bled away in violent spasms, vomiting blood onto the grass. As evening fell, armed with flasks of tea and boxes of sandwiches, we drove the stationwagon to the paddock, settling down 50 metres from the still warm sheep's carcass. Positioned on a rise near a tree line we rolled down the only uncovered window and poked out the barrel of the rifle with the scope attached. Then we waited.

On the roster system we patiently saw the night through, speaking very little. Uneasy in such uncomfortable confinement, I fought for sleep when Earnshaw and Eliot took their periods on duty. Nothing happened.

In the first light of morning we gave up the effort and drove back to the farmhouse. In splendid sunshine at 7.00 a.m., Ross Earnshaw drove over to inspect the carcass. Its entrails had been eaten away.

🐾 🐾 🐾

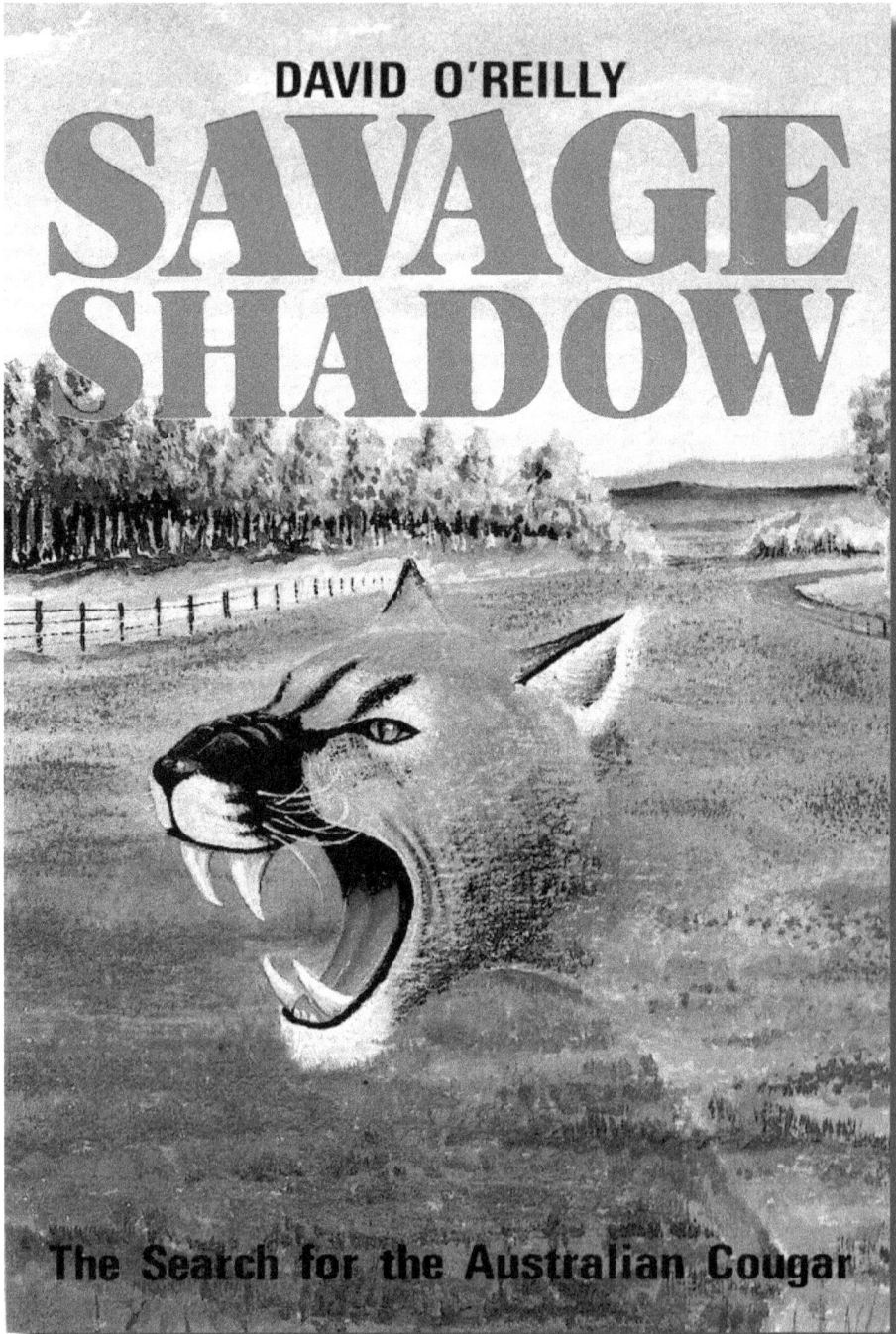

The original cover of the 1981 edition of Savage Shadow.

Chapter Six

I T SEEMED INCONCEIVABLE, as I stared into the cage, that an animal akin to the one prowling the other side of the fence could be running wild in the bush. I was on my way to a long-overdue interview with Des Gooding at the Department of Agriculture offices when I decided to stop off at the Perth zoo and seek out its cougar cage. The zoo had two animals, both females, locked inside a cramped two-tiered concrete pen.

Words I had heard spoken a dozen times came back to me--'You can't move a muscle when you see it because it looks so unreal, so out of place,' . . . 'they just don't belong in our bush, so at first you don't believe what you've seen,' . . . 'they're so foreign to what you know about the bush that you can't believe your own eyes.'

As I stood before the cage it was preposterous to think that such animals could be ruling a huge parcel of the Australian wilds. The larger cat lay on her side, panting in the afternoon sunshine, lazily oblivious to the passing tourists and noisy schoolchildren. The other was stalking back and forward in worried agitation at the rear of the cage. Both wore heavy grey coats that disguised their savage physical power. They looked overweight and under-exercised yet their noble pug faces and alert ears were solemn testament to their murderous potential. Long curling tails with darkened ends unfurled giddily behind them and their feet were almost too big - blunt mittens of heavily furred skin.

Everything about the cats looked too big, too powerful. How could such animals remain as invisible as the wind? And where were the outward manifestations of the cunning and cruelty attributed to them by men?

As I gazed transfixed into the cage I determined that I should approach the dilemma from another point of view by learning as much as I could about cougars in an effort to establish inconsistency or contradiction in what I was being told by the farmers. Some of them were insistent that the animal they had seen resembled an American mountain lion. My job, then, was to find out as much as I could about this animal to discredit their argument.

I glanced at my watch and realised I was suddenly late for my appointment with Gooding.

The administrative heart of the Western Australian Government's Agriculture Department sat in grassed bungalows in a building complex in the Perth suburb of Como. Sprinklers coughed bursts of water onto the lawns around 'C' block in which Gooding's office, 'room 144', would be found. I climbed the staircase to the second floor and discovered Gooding wasn't in his opened office, one of dozens peppering the long, sun-lit corridors of the hospital-style complex.

I wandered further down the corridor past the offices of sundry other Agriculture Protection Board officers. On one door I suddenly recognised the name of John McSwain, the man Tomlinson had mentioned in relation to the alleged circus accident near Donnybrook.

McSwain sat at his desk, attending to a mass of paperwork. I quickly introduced myself, captivated by the unexpected prospect of extracting more information about the accident allegations. I needn't have bothered. McSwain was far from helpful. He was highly sceptical about the entire feline predator theory. He insisted that he knew nothing himself of any accident. It had merely been a hazy chapter in the bush mythology of the state's southern regions for many years - the gossip of old-timers over a beer when they had nothing better to talk about. McSwain became uncomfortable at my questioning, repeatedly insisting the theory was nonsense. I was confounded by this agitated attitude.

After a brief unproductive chat I sauntered up to Gooding's office to find the key A.P.B. man at his desk.

Gooding seemed, initially, a lot more receptive to the farmers' claims. But I sensed from the start that he was a shrewd and cautious man. As I questioned him I realised that he was testing me from a defensive posture aimed at extracting as much information as he could while giving away the bare minimum himself. He repeated the basic stand he had assumed on each of the few brief occasions we had talked on the telephone. Until more concrete evidence was brought to him, Gooding was obliged to accept the word of experienced bushmen and doggers employed by the department who were adamant that the farms of the south west were under siege from nothing more insidious than the orthodox animals of the bush. Gooding struck me as a pragmatist - bent on logical evidence and determined not to be taken in by an argument that could be irrefutably proved.

I was becoming increasingly frustrated by the weaving complications of the phenomenon. It began to show. I put to Gooding the integrity of the people I'd met in the south west - their sincere and unflappable belief in what they were saying. Our conversation became a little tense until Gooding finally gave ground.

'Look, I know all that,' he said explicitly. 'I've been down there too and I've met these people and I understand what they're saying. But we need more than that. We just can't start sending dozens of men down there without something more concrete. Government departments don't work like that,' he said, pausing and leaning forward in his chair. He removed a pair of black-rimmed glasses and tiredly rubbed a hand back over a balding head.

'With all that though, sometimes I think there could be nothing more fascinating than for what they're all saying to be right. It would be our job, I guess, to do something about it and I'm not sure what we could do but, by God, it makes life interesting,' Gooding looked at me soulfully. 'For the moment, though, the people down there have got to understand that there's only a certain amount we can do until they give us something more substantial to go on. There's nothing in the samples they've sent to tell us that there's something killing stock that's out of the ordinary. I'm sorry,' he said.

My inquiries then changed direction to focus on the reference library facilities of Perth. On the shelves of the libraries I sought an alternative doorway to the truth. Dozens of people had not only claimed that they had seen a strange animal lurking in the bush but that it displayed what they understood to be the physical features of an American mountain lion. I was aware that in the age of television, there were few people not familiar with the superficial physical characteristics of the world's popular wild animals. The question remained - under the influence of some kind of community hysteria, could so many people mistakenly superimpose upon orthodox bush animals the characteristics of a totally foreign animal?

I had to find out how much was commonly known about cougars. Would such detailed knowledge as was stored in the books contain anything to dissuade me from the cockies' preposterous assertion? I gathered together every wildlife book I could find with reference to the cat family and in particular, the cats of the Americas. From all these sources a picture began to emerge of the animal called *felis concolor*, mountain lion . . . cougar . . . puma . . .

I learned that the cougar has a greater geographical range than any other member of the cat family and, in fact, any species of native animal in the Western hemisphere. It is found in every area, in the Western Americas from British Columbia in the north to southern Argentina. In past years, it was widely distributed throughout the entire Americas but in recent times it has become almost extinct east of the Rockies. Throughout the U.S.A. the cougar populates a sweeping margin through many coastal fringe and western states including Washington, Oregon and California. It is widely spread throughout Mexico and has even been found living in the swampy lands of Florida and in southern states on the Gulf of Mexico including Louisiana, Mississippi and Texas.

A survey conducted by the New York Zoological Society in 1964 found around 300 present in Florida, 25 in New Brunswick and around 300 in Texas. The survey indicated a minimum population of 4000 in the Rocky Mountains and Pacific Coast states, with the greater number in Arizona. Canada is believed to have between 3000 and 11,000, most of which are in British Columbia and Alberta. In the Americas the animal lives in virtually any type of country where deer abound. It prefers mountainous or hilly woodland, but can also live happily in bushy swampland. It has been found in regions extending from sea level to areas of up to 3,300 metres elevation. Mexico is regarded as a stronghold of the puma: in central and south America, although distribution is not continuous, it extends to the Straits of Magellan. The animal shows remarkable adaptiveness in the gamut of climates found in the Americas - sub-Arctic regions of Canada, alpine forests of the Rocky Mountains and tropical climates. Within this there are also great variations in habitat - from mountain to forest, desert scrub, swamp or jungle.

The fourth largest member of the cat family, the cougar is described as a big, tawny animal characterised by a very long tail, heavy legs and proportionally small, round head. It is the second biggest of the cat family in the Americas behind the jaguar, but gives the impression of being larger because of its longer legs and rangier build. A fully grown male cougar can weigh up to 130 kilos, however the average weight is around the 70 kilo mark. The male averages between two and three metres in length and up to half of this can be taken up by its long curling tail. It stands between 60 and 75 cm tall.

Theodore Roosevelt held, for many years, the record for having shot a 115 kilo male in Colorado, but there have allegedly been many far larger animals killed since. The female is roughly two-fifths of the male's physical dimensions, according to some hunters. She can be up to over two metres in length with an average weight rarely exceeding 45 kilos. The colouring of the animal varies considerably throughout its geographical spread and according to the time of the year. One of the reference books described the animal's colouring as grizzled grey or dark brown in the upper parts with shades of buff, cinnamon, tawny, cinnamon-rufus or ferruginous. The colour is usually most intense along the mid-dorsal line from the top of the head to the base of the tail - its shoulders and flanks a lighter colour, its underparts a dull white, overlaid with buff across the abdomen. The sides of the muzzle are black externally, with greyish medium patches on some. The tail is black above and light below. The young are spotted with black on a buffy ground colour. There is considerable colour alteration in the animal's coat as the seasons change. They are much greyer in winter and more tawny in summer.

There appears to be no regular mating season, and cubs are born at any time of the year, though often in spring. There are usually two and sometimes three kittens in a litter and there have been odd cases of four. The female begins breeding between two and three years old, and mates are together for a short time only. The den is usually a natural cavern or dense wood growth. Gestation requires 90 to 93 days and litters may be spaced at intervals of two to three years. At birth the kitten is between 20 and 30 cm long, weights about half a kilo and is well furred. Its eyes open in between 10 and 14 days. It is weaned in about three months. In six months it weighs up to 22 kilos and has shed its spotted coat.

The mother assumed the full burden of rearing the kittens, especially in rare circumstances. If zoo captivity is an indication the mountain lion lives to about 12 years but rarely beyond 18 years. At eight months of age the kitten is up to two metres long and weighs up to 25 kilos but is not really independent until it is about two years old and ready to begin its own breeding cycle.

The existence of "leones" in Central America was first reported by Columbus, and for many years it was assumed the New World shared the conventional lion with the African Continent. The supposition was that all skins of the cougar that were brought into settlements by the Indians were the skins of females; for the early settlers the familiar coloured skins without manes, could only belong to lionesses. As the Americas were developed and settled the mountain lion grew in the folklore as one of the nation's most mysterious animals. Bearing dozens of Indian names it became known in various shrouded guises as the Puma, Cougar, Catamount, Red Tiger of Conquistadors, and the North American Ghost. It was probably the subject of more misinformation during the years of colonisation than any other animal in North America. It was also known during those day as a Painter, but names such as Painter and Catamount have now faded from use. The reference books told me there was only one successful method for hunting mountain lions - preferably on horseback, armed hunters would rely on specially trained packs of as many as six, but sometimes as few as, two hounds.

American hunters insist that the work of a good cougar dog in unravelling scent is amazing to witness. So rare are good dogs that it is claimed only one out of 100, regardless of species, will ever become the exceptional chaser required to lead a good pack. Such a lead dog is even today regarded as priceless by the hunters of the Rockies. It will pick a cold scent, identify the species of animal it detects, determine the direction and then give chase, refusing to be sidetracked to chase deer, bobcats, bears or small game whose fresher tracks may have cut across the lion's spoor. It will unravel the cat's tracks for anything up to 10 hours without flagging, gradually homing in on the tiring animal until it trees in panic. From there the dispatching of the cat to oblivion of the zoos of the world is a relatively easy task, if the hunter has had the endurance to keep up with the chase.

The cougar is regarded as the most private and shrewd member of the cat family, its guile in remaining an unseen mystery now being an historic, indisputable fact. In his book *Cats of the World,* I found Armand Dennis has this to say:

> *I have come to the conclusion that the puma is still largely an unknown quantity, even to the indefatigable Americans, although it is the most widely distributed mammal in both continents of the New World, found even today over 100 degrees of latitude from the deserts of Patagonia to the mountains of British Columbia. Although hundreds of thousands have been hunted to death by man and his dogs since the coming of Europeans, although I dare say the puma skins in museums would, if laid head to tail, stretch most of the way from New York to Chicago, no-one has yet been able to watch pumas living their lives as we can watch lions in East Africa.*

And in his book *Animals of the Canadian Rockies* Dan McGowan said:

> *Were it not for man with his dogs, guns, traps and poison most of the cougars would die of old age. Man is the enemy*

who is greatly feared and against whom precautions have to be taken. In Eastern Canada, suddenly confronted by white settlers, the cougars apparently did not have time to learn new lessons in life-saving and were either slaughtered or driven off. Those resident in the mountains of Alberta and British Columbia where rifles gradually replaced bows and arrows quickly adapted themselves to changed conditions, concluding that discretion was the better part of valour and absence of body more desirable than presence of mind.

Thus, beyond all creatures in the western wilderness these animals have mastered the art of taking cover as a means of avoiding mankind. Ernest Thomson Seton said that in 30 years of wandering in the wilds of North America he had not seen a cougar. Lloyd Thomson of Hamilton, Montana, a successful hunter of these animals, killed seventy of them and never saw one of his prospective victims until dogs had driven it into a tree top.

He is such a successful private predator because all is grist for his mill - he will eat anything from horses to small bush birdlife. In the Americas he will kill on average one deer a week the year round. In ranching areas of the Americas he will eat horse meat and will on occasion attack and dispatch fully grown horses which display an almost pathological fear of the big cat. But he also kills cattle and sheep in abundance and has been known to drag off large pigs. In one recorded incident in Florida a cougar killed and dragged off a 100 kilogram boar which had tusks 10 cm long. The cat never sustained a scratch in the brief, brutal encounter. The cougar is primarily a nocturnal animal, hunting by night, making its nightly kills by stalking its prey to within a short distance then overtaking it with a short, swift burst of acceleration. It will return to its prey over coming days to feed but will not eat once the meat becomes putrid. According to Clyde Ormond in his book *The Complete Book of Hunting*, cougars do most of their hunting by night and bed down in the high sunny rimrock crags by day. 'Because of their habit of bedding down during the day in such inaccessible places man seldom sees a wild cougar until it has been coursed by dogs and treed.'

Unlike wolves, cougars rarely kill just for the sake of killing, although a few such individuals have been reported. One incident in the U.S.A. involved an old tom which killed and maimed 19 sheep in one night. As a rule, though, the animal will kill and remain in the area to return to feed for a few days till the meat is gone or putrid, then leave the vicinity. It is believed that the cougars live in large, loosely related communities. The big tom will range through an area which may extend over a 160 km in which there may be half a dozen females. He makes regular visits through this area, meeting and staying for a short time with each in his harem. He has no interest whatsoever in his offspring, and will in fact kill them if he has a chance. The females do not travel far from their dens, especially when the cubs are very young, and they will fight savagely in defence of the cubs, even driving off the male if necessary. As the young grow older the mother takes them on hunting expeditions where she teaches them to kill. Sometimes the cubs remain with her until they are a year old.

There are records of cougars killing or eating other predatory mammals, martens, skunks, racoons, foxes and even coyotes. But there is no active cannibalism - occasionally a cougar will eat part of a dead mate, and of course the eating of his own family by an insensitive male is common in the animal world.

There is much argument about whether a cougar will attack man. They have been known to do so on rare occasions. Generally the animal has a strong fear of man and will avoid him at all costs. They will not attack even when cornered or treed. Some hunters will kill them by actually climbing up high into the trees with them to use a pistol at close range. In spite of this fear it is well documented that cougars have followed farmers and ranchers for many miles apparently out of nothing more than curiosity. It is established that they observe man and learn from that observation. There are very few authenticated cases of man-eating cougars. Some attacks have been due to rabies or extreme sickness in the animals, others due to genuine mistaken identity - trappers walking through the forest with piles of furs covering their backs, giving the impression of a moving animal. Some cubs are believed to be dangerous when first left by their mothers to fend alone and suffering the pangs of hunger. One Phillip Tanner died in Pennsylvania in 1751 after being attacked by a puma. In 1924 a young boy was killed by a savage puma in Washington State. The animal was found to be suffering badly from an injury and was killed. In recent years there have been accounts of attacks in parts of Canada but were mainly linked to the shortage of available food at the time.

According to the books, the training of a pack of dogs to capture a cougar is a specialised and time-consuming job. The cougar is one of the fastest animals on earth over three hundred metres, but it has very small lungs and gets short-winded. Often, when surprised by hounds it will climb the first sizeable tree it can find and in any event rarely runs far once the hounds are close. The knack would appear to be getting close enough to be able to panic the animal. Numerous fruitless hunts have taken men and hounds over thousands of hectares of territory for days on end. But once the dogs are lucky enough to come on the scent close to the animal, the hunt can take as little as ten minutes before the cat is treed. There are many cases of it being chased by just one dog - German shepherds, mongrels, Airedales and even wire-haired fox terriers have accomplished this feat. But something like 90 percent of cougar trailing is done the hard way, following a cold trail.

When a cat is treed it can often be many hours before the hunter hones in on the dogs' barking. It is an essential quality of the dogs that they maintain their place at the base of the tree calling in their masters. There are accounts of some dogs keeping cats treed for up to 14 hours. The hunter must be prepared for many long days in the bush when he goes hunting cougars. It is best to hunt in the morning before the sun has burned off the dew. Moisture intensifies the scent. A little-known fact is that in areas of hard footing the scent glands in the cougar's footpads will close up entirely and leave no smell whatsoever. In rocky areas the trail can only be found by casting around and cutting across where the cougar has left the hard footing, and where his scent glands have started working again. Often good dogs will lick the ground to pick up the faint scent.

Although there is generally little danger in the hunt, the cougar is a big powerful killer and can do much damage to the unwary hound.

If a cougar falls out of a tree injured, the dogs will blindly rush in with disastrous results. The cat can kill a dog by biting through its skull or disembowelling it with its hind legs. A head or neck shot from the hunter is preferable because it will kill instantly. Cougars are often taken alive and though this is not particularly dangerous it is a job for more than one man. If the treed cat goes to ground he will only go a short distance before going up another tree if the dogs are in pursuit.

After completing much of this library research, an image began to form in my mind of exactly what kind of animal the cougar was. I could, of course, only rely on the resources at hand to give me an accurate and up-to-date picture. However, to say that I was impressed by the significance of what I had read would have been a comprehensive understatement. I had in fact been catapulted by it onto the new stage of my enquiries, my appetite for an answer whetted yet again by a totally engrossing mystery.

I tried to analyse the import of what I had discovered from the books. Overwhelmingly it appeared that nothing I had found substantially undermined the theory. If anything, the reference books had grabbed the theory and lifted it, a formless possibility, out of a mire of improbability till it stood before me, a rickety structure of entirely conceivable but admittedly tenuous argument. I quickly thought back over the major streams of argument proffered by the farmers, aligning them with the information stored in the books, to establish that elusive inconsistency. On the face of it I could find none.

The authorities had queried why it was that so few people had seen the animal and even then for such short periods. But the books showed the cougar to be extraordinarily private, and obviously determined to stay away from man. Several passages illuminating this piece of argument, were stunning in their directness.

> *Although alluring to a bait is practised in America, the much more common method is pursuit with dogs. Indeed Jay Bruce, a great hunter of the puma, revealed after travelling 40,000 miles and killing nearly 700 of them that all the living pumas he had seen, except one, had been after they had been treed by his pack.*

Other books refereed to the animal's perceived need for isolation. Part of the conservation problem in the U.S.A. was based on the gradual encroachment of civilisation into the remote areas which were the only place the cougar could thrive . . .

> To this day the animal is found only in small islands of terrain that offer them the great degree of isolation they require.

According to the books, so stealthy is the cougar that he has been known to come very close to major population centres without being long observed or captured. A new York zoologist, James Ellsworth DeKay, recorded the appearance of a mountain lion within a few miles of New York City at the end of the nineteenth century.

Equally stunning were the books' detailed accounts of how cougars kill in the wild. I recalled farmers hypothesising that their stock appeared killed, their necks broken, by the force of some type of paw "punch". This speculation has been strongly ridiculed by A.P.B. officials, including Des Gooding. To read, then, the following account in an American wildlife book was a revelation:

> The usual method of killing is by stealth, the great cats lying in wait for, or creeping up silently on, their victims. The neck of the luckless captive is broken by a violent blow or by a powerful wrench with the paw, even large animals like the elk or caribou being killed in this fashion.

The authorities had questioned the farmers' claim that they were losing stock which had been struck down savagely in attacks that broke their necks. The farmers claim that no indigenous animal of the Australian bush killed in this manner. There was no doubt from my research that the cougar did. In killing deer, for example, the animal could leap up to 8 metres in making its strike:

> . . . the cougar springs upon the animal's withers and bites into the neck at the base of the skull. The big teeth sink deeper and deeper until the spinal cord is wrenched and severed.

I also found a primary source account of a killing, narrated by the American, Victor H. Cahalane:

Only sixteen feet away a buck picks at a seedling Manzanita. Immediately the cougar's muscles, like taut steel springs, release the pent-up energy. A swift cold fury, she makes two tremendous leaps then a final short one. The victim has only time to hear a rushing sound and to throw up its head. Then it is struck by the avalanche. With more than a hundred pounds' weight behind them, the great four paws strike the deer's shoulder. They drive the front quarters violently away. The head and neck snap around against the cougar's body. Like a sack of bones and flesh, the deer crashed to earth fully twenty feet off - he is dead, neck broken.

From my research there was no disputing it was cougar behaviour to eat the internal organs, often entering the belly after the kill to take its pick of the more succulent entrails. In some cases the flesh meat is not even touched. The bodies of countless sheep and kangaroos, their offal eaten away, bore graphic testament to this part of the greatest mystery in the Australian wilds.

I found a fascinating account of a typical cougar feast:

It usually opens the belly and removes the intestines, burying or covering them over. But it is fond of some of the smaller organs, and the liver is a particular delicacy. Next the ribs and loins are eaten and the first meal may amount to six or seven pounds of entrails.

I recalled the many sheep, lambs and kangaroos on the farms of Cordering and further afield, their entire rib cages and contents eaten away. And on the question of the partially-eaten sheep, lazily part-covered with twigs, leaves and broken soil. I did not have to look far to find it a well-documented part of cougar behaviour patterns:

The big cat eats its fill of the deer, then rakes pine needles, oak brush twigs and leaves over the remainder.

Sensibly, Charlie Sumner had gathered crucial pictorial evidence of dead 'roos and sheep found on and around his property, their necks broken, and partially eaten bodies obscured under a blanket of green rakings.

According to the reference books, one striking illustration of our ignorance of the animal's behaviour is confusion over the various noises it is alleged to make. This was crucial in the Australian context, for some farmers, including Dennis Earnshaw, claimed to have heard unidentifiable noises ranging from throaty growls to piercing screams. The books indicated that there are some cougar hunters in the Americas who stoutly maintain that the animal never makes any call above a low growl or spitting noise at hounds when cornered. But there are recorded instances, both in captivity and in the wild, where the animal has made a variety of sounds. The great naturalist and pioneer of wildlife research, Ernest Thomson Seton, claimed the cougar repertoire was that of a house cat, only largely amplified. Armand Denis wrote in *Cats of the World*:

> . . . *in spite of its size, (it) is not one of the roaring cats, whose only American representative is the jaguar. William Beed once heard a long, loud, drown-out quavering cry from a puma in the Bronx Zoo. On the other hand Robert Bean of the Chicago Zoo stated from long, long observation that all the females he had studied screamed but not the males, who uttered a whistle, and that the scream only occurs at mating time. Finally, Victor H. Cahalane heard a female in Washington Zoo shriek repeatedly.*

Cahalane commented:

> *I never heard a woman being murdered but I think it likely she might be a whole lot more quiet about it.*

The problem of the shortage of clear footprints, and the complication that the theory was beginning to prompt over-enthusiastic farmers into making claims about the pad marks of indigenous bush animals, was very real. Again, the reference books were informative, stressing that, overwhelmingly 'except in snow, the cougar sign is invisible.'

In short, nothing I had read significantly endangered the theory's continuing, frustrating, existence. In terms of the physical dimension and apparent behavioural characteristics reported in Australia, there appeared to be a strong thread of consistency. Given the general level of public awareness of what the animal looked like in the U.S., the physical consistency could only be taken so far. It was true, though, that the theory was nothing if not enhanced by the close approximation to detailed behavioural characteristics documented in books. It was also clear we were talking of an animal about which very little was known in Australia, and from all accounts, even in its home environment - but it also appeared to be an animal entirely suited to life in Australia. Without natural predators, and with all its food requirements easily procurable, it was entirely feasible that the animal could enjoy a relaxed and relatively anonymous existence in the millions of hectares of virtually unexplored scrub extending across Western Australia.

The one major complication I found bewildering was the question of sightings which involved a black animal. Many people, including Ian Offer, were insistent they had observed a black - often 'jet black' - animal. Nowhere in the literature was there mention of the American puma or cougar being entirely black in its body coloration.

Could Offer himself have been correct when he speculated about the possibility of Australia having its own indigenous big cat species - an animal which bore the apparent characteristics of the cougar, yet could be totally black in colour?

Despite, and in part, because of this one complication, a very real sense of excitement engulfed me as I struggled to make these arguments and counter-arguments stand up to searching analysis based on the reference book documentation. As I sat in the library I resolved to return again, within days, to the bush to press other lines of enquiry.

Sharp, large lights moving gracefully in the dark haunted me. My eyes dropped for the last time onto the open pages before me. They came to rest on an account of experiences in the pine-treed forests of America in another century:

When the benighted traveller or wearied hunter may be slumbering in his rudely and hastily constructed bivouac at the root of a huge tree amid the lonely forest, his fire nearly out, and all around most dismal, dreary and obscure, he may perchance be roused to a state of terror by the stealthy tread of the prowling cougar: or his frightened horse by snorting and struggles to get loose will awaken him in time to see the glistening eyes of the dangerous beast glaring upon him like two burning embers.

🐾 🐾 🐾

Strange prints, big and small, found on the Earnshaw property - aside from the animal kills, it was the only evidence of the mystery predator's presence.

One of the 'roo shooters who worked on the Earnshaw property.

Dead lambs believed to have been killed by the mystery predator.

Cat-like prints photographed on one of the farms.

More suspect prints found near where the cat-like animals were seen - this one appears to have five toes.

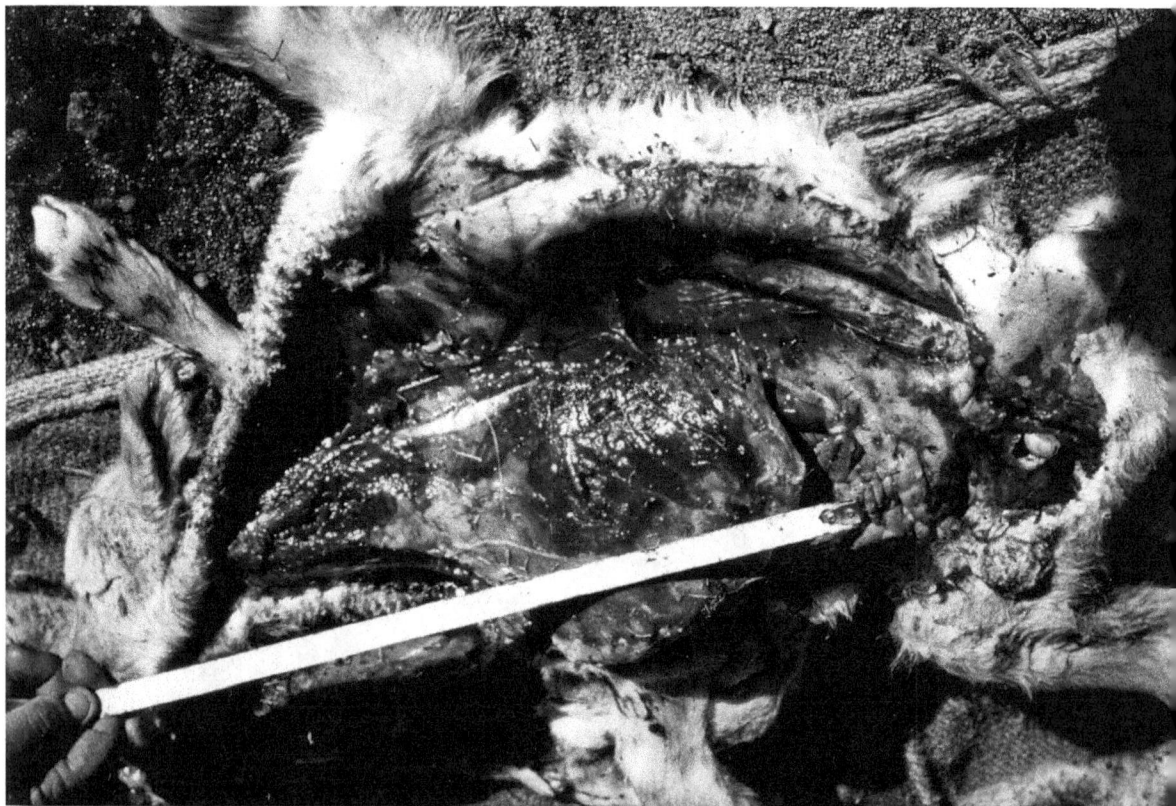

A classic mystery kill - the skin of the animal carcass has been peeled back in the manne
a big cat.

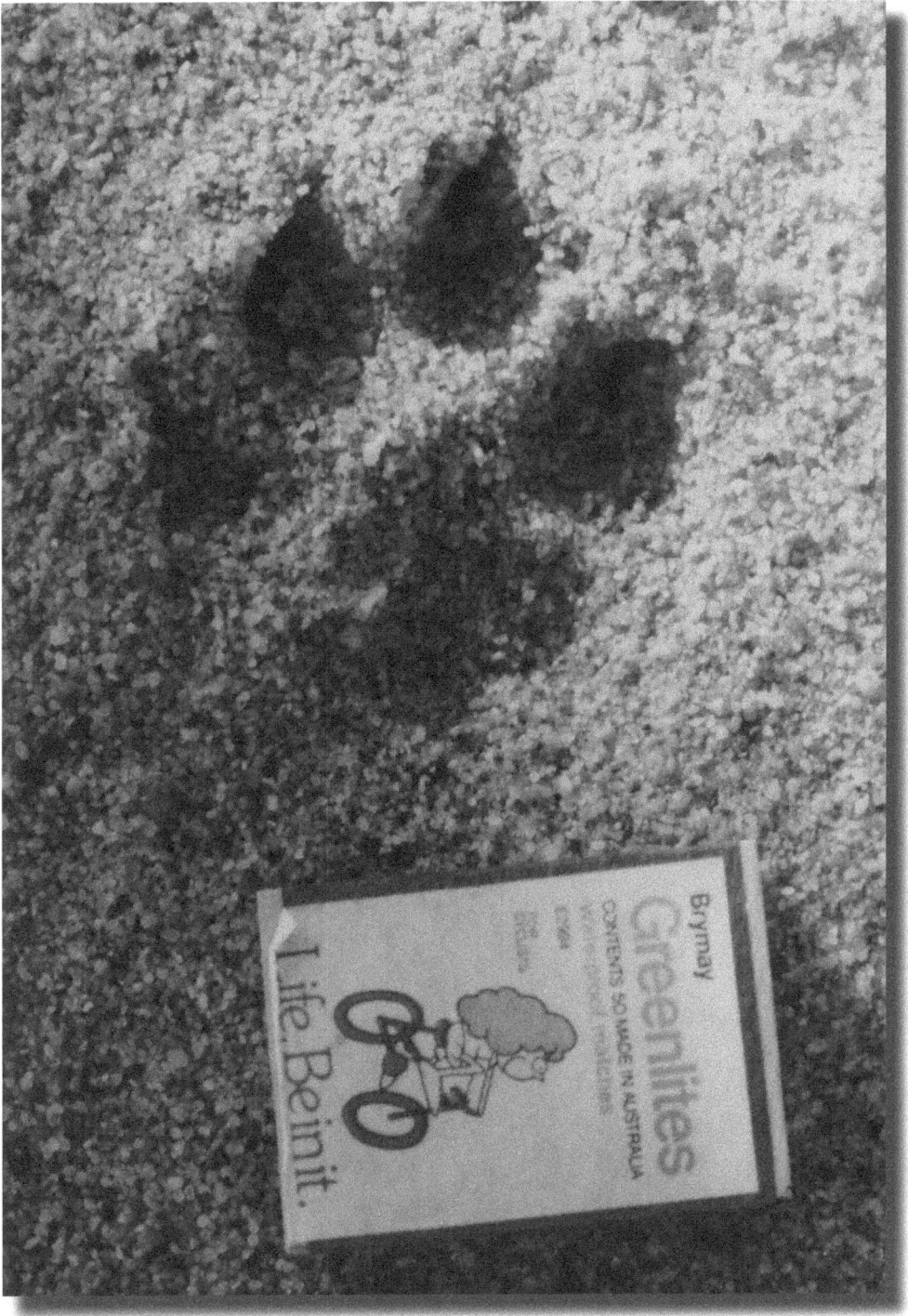

Another unusual print photographed on the farm.

Dennis, his wife Henny and their three children.

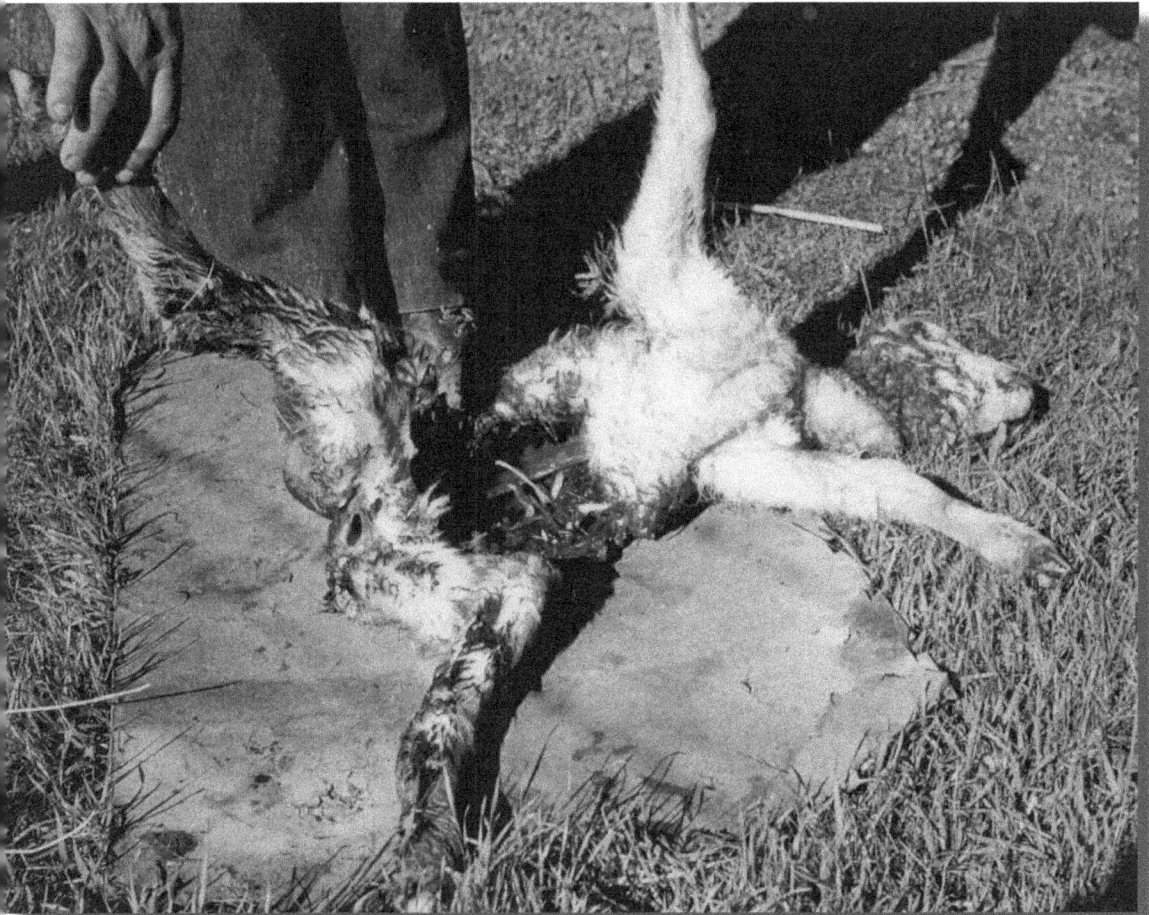

Another livestock kill on the farm.

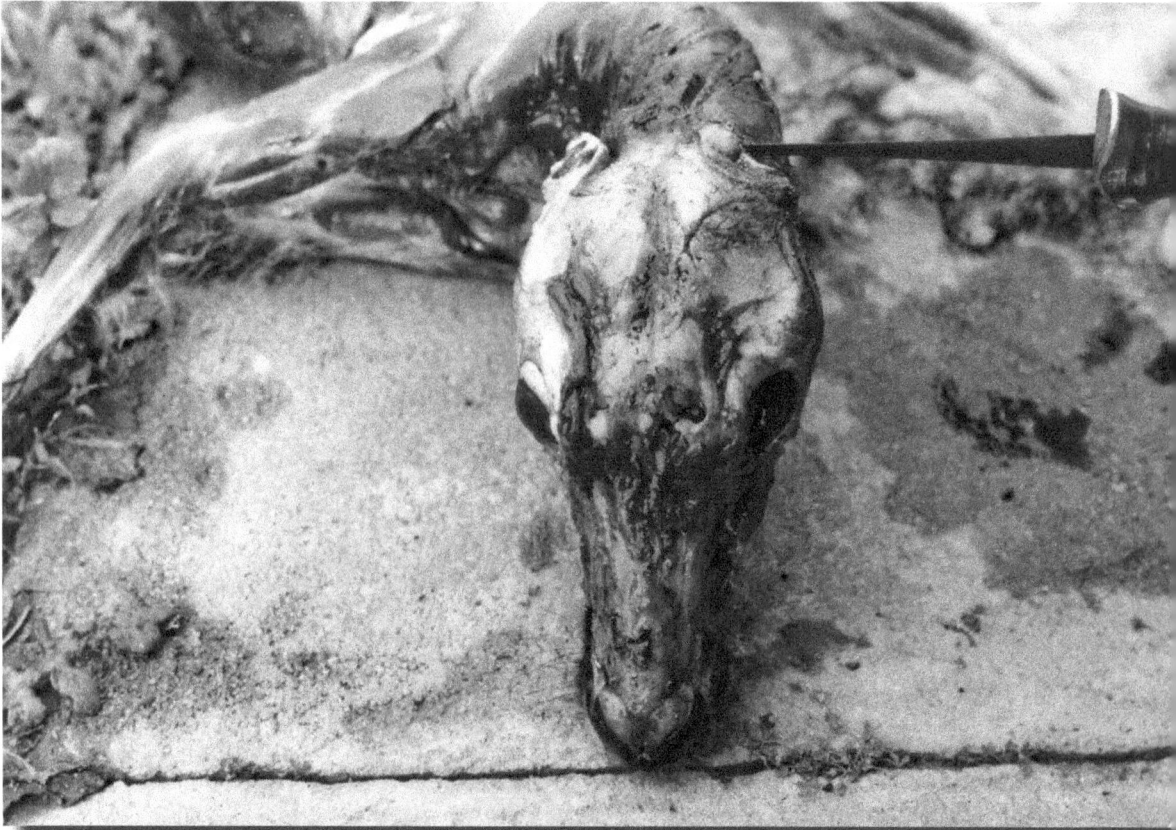

A view of a skinned kangaroo with puncture marks in its neck and bruising.

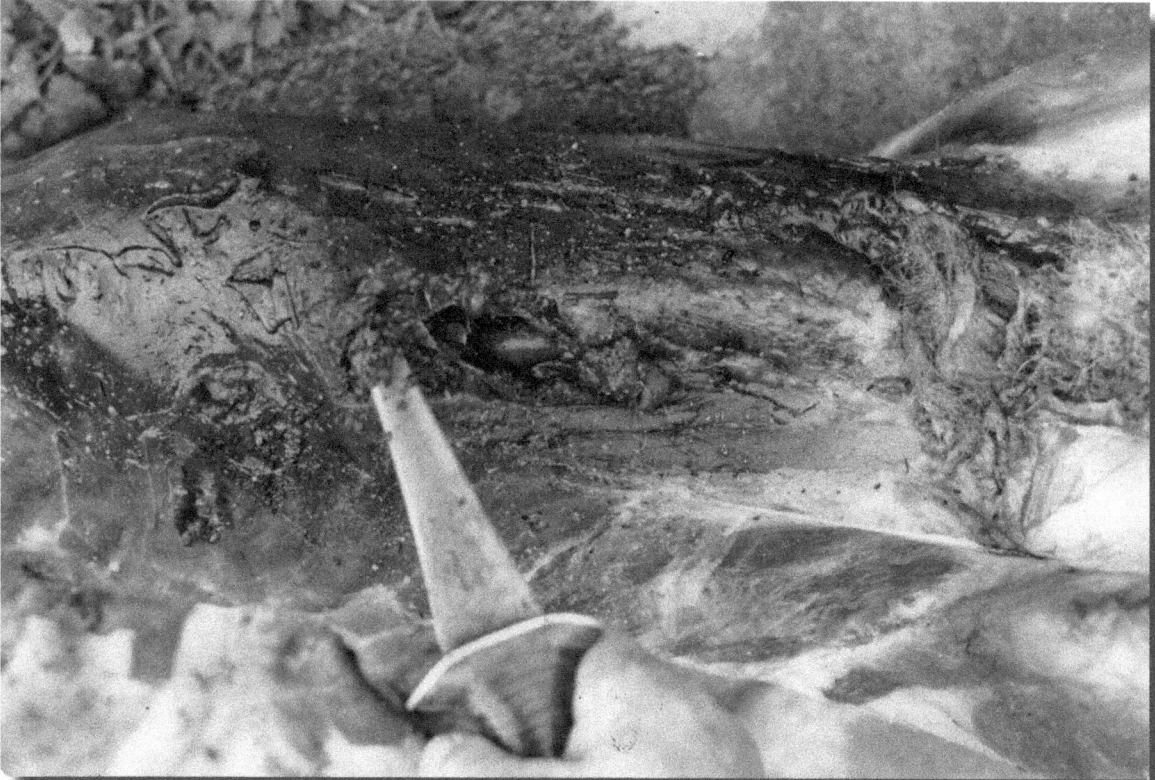

Another view of the skinned kangaroo with a knife blade indicating puncture marks.

A gutted kangaroo with a possible broken neck.

White sticks indicate puncture/scratch marks on this skinned kangaroo carcass.

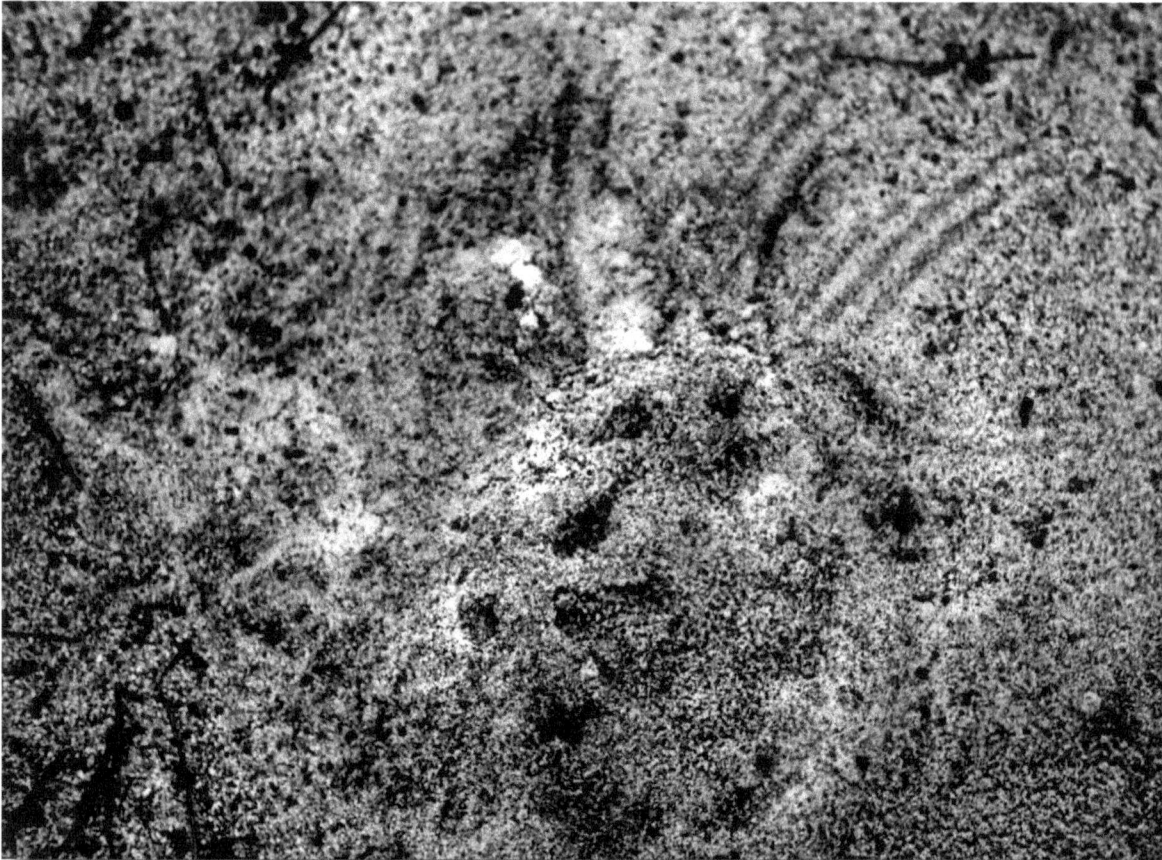

More cat-like scratches seen on the farm.

Dismembered lambs discovered by the Earnshaws.

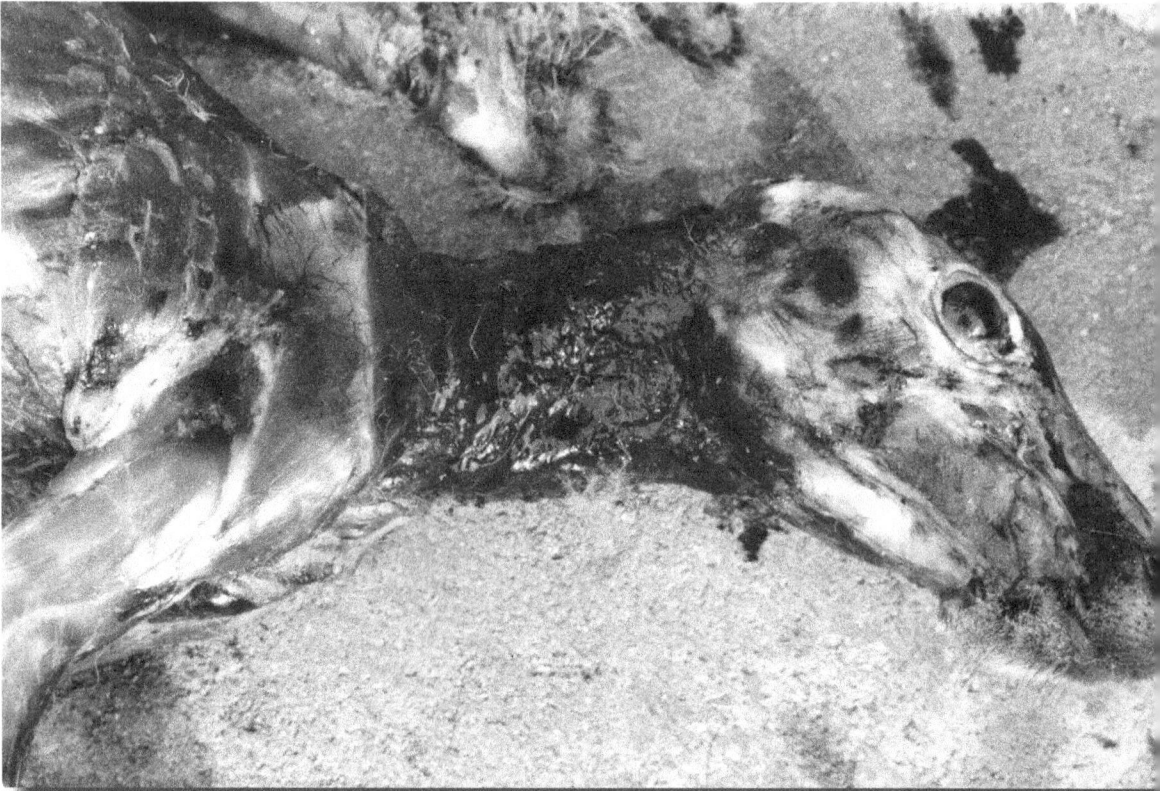

Another kangaroo skinned for a 'bush autopsy' to ascertain how it died.

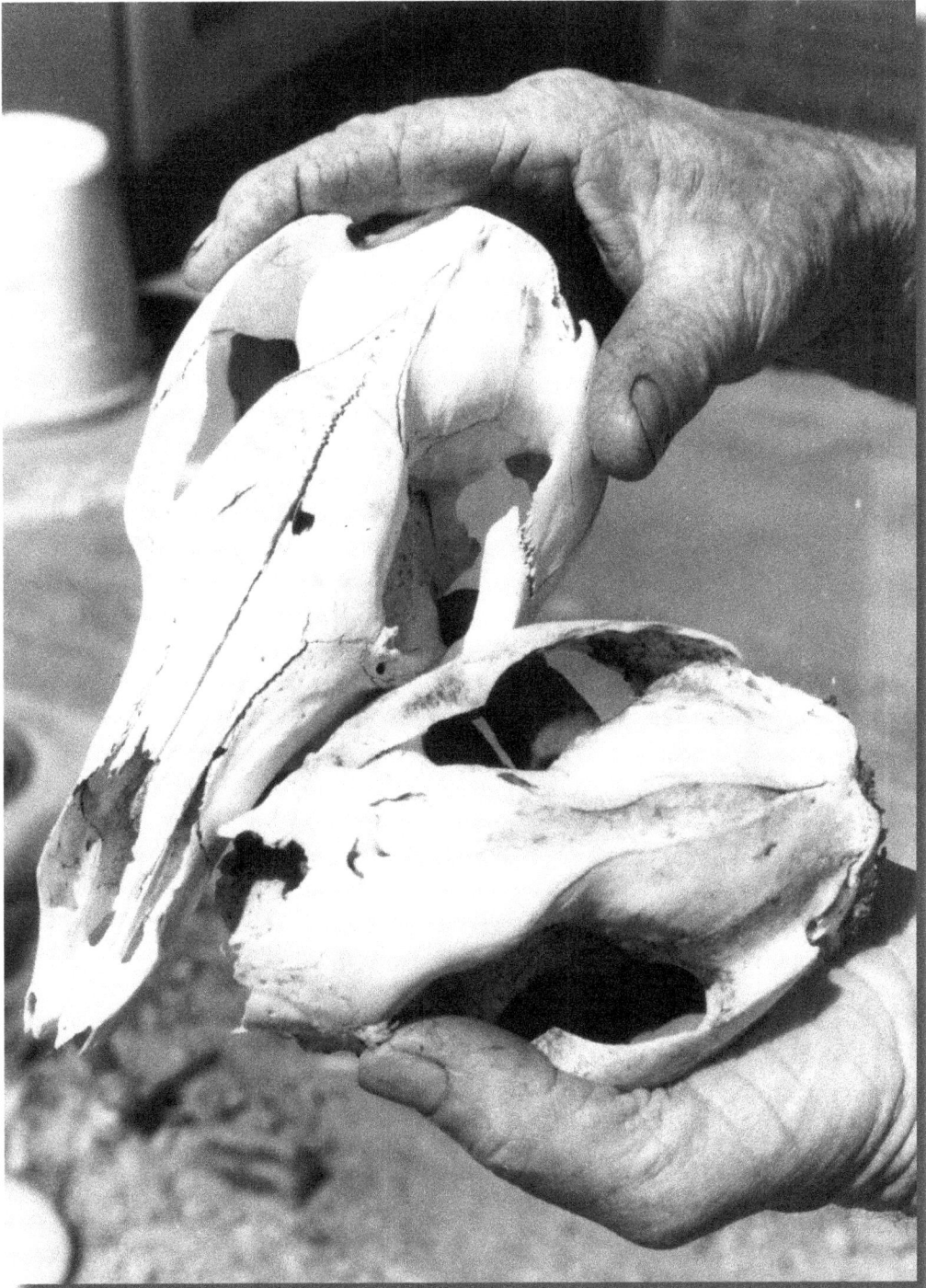

The punctured skulls of two kangaroos - what predator caused this kind of damage?

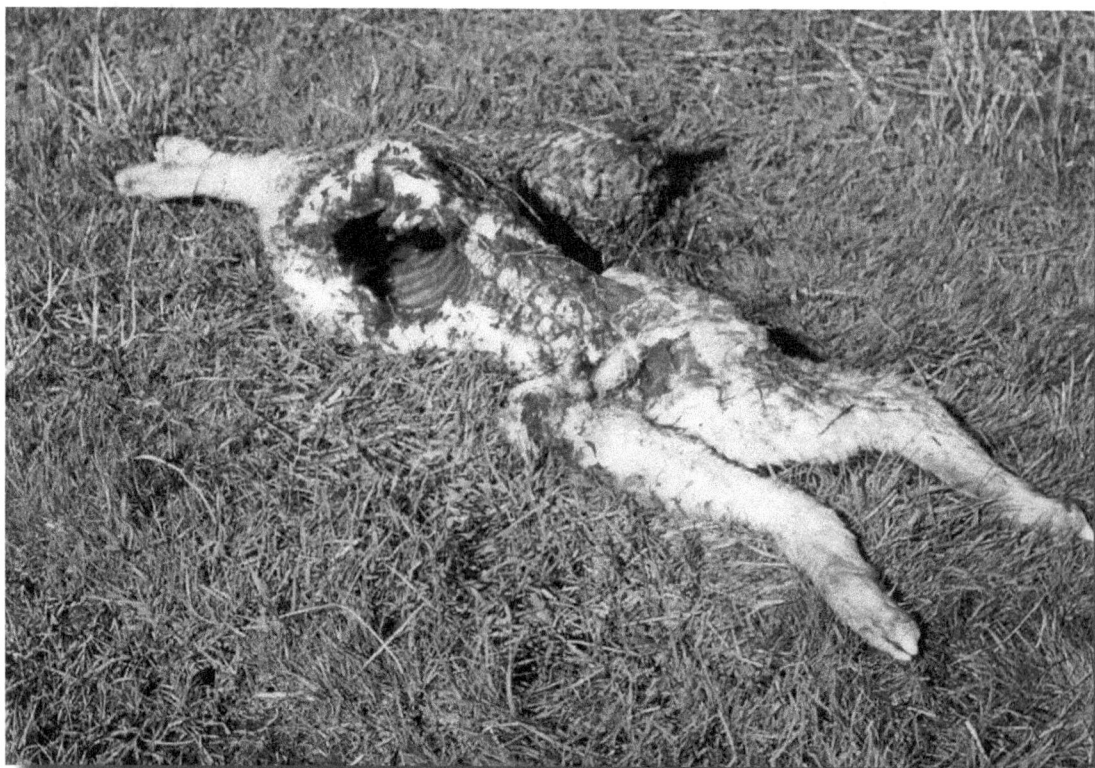

A sheep carcass neatly stripped of flesh.

Chapter Seven

THE LIBRARY FORAY WAS A WELOME BOOST for my enthusiasm in what became, at times, a desperately tedious exercise. I was in regular telephone contact with the key properties in the south west, but after much consideration I decided I needed to spend more time there chasing different leads. I was informed, for example, by one farmer that a local M.P., Mr David Evans, the Labour Party Opposition Member of the Legislative Assembly for the seat of Warren, alleged he knew of a circus accident near Donnybrook in the early 1960s. I contacted Mr Evans by telephone, and realised he had a long-standing interest in the matter. His constituents had periodically brought the question of mysterious stock losses to him. Evans grew to believe that the issue would eventually have political mileage for him in State Parliament. He informed me that his wife vaguely recollected observing, through a rain-blurred car window, a circus truck overturned on a narrow bush road one blustery winter's night in either 1961 or 1962. They had been travelling back from Perth to their country home after a short spell in the city during their children's school holidays.

Mr Evans could not recollect the incident himself, but that was because he was concentrating intently on the hazardous drive. His wife insisted it was one of the two years, and probably in August or September because of the regularity of their Perth holidays at that time. At my request the Evans' gave much thought to recalling as accurately as possible where the accident occurred. In a subsequent telephone conversation, Mr Evans informed me they had decided it had happened near a rail crossing on the Donnybrook to Bunbury road, 10 km west of Donnybrook.

It was clear that as *The Australian's* operation was picking up momentum I could not afford to spend a great deal of the company's time investigating the story unless I could provide new hard copy for publication. So it was obvious the only way to manage much of the nit-picking investigative work was on my own time - over weekends and on the occasional overnight trip into the bush. On four or five separate weekends I left work late on Friday evenings and drove south to join Earnshaw and the other farmers in attempting to pick up some of the leads, such as the one David Evans had provided. Working from the premise, however unlikely, about a circus accident, I surmised that even if it had occurred late at night on a remote road, someone in the local region would have known about it via the bush telegraph. It was crucial to find anyone who may have remembered the accident.

It also occurred to me that any such accident could have been recorded in one of the small provincial newspapers sprinkled throughout the bush.

The lady at the counter of the offices of the *Collie Mail* newspaper gaped disbelievingly when I asked if I could examine all back-copies published in August, September and October in both 1961 and 1962. The hunt then through thousands of pages of old newspapers was a dry and fruitless one. After hours of scanning the papers for what could have been, in the end, merely a two or three line reference to a local automobile accident, Earnshaw and I gave up, handing back to the still incredulous lady her bound volumes before retreating to the Collie Club Hotel for lunch. From the inconclusive pursuit we turned our endeavours to seeking out the scene of the accident witnessed by Mrs Evans.

She recollected seeing a trailer with a cage atop, on its side by the roadside in the rain, as her husband eased their vehicle through congested traffic at the accident site. The M.P.'s memory of the piece of road was hazy, but based on his wife's description, he had narrowed it down to a section which, years before, had had a sharp right bend some hundred metres from a railway crossing just outside of Donnybrook. Mr Evans recollected that, in later years, the road had been by-passed when a straight piece of highway was put through within metres of the old bend.

Earnshaw and I located the railway crossing, a simply marked road and rail intersection like so many that punctuate the Australian bush byways. A hundred metres back long the highway we left our car and began searching through the brush by the road. Suddenly Earnshaw yelled out.

I struggled through scrub to where he stood in the middle of two hundred metres of overgrown bitumen, the remnants of a degenerating piece of the old highway. At the end closest to the distant railway crossing the road arced in a vicious right hand bend. It was suddenly conceivable that we could have found the site of the accident witnessed by Mrs Evans. The prospect of such a sharp bend suddenly materialising out of a dark and wintery night, made the chances of a nasty accident seem all the more credible.

Within minutes Earnshaw and I had excitedly plotted a mental picture of how the accident could have been taken place. Everything seemed to fit the rough outline provided by Mrs Evans. As I peered around I noticed an old farmhouse some distance back, on the other side of the stretch of modern bitumen.

'I wonder if the people living over there were here in the early sixties?' I said to my companion, pointing to the distant farmhouse, as Earnshaw's face lit up with expectation.

'Well, why don't we just toddle over there and find out?' he said brightly.

From the direction the circus was travelling and the location of the cage recalled by Mrs Evans, Earnshaw and I believed we had fairly accurately painted a picture of the accident site. Now we needed someone living nearby who could fill in the details. We needed a more reliable account of the accident before we could begin to make meaningful assumptions about the possible escape of animals.

At the nearby farmhouse we were met by an elderly Italian man who initially had great difficulty hearing me, and then problems understanding me when I loudly introduced myself. My explanation degenerated into monosyllabic gesticulations until, finally, his wife loomed behind a screen door at the front of the farmhouse. With her better grasp of English rescuing the situation, the old man sullenly withdrew to his gardening.

Yes, her family had lived on the farm for many years, the woman confirmed, dragging whispy, long grey hair caught in the wind, back around her ear. But, she said, if anybody could remember such an incident it would be her son. He was working back down the highway picking apples in a sun-drenched grove. Earnshaw and I drove off the highway and down a grassy path into a field where plantation workers stood knee deep in sodden shrubbery, filling buckets with fruit.

'Yeah, I seem to remember a problem one of the circuses had on that stretch of old road,' the young man said as Earnshaw twitched a nervous sidelong glance at me.

'Yeah,' he repeated, rubbing the thighs of his jeans with muddied hands. 'It was a circus and I think they used an elephant . . . Yeah, that's it. A van had turned on its side in a ditch and they used an elephant to right it.'

'Show us,' I implored, nudging the young farmer towards our car.

Dennis Earnshaw stood by shaking his head, his face full of foreboding. Our companion was busily outlining what he recalled seeing so many years ago as a youngster. On a patch of the old road about 50 metres from his parents' farmhouse, a van and not a trailer had overturned in a gully. An elephant had helped hoist the van back into an upright position from where it was driven back to the road. But no, the farmer insisted the accident had happened nowhere near the bend described so accurately by Mrs Evans. At our urging the farmer again went through every detail he could recall, but in the end, nowhere did his account coincide with that of Mrs Evans. He was, in fact, far surer of his facts than many of the people I had questioned over aspects of the cougar controversy. Not only was his account at variance with Mrs Evans' on questions like the type of vehicle and the site of the accident, but he was also of the opinion that the circus had been travelling in the opposite direction to that suggested by the M.P.'s wife. And he could give us no real idea of approximately when the incident had taken place. Unlike Mrs Evans he had no immediate reference point in time with which to associate it. She knew quite well that the family had gone on holidays to Perth at certain times in the specific years.

Like a whisper on the wind, the explanation to the mystery was eluding us again. The accounts we drew together from talking to people in the Donnybrook area were either too vague, too generalised or too damnably complex for me to make any definitive assumptions about this alleged accident. No one else we encountered in the region could provide us with any helpful information. Many of them had, of course, heard these stories of a circus accident many years ago, and a few even knew of rumours that animals had escaped, but then they were only old bush stories, weren't they? I wondered whether it was possible that there had been two separate circus accidents within a few years of one another, within a few hundred yards of one another, on the same piece of highway.

The focus of my inquiries then turned to the town of Bridgetown, 50 kms south east of Donnybrook. One of the farmers had heard that in the early 1960's a circus trailer had been repaired in Bridgetown at a local engineering works. Inquiries in the town revealed that the largest plant capable of handling such a welding job would have been the firm of Armstrong and Cutmore.

In the period in question Bill Cutmore had been the company's proprietor. At his home in a shaded Bridgetown street, Mr Cutmore was, unfortunately, unable to provide me with anything beyond more rocks upon which my inquiries floundered. Almost unbearably, he could vaguely remember welding a gate back on to a damaged circus cage which had come in on a vehicle in the early sixties. But Cutmore's memory was faded. And it took considerable persistence to keep the gentle old man on the track in my questioning. He digressed slowly and disjointedly on to all manner of incidents that had occurred over the years at his factory but he could be no more specific than to agree he had done some kind of repair job a long, long time ago. It was pointless pursuing further details.

For years, Aubrey Chugg ran a fauna park at Dunsborough, east of Busselton, virtually on the coast near Cape Naturaliste. One weekend I was driving with Dennis Earnshaw through the area and we decided to approach Chugg and discuss the mystery with him. A lean, wrinkle-faced man, he had little patience with the stories. Like Ian Offer's, Chugg's fauna park provided him with an adequate income, attracting large numbers of tourists during the summer months. When I introduced Earnshaw and myself at the front of his residence near the park, I realised at once he had not absorbed either of our names once he sighted the marked press car I was driving. But he made no secret of his contempt for anyone who spoke about cougars in the bush.

'Some time back some local people swore they'd seen this yellow animal in the back scrub. Everyone was jumping up and down about this "creature". I told them it was a dog,' Chugg said.

'But no, some of them just wouldn't have it. I reckoned it was one of the neighbour's big dogs on the loose. I went to see him but he was adamant the dog was tethered in a back shed every night. He claimed the dog wouldn't kill a fly, let alone stock. Then there was a blow up one night when this yellow thing was sighted again. I went straight out to the neighbours and told him I thought the dog had been out. He got very upset and rushed out to the back shed. The dog wasn't in it, of course - it had slipped its line and was out into the local stock.'

'So you don't give any credence to these claims of the big cat?' I asked him.

' God, no,' he said. 'I just can't understand people like those folks over Cordering way and what they are saying in all this. Them Earnshaw blokes, for example, have been talking about this for a long time now and I just can't understand it. I read in the paper where they were saying . . .' It was obvious Chugg had not fully heard our introductions, such had been his initial apprehension at the sight of the car with *Sunday Times* and *Australian* advertising painted all over it. I interrupted him as he continued his references to the Earnshaw family by pointing out that it was, in fact, Dennis Earnshaw he was addressing. The park owner reacted with a start.

'Well, no offence intended, but I'm sorry, I just can't accept all this business. You blokes say you've seen what you reckon, but I've spent a lot of years in the bush and running this place, and I've never seen anything resembling what you describe.' Chugg then went on to talk about speculation over the years about "phantom" animals marauding the bush. Wherever an animal existed, he said, he believed a rational explanation could be found.

'But they just keep coming in with all these stories. Like one year an American fellow and his family were camping in the bush nearby and they drove their camper van in one morning, all excited. He was jabbering about seeing this big cougar in the early morning light, on a rock . . . Said it made some horrible noise at him, but it was obviously tommy rot.'

Earnshaw and I glanced at one another, but Chugg continued. 'And then there was the time when one of our neighbours came here screaming and yelling about seeing a big cat in the bush, out past the park. I never would have thought she'd be silly enough to start talking about it, too.'

The three of us were now on our haunches in the sunny front yard of Chugg's home. Earnshaw stared blankly away to the bush, dreamily biting on a tuft of grass, musing at Chugg's comments, the slightest suggestion of a sardonic smile on his lips. His face was covered with fatigue and frustration.

Chugg took a brief respite and I bought in. 'Mr Chugg, you say there's no possibility of any such animal being out there, basically because you've never seen it, right?'

'Yeah,' he said cautiously.

'Yet in the next breath you tell us about occasions where people have come in to ask you about incidents which seem to involve the same type of unidentified animal. Doesn't that tell you that although you might not have seen it, there still could be something there?'

The park owner paused for a moment before launching again into insistence that he knew the bush too well to be "conned" by stories of mystery animals.

'But excuse me,' I interrupted, 'you say it's not possible because you've never seen it yourself?'

'That's right,' he said positively.

Dennis Earnshaw and I later located the Williams family, on a tree covered orchard farm just outside Donnybrook. While Arthur Williams managed their farm and fruit-picking business, his son Bob worked for one of the freight companies, driving heavy lorries back and forward from Bunbury and Perth. The two men had each experienced their own sighting of an animal they could not explain in the Donnybrook area. It was Arthur Williams who made the bees' wax impressions of a series of large unidentified footprints, plaster casts of which had been rejected by the A.P.B. as dog tracks.

'One morning the cows were kicking up a terrible fuss,' Arthur Williams explained. 'I woke up just at daybreak and there was this commotion going on. I went out into the paddock and it was still reasonably dark. Anyway, all the cattle were herded into the centre of the paddock and making a hell of a racket. Then in the dimness I saw this thing come ripping in towards them. Each time it came in the cows went wild, almost trying to fend it off and away from the calves. Well, it seemed to make three runs. The first time it charged into the herd and then turned on the run and swung off over towards our tee-tree swamp. All of a sudden the stock started bawling again, and I saw it come sweeping in for the second time. Then, the third time it came running out of the twilight from another direction, but kept going past the cattle and out of sight. The last time it didn't get as close because it veered off. It would have been about 200 metres away. I could see it was a big grey animal - I could make out the cattle and I could see it sweeping in, but each time it went away I lost sight of it because there wasn't enough light. It had to be something strange, because them old cattle never pay any mind to foxes or anything. And our brown kelpie had come out there with me. As soon as it saw this thing charging around the dog dashed back to the house. It scared the life out of me too. I was shaking.'

While he could not make out precise details because of the limited light, Arthur Williams said the animal was 'long, big and grey, and it took long lopes.'

172

Some months later Bob Williams was driving to a neighbour's property at 9.00 a.m. one morning. 'As I came to the top of a hill, I saw this thing just standing there in the middle of the road. It was looking ahead in to the bush side on to me, but when it heard me coming, it turned to look at me and leapt away in one bound.' Williams claimed it was jet black in colour, and definitely a large muscle-bound cat with a long tail.

'I guess it was 80 to 100 metres away when I saw it, and I was travelling at around 75 kilometres an hour. I took just a few seconds to reach the spot, but it had disappeared by the time I got there.'

The Williams family had previously heard a throaty animal noise in the orchards while working, but shrugged it off. Ironically Arthur Williams recalled saying to his son at the time, 'If I didn't know better I'd say that was a tiger.' But after their sightings, they, too, began to piece together a tapestry of understanding about the predator's movements and style. Their previously unexplained dead stock took on a new meaning. Previously they had been at a loss to explain dead sheep and calves, their internal organs and chest cavities eaten away, the bones eaten clean, with no mess on the ground around the kill. For the Williams', the deep tooth marks on the kills told them something efficient was at work - and an animal totally foreign to the environment. They, too, were told by the A.P.B. that the stock losses were due to fox and eagle predation.

'They must have thought we were fools,' Arthur Williams said. 'We've seen the way foxes kill. But the stock and the 'roos have had their entrails eaten out, clean as a whistle. The killing style is the same all the way through - totally unique, and I reckon only a cat would do it,' Williams said.

I hauled the car into a dusty, single bowser service station, on a side lane corner in Nannup, 32 kms due west of Bridgetown. Inside, Earnshaw and I sipped Coca Cola to relieve the summer heat, and inquired where we could find George Cochman's home. His neat, tin roofed cottage stood in a quiet street, several hundred metres from the centre of the small township. It was set low in a bracket of rose bushes, hidden from the outside world. I pushed through a creaky front gate, and knocked at the entrance to the weather-board house. There came no answer.

The flyscreen door snapped back, and I wandered to the side of the building, where I could sense movement at the back. With a file of newspaper cuttings and photographs under my arm, I strolled down an overgrown driveway, past open windows, to where the back of the house was enveloped by a wide, sunlit, wooden-floored verandah. Below and behind, a green yard of vegetable gardens and grassy slopes slid away to the creek. A spindly staircase wound its way from the verandah, down into the yard where an impish teenage girl stood staring blankly up at my approach.

I looked into the darker air of the veranda. An aged sheepdog of dubious lineage, covered in flies, slumbered harmlessly in one corner. I stepped on to the verandah and called out Cochman's name. The girl in the yard below stumbled forward and yelled something unintelligible in a strained voice. Struggling up the slope to the base of the stairs, she made no effort to join them, merely staring at me, taking thick, troubled breaths.

I called again for Mr Cochman and this time won a reply.

'Hello?' he called. A spindly old man appeared in the doorway which led from the verandah into the kitchen. I blurted out my introduction, and after he looked me over for some moments, Cochman finally gestured me to cross the verandah. In the grubby kitchen I outlined the reason for my visit, but he stood by, reactionless. Then he abruptly interrupted with an offer of a cup of tea. I nodded, and he motioned for me to sit at a laminex table, the kitchen's centre piece.

I began: 'The A.P.B. told me that if I wanted to know anything about the bush in this part of the world I should find George Cochman. So I have. There are all these stories about animals and tracks and sightings. What I want to do is to talk to someone who knows tracks - who can say definitely, one way or another, what a certain track is.' I steadied myself as Cochman finally gave me his full attention. 'Now, these people say there is a big cat in the bush . . .'

'It's bullshit,' the old man barked. 'I've heard all this, and I tell you it's bullshit,' he repeated. There was a short silence then he resumed. 'Son, you want somebody who knows tracks - well you've got him. I've spent more years in the bush than you've been alive, and I've seen it all. There isn't very much I don't know about its animals, or the marks they make. These people are just talking through their hats about this cat business.'

'You don't believe there's anything at all in it, then?'

'No. I can honestly say I've never seen anything that resembles a big cat, and if anybody should know it would be me.'

'So that means that if I showed you pictures of tracks you'd be able to tell me what made them.'

'Yup,' Cochman said, scouring the room for the evasive teapot. 'I've seen everything that there is to be seen in the bush,' he said, shuffling across the room in a battered pair of bedroom slippers, their heels trodden to the ground.

'Alright, I've got these pictures and I'd like you to look at them and tell me what made the tracks featuring in them,' I said, drawing a pile of prints from a manila folder. There was a group of photographs Neil Eliot had taken, and some I had taken of tracks in the Cordering area. Unfortunately, I had not used a cigarette box or a set of car keys to illustrate the relative size of the different prints. And in fact, I had two or three photos of one very good footprint that I had taken from different angles and heights, while hunched over above it. It was one of these pictures I first handed to the old man on his return from the kitchen sink.

He grabbed it and frowned hard. He then moved it away from his eyes to full arm's length, and dropped it to the table. Pinching an itchy ear lobe, he seemed to glare at the print before him. Then he took it up again, and walked into the doorway, where the sunlit verandah gave better light. He turned the picture from side to side, squinting at it through a brow creased by years in the sun. Snorting like an old bull, he finally walked back across the kitchen and threw the photograph on to the table.

'Kangaroo dog,' he said triumphantly, ' a big one too. A kangaroo dog make that track - that's what it was. I was a dogger for years and I know a kangaroo dog track when I see one,' he said.

'Are you sure?' I asked.

'Positive,' he asserted, taking the picture up again, his head bent sideways, reaching for light in the dim kitchen. Cochman then outlined all the conformation of the pad mark that told him it was a big dog.

I scratched my forehead and stared at the pile of pictures and newspaper cuttings. On top sat another picture. It was, in fact, another print of the same mark, only photographed by me from a slightly different angle. It was the same footprint that Cochman was ruminating over. Realising this, I spontaneously grabbed it and thrust it at Cochman, who dropped the first photograph to the table.

'And what's that?' I asked breathlessly.

The old man went through the routine again. He walked out into the light, and then turned back to the table. 'Well, son,' he said, 'I'm sorry, but that ain't no big cat either. That's a fox. Just a little bloke, but it's definitely a fox.'

I was speechless. This was a man whose expertise on animal tracks underpinned, to a large extent, the contempt of some less experienced district A.P.B. officers for the big cat theory.

'Mr Cochman, I'll ask you once again,' I said slowly. 'Look at both these padmarks again and tell me what animal made them.' I placed the two pictures side by side on the table. The footprint sat at different angles in the frame of each print, and appeared to the naked eye to be of slightly different sizes. I began to gather up all my material. More animated now, Cochman thumped the table with an index finger.

'That's a kangaroo dog and that's a fox - no doubt in the world about it,' he said indignantly.

I grabbed the two pictures and pushed them into a manila folder. 'Well, thanks Mr Cochman, you've been a great help to me, but I really must go,' I said, quickly spinning through the doorway of the verandah.

The old dog still hadn't moved from where it lay on the greying floorboards. I glanced over the verandah edge, and the girl was nowhere to be seen below. My abrupt departure was certainly offhand, and probably rude.

'Well, aren't you going to stay for a cup of tea?' Cochman called after me from inside, teapot in hand. I made no effort to answer as I swung off the verandah, and up the driveway to my car.

🐾 🐾 🐾

Barry Morris' cat picture, showing the silhouette of a cat-like animal on a ridge.

Chapter Eight

TOWARDS THE END OF A HECTIC DAY in the office, my phone rang yet again. The caller calmly informed me he had taken a photo of an animal in the bush which he believed I could be interested in examining. He said the animal resembled an enormous cat, and wondered if *The Australian* would be interested in purchasing it. Battling to conceal a sharp surge of excitement, I suggested he come to my office, adding the rider that I would only consider a purchase if he guaranteed my paper would have first option. He said he intended offering the picture for the best price, but agreed to see me before talking to any other papers in Perth. Some hours later I ushered Barry Morris, a tall, well-dressed local businessman to my office desk.

He produced a slide transparency, which he claimed was a picture he had taken from the window of his car while travelling on a property in the north west of the State. I was startled when he revealed the picture was taken on a station outside Carnarvon, over 1000 kilometres north of Perth.

'I was travelling with my wife and my parents in our car when we noticed this big cat just loping along a rise. We stopped, and as it headed over the hill, I took out my camera and snapped the picture,' Morris said. He had learned of my involvement through the newspaper stories that had appeared under my byline, and he candidly admitted he wanted to sell this picture to the highest bidding news group. I was confident I was the first newspaper man he had yet approached, but I was finding it difficult to disguise my enthusiasm in the face of such an important breakthrough. Henry Kissinger observed that negotiators should never betray any emotion, but I could not help but wonder whether this was the crucial development - the first photographic evidence confirming the existence of some kind of large feline predator in the Australian bush. On the slide transparency it was difficult to ascertain the exact shape of an intriguing black figure on the horizon of a fairly typical outback scene.

I alerted Neil Eliot in the photographic department downstairs, and then led Morris through the honeycombed *Sunday Times* offices, to where the photographer was waiting expectantly.

Eliot set about 'blowing up' the transparency by making a negative of it and then turning it into a black and white photographic print. We needed to keep as much detail of the animal's outlines as possible, so he placed the transparency virtually on the floor, and stretched the enlarging machine to its maximum setting, succeeding eventually in magnifying the relevant section of the transparency to around one hundred times its original size.

Interestingly, Morris insisted that the transparency, and all the prints produced, never leave his sight. His brutally obvious suspicion disturbed me. While professing to be a total photographic amateur who stumbled onto a lucky picture, he seemed solemnly intent on not allowing any copies of it to slip from his grasp. Clearly he was seeking to establish a negotiating price. And I began to play down the significance of the picture to dispel his hopes of a high price. I urged him to indicate his figure, and he finally admitted he wanted $1000 for the photo. I scoffed at the suggestion, and calmly walked from the photographic room, trying to maintain a semblance of faint derision. Once outside I scampered upstairs to talk to my editor in Sydney. He urged me to liaise with the Managing Director of Rupert Murdoch's Western Australian operations, Mr Murray James. James was a newspaper proprietor of immense experience and considerable power inside the Perth establishment. While he and I enjoyed a very friendly working relationship, he occasionally tempered my enthusiasm with the cooler head of experience. I was often thankful to be guided by his advice. He was extraordinarily sceptical about the entire cougar theory, while at the same time not the least perturbed if legitimate stories about it helped sell *The Australian* and *The Sunday Times* in Western Australia.

When the slide was enlarged as far as possible, with a minimum blurring of clarity, it revealed a jet-black, cat-like animal, its tail leaping high in a semi-circle over its body, the lower part of its legs lost to sight as it disappeared on the horizon. Murray James was suspicious of it from the first, and initially refused my entreaties to allow me to negotiate a price.

He feared con-men were at work. But I insisted he allow me to attempt to beat the price down, and finally he gave ground only to that extent. Morris insisted he wanted $1000, and promptly left the building, having made sure he had collected every picture and negative the photographers had made from the transparency. I would learn later that he had negotiated, without success, with other Perth-based newspapers before giving up. But at that time I could scarcely endure the frustration. While I agreed with Murray James's doubts about the monetary value of the picture, I was, however, frustrated that what could, conceivably, have been the first photograph ever taken of a new, national wildlife phenomenon, had slipped through my fingers.

By now my grasp of the controversy was becoming confused in an embroilment of claim and counterclaim. I felt I could have been losing the touchstone of objectivity that allowed me to make dispassionate judgements. That, of itself, was beginning to make me wary. I rationalised the loss of the picture away by telling myself, in a somewhat depressed moment, that the whole thing was preposterous and totally unscientific. The pressure of public ridicule, coming as it did even from some close friends, was also wearing. Quite validly, everyone wanted to know why the animal had not been shot or captured. There were so many questions that remained unanswered and I was becoming inpatient with the time and effort needed to explain to people the detailed background that seemed to support the theory's conceivability.

The next day I had an appointment with Des Gooding and I intended taking to him the box of "evidence" that I brought back from the farms, including plaster casts and photographs. I met Gooding and John McSwain in Gooding's small office, but after friendly chit-chat the session became a little heated when I rehashed the entire theory again with the A.P.B. officials.

Their doggers in the south-west were insisting that dogs were responsible for the killings and the footprints. McSwain mentioned the possibility of dingoes, and Gooding alluded to reports that wild pigs had moved through the district. The fact that the farmers, the people who lived their lives in the bush, and depended for their livelihoods on knowing their environment, had bitterly derided these suggestions left Gooding and McSwain intractable. I put it to them that surely the people who lived in the south-west knew better what sort of animals were there than the A.P.B. Gooding retorted by saying that highly skilled and experienced department officials were paid to know what went on in the bush. He fell back again on the claim that wild dogs were responsible, and that his men had been unable to come up with anything out of the ordinary. They had set baits and traps, and come up with no strange animals in the Cordering region. I then threw a cat among the pigeons, so the speak, by asking why it was then, that all this extra work had not even produced one of the "pack" of dogs allegedly responsible for the wide-spread stock losses.

'The Government has conceded that something is wrong - that there is some animal marauding and killing stock, so where are the wild dogs that your men are so skilled at catching?' I asked. With that, John McSwain became visibly agitated, and making his apologies he stalked from the room, apparently angered by my persistence. It seemed to me extraordinary that weeks before, the A.P.B. Executive Director had gone on public record to admit that an officer of his had some recollection of a circus accident in the early sixties. It amazed me to think that this officer had just stormed out in anger because I refused to accept the easy options being presented by the authorities.

Despite McSwain's discomfort I believed that Des Gooding was trying very hard to maintain total objectivity in his inquiries. He was clearly imposing the most rigid evidential conditions on the theory to test it for flaws to the last detail. It was significant that he was using a disciplined scientific base in his inquiries. He was working from the premise that responsibility for establishing a case with emphatic evidence rested with the farmers. He rejected the plaster casts, on the advice of his officers, as the markings of dogs. However, I showed him a set of pictures taken of a kangaroo, found partially buried under twigs, with its neck broken, deep fang marks to its throat and skull, and its heart, lungs and liver eaten away through an almost clinical incision into the lower body. McSwain said this was killing behaviours of wild dingoes, But Gooding was clearly mystified.

As the conversation became more and more brittle, Gooding finally gave way. I sensed each time we talked that he was as much in the dark as I. So I determined to pursue him from the same premise he was using. I wanted him to prove to me that the animal did *not* exist. So far he had failed to do so.

'Look, if one of the farmers came in here today with the footprint of a real cougar, I would definitely be able to identify it,' he said confidently, after a long pause.

"How?' I asked despairingly.

'That doesn't matter,' he continued, 'but we've been looking at the animals in the zoo, taken samples from them, and we know what a cougar's footprints look like. If one comes in, I'll know it.'

'How can you be so sure?'

Gooding shifted awkwardly in his chair. 'Look, this is a difficult area . . . you can't expect me to say too much. Suffice to say we know enough to be sure that what these farmers have got are not cougar footprints,' he said, pointing to the box of plaster casts close by on his desk. When he said the A.P.B. had established a "key" piece of evidence, I asked him to reveal it to me.

'To be frank with you it's quite clear yon have been working very closely with the people down there,' he said. 'I can't say too much about it, otherwise next week they'll all be coming in here with the right footprints.'

With that I reacted with some anger. 'Excuse me,' I said emphatically, 'but I resent the imputation that I would run confidential information back and forward to the farmers. I accept that they have been feeding me in all this, but you well understand that's part of my job. However, I am a professional journalist, Mr Gooding, and I have been spending a lot of my company's money, not to mention a hell of a lot of my own, on investigating what I believe is potentially an important story. If you have any such piece of key evidence that indisputably destroys the farmers' claims, then I would ask you to explain to me so I can withdraw from these enquiries and stop wasting both your time and mine.

'What I am saying,' I continued more diplomatically, 'is that you have my personal assurance that any confidential information you tell me will not be relayed to anyone outside this room. But you must put me in the picture so that we can stop wasting one another's time.' My indignation did the trick. Gooding first fixed me with an inquisitive stare and then relented. He agree to divulge the details of this key evidence on the understanding that I would not reveal it to anyone.

From a filing cabinet behind his chair he pulled a photostat of a series of animal footprints. I didn't mention that the photostat diagram was from one of the books I had uncovered in my own inquires in the reference libraries. The diagram indicated a cougar footprint was between three inches and three-and-a-half inches in width. The print was made up of four, roughly oval-shaped toe marks, without any toenail indentations, and a roughly triangular heel pad, the rear section of which divided into three quite distinct circular nodes. Gooding claimed that when cougars' feet, and in fact, all members of the cat family, were examined, they revealed this quite distinct triple node effect on the rear pyramidal pad. He said dogs did not have this characteristic in sharp detail, and this was the major difference. Canine animals did not share this feature, yet a simple examination of a tabby cat's feet would show the felines did.

'So until we've seen prints with these nodes we haven't seen cougar prints,' he said decisively.

On the face of it, Gooding had revealed to me details about the animal which cast serious doubts on the farmers' claims. Despite all that had gone before, the Government's officer with responsibility for the official investigation had confidentially explained to me a significant evidential detail which seemed to undermine a crucial part of the farmers' claims. Gooding also informed me he had made extensive inquiries through his Department in an effort to shed light on the question of the alleged circus accident.

'But I thought there were no longer any records left going back far enough to help us?' I said.

The A.P.B. man told me that although this had earlier appeared to be the case, further enquiries had turned up relevant details locked away in a disused filing cabinet. 'So now, let's hear you guess how many cougars came into this state between 1958 and 1974 in circuses,' he said. 'Hundreds, you think? Well, the records show that only one came in during that time - it left with the circus, and would have found it difficult breeding by itself had it got away.'

I was satisfied, as I left Gooding's office, that despite a mass of nagging and, as yet, unexplained questions, he had provided me with tangible and crucial new evidence.

🐾 🐾 🐾

At the end of the 1960s Bob Neuman had come to Perth seeking his fortune. An ex-rancher from the backwood mountains of Montana in the United States, he had heard much about Western Australia, and decided to investigate its potential. He and his wife fell instantly in love with the place and began planning to build a business. Ten years later the prosperous Dakota stud farm at Muchea, Bullsbrook, 50 km north of Perth, bore witness to his success.

The rambling corral network on the ranch was a strong summertime drawcard for tourists and Neuman quickly found a niche among Western Australians keen to make us of his expertise as a horse breeder and handler. He gradually built up one of the state's finest strings of Appaloosas and quarter horses.

Neuman had been devoted to the outdoors from his earliest childhood. He was obviously a product of a genuine American mountain cowboy lifestyle. Balding, with a massive physique developed through years of handling horses, and bronzed by the Western Australian sun, he was happily learning the intricacies of the Australian bush, just as he had come to understand the forests of Montana. There was little he didn't know about life in the snow-covered Western Rockies. He was also an experienced cougar hunter.

Through a mutual acquaintance Neuman met Don Hart, an Agriculture Protection Board research officer, who was surprised to learn about Neuman's knowledge of, and interest in, Montana's pumas. The ranch owner proudly displayed photographs of himself as a young man, surrounded by the accoutrements of the hunt - high powered rifles, ammunition belts, rangy and powerful hunting hounds, and dead cougars.

Hart quickly informed Des Gooding, and soon after Neuman was asked if he would go to the south west to consider the farmers' claims. The slow-talking rancher with the quintessential American drawl happily agreed, and drove to Cordering with a couple of horses in a trailer. He spent three days riding through the region and meeting Dennis Earnshaw, Charlie Sumner and the other farmers. The A.P.B. had agreed to pay for his petrol for the round trip.

The farmers showed the American dead stock, mostly lambs, their throats savagely mauled, and their chest cavities and stomachs often cleanly eaten away. Newman was astounded. After a few days, Dennis Earnshaw summoned the courage to pop the question.

'Well, what do you think it is?' he finally asked the American late one afternoon after more dead stock had been found in a paddock in the district.

'Man,' Neuman said, lingering over the word, 'you sure got cougars.'

In fact, from the moment he first examined the dead lambs, Bob Neuman was certain that a big feline was responsible. The ravaged bodies bore all the hallmarks of a cougar attack. It was the clinical sureness of the assault, and the almost delicate removal of various organs and whole sections of flesh and bone from different parts of the bodies, that told him a large feline was at work. As well, he pointed to the critical puncture marks, often obscured under rolls of wool, or hidden in the bloody gore of the substantial bruising of the animals' flanks and necks.

'It's gotta be cats,' Neuman told Earnshaw. 'A cat is the only thing that will kill a sheep this way. They don't make a mess and they don't tear the wool out in big lumps and leave it scattered around like dogs do. I've seen rabbits and sheep and deer in the States just eaten out like here - nothing left. Clean as a whistle - picks 'em clean, does cats. What you got here is the style of the kill all the way through.'

Newman's arrival on the scene in Cordering was important because he began to give the farmers, for the first time, definitive insights into what was happening around them. They showed him various photographs and plaster casts of footprints. Some of these, he was adamant, were not from the feline animal. He believed that distorted fox tracks, and other "natural" phenomena, were being mistaken for signs of the cat by some of the more over-zealous farmers.

'The problem here is that you've got so much rocky and stony ground. It's all pretty hard country in that bush, and you just ain't gonna see the tracks very often. Like, the mamma cat - well, she'll lead you a great old dance. She might come upon a crik. She'll stop and look at the muddy sand around the crik and she'll stay on the dry, and move down along the water for maybe a mile, till she finds a tree fallen down over a narrow part where she can cross. She won' leave no tracks.'

'And your trapping's no good either,' Neuman counselled the farmers. 'I've never known anyone to ever catch one in a trap - a lot of people been setting these ole traps, and they come back to find the ole cat's eaten the bait, and it ain't sprung.'

Neuman told the farmers he believed they were working under a massive disadvantage, compared to hunters in the U.S.

'Over there they got plenty of snow in a lot of these rocky areas. The cat comes in, makes a kill, eats and gets away, but you always got his tracks in the snow to start with. Here you can't see too many tracks.'

The farmers were immensely buoyed by Neuman's observations. Some were jubilant. Des Gooding had brought him to the district to examine the phenomenon, and his findings categorically supported their claims. They enthused that it would surely prompt more Government action - a more serious attempt to deploy men and money to examine the details of their claims.

Dennis Earnshaw asked Neuman, 'Is there any doubt in your mind, based on what you've seen, about what kind of animal it is?'

Neuman replied: 'There's no doubt. In fact, I'd be willing to go so far as to bet a lot of money that you got big cats running wild here and doing a lot of this damage. I'd be willing to bet $1000 here and now that you boys got a big cat of some sort.'

After his few days in the region, Neuman again talked to the A.P.B. officers. They asked him what he thought about the farmers' claims, and he told them it appeared the predator was indeed a big feline.

Neuman and Dennis Earnshaw became very friendly in the months following the American's initial involvement. Coincidentally, Earnshaw received a letter from a Perth resident who informed him that he had the only male bloodhound of breeding age in Western Australia.

The dog, out of an American-British breeding champion which had itself won a number of show awards, including the Perth Royal, was for sale, because its owner was being transferred to Canberra in his employment. The dog had done some minor hunting in the Western Australian bush, and his owner offered the dog for training by Neuman for the cat inquiries. The stud rancher put the bloodhound through its paces at Bullsbrook, but reluctantly came to the conclusion that it would be unable to help in the Cordering inquiries. It was returned to its owner.

Neuman told Earnshaw that a pack of dogs would be more appropriate if the cats were to be successfully hunted. A friend of Earnshaw's in Perth bred fox hounds, and he agreed to procure and train two such animals.

Neuman began working with the dogs on his stud ranch, but the experiment also proved to be a disaster. In secret, he used domestic cats and their scents to train the dogs to chase. As long as the dogs could see the cat they would follow until it was treed. When Neuman tried to train them to chase purely on scent, however, without sightings, the dogs lost the track and floundered badly, while the cats made an easy escape.

The fox hounds were obviously unsuitable, and Neuman informed Earnshaw that they could not be trained for the job.

Some weeks after his first visit to Cordering, two Americans, Estin Jones and Casey Collins, who, like Neuman, had migrated to Australia, visited his stud while on holidays from The Eastern States. While on the farm they noticed the dogs tied up in the yard and enquired of Neuman about their breeding.

Just by chance, both had also had extensive experience of cougar hunting in the United States. In fact, one of the men's father was one of the most famous professional hunters in the U.S., a man who had built up a successful international business by organising and hosting safaris for businessmen millionaires through the American mountains. He also took parties to South Africa and part of Asia to hunt other big cats, including black panthers.

Both the visitors were astounded when Neuman related the theory of the Cordering cougar. They immediately insisted they visit the region, so the next day they all drove to the south west for the afternoon to look into the matter.

After a tour of the properties, during which they talked to the farmers, the three Americans were unanimous - Australia, like other continents of the world, could boast its own species of big cat. Earnshaw, Neuman, Collins and Jones began discussing the need to import packs of good cougar hounds into Western Australia.

Later they made extensive enquiries, but it was clear that the landing costs alone could be over $2000 per animal, and with quarantine restrictions it could be over a year before the animals were released in Australia. At a time when the prospects were high that a lucky shot by a Western Australian farmer could suddenly substantiate their claims, a year-long wait, and the growing costs of importing the dogs and then maintaining them, seemed out of the question.

'It's a shame,' Neuman told Earnshaw, ' 'cause with just one of them old dogs you could get out early next morning after a kill, put him on the track before the dew's melted, and you'd get one in no time. You start to push these lazy ole cougars down here with a good dog and they'll be up a tree in no time,' he said. 'They only got them little lungs, and with a good hound after 'em a-bellowin', they'd go to tree quick-smart.

'You got to remember though, them cats are good. Like when I was in the mountain country, I went out one year after a female who'd been coming in from the forests, killing, and going off again. The hounds got the scent and I could see from the tracks in the snow she had kittens with her. We got on after the little ones, but then the old lady came down and cut across the kittens' trails to lead the dogs off. She played the dogs out for a full day till they couldn't go no further. The kittens' tracks had disappeared and we was just chasing her, but then we gave up. I didn't get no kittens, and I didn't get her - that's how it is with 'em sometimes.

During subsequent visits to the south west, Neuman was mystified by the apparent killings for the sheer sake of killing. He knew the cougar to be an animal which killed to eat and to educate its young. But the number of stock losses with no food motivation perplexed him. And he could proffer no explanation to shed light on the frustrating incidence of sightings of the apparently bigger, jet-black animal.

'It could be that somehow there was also a panther or something involved, it would be killing just for the hell of it,' he said. 'But I can't understand it. Why would you have two types? Sometimes the old cougar tom can be very dark brown,' he told Earnshaw, 'but too many of your people say they've seen this black one. Why are they so insistent it's black?'

'By hell, if it's a panther, then you got problems. The old cougar will run till its treed and then you can just shoot him or pull him out and bag him for the zoo or whatever. But the black one might be different. If the dogs chase him and corner him he could just a easy turn on them and then you'd be picking up pieces of dog everywhere. Them cats' nails are like knives and when they reach to swat a dog, they lay him wide open.'

Through early 1979, the A.P.B. maintained the belief that either dogs or wild pigs were responsible, but Bob Neuman scoffed at this argument.

'In all the time I rode through this country, I never seen no signs of pigs - I never seen nothing to say it were wild dogs, but I never seen nothing except the way they kill to say its big cat either,' he told the A.P.B.

After a time, Neuman began developing fairly strong personal theories on the cat's behaviour.

'There's getting to be a lot of them out there,' he told the farmers. 'You got a different country and climate here. In places in the States they had a $50 bounty on them thirty years ago, when $50 was a lot of money. With years of hunting with hounds, they were starting to get down in numbers. But then when they lifted the bounty, there got to be more and more of them in some parts. Then they started coming in closer to the ranches, when the snow drove them down from the high country. And that's what's happening here.'

'They been livin' happily without no problems up in the bush, but now their numbers is getting up and they're spreading down onto the cultivated land, and you're seeing a lot more of them. They've lived on kangaroos now for quite a while 'til they realised there was somethin' easier. An' so they've moved on to your sheep and cattle, and you'll see more and more of them comin' onto the stock, more and more often.'

'Hell, they just sneak up down wind, then they just get them old 'roos so fast and easy. There ain't no dogs or pigs that kill that way, and then eats them out as clean as you like - dogs get in there and leave 'em all chewed to hell!'

The more he saw of the growing bitterness among the farmers about the authorities' attitudes, the more Neuman tried to counsel caution. He recognised the farmers were over-zealously ascribing incorrect signs to the work of the cat.

'There's quite a few of them tracks that I just don't believe the cat made,' he told Earnshaw. 'But some of them are cats for sure and only a cat kills that way.'

Being a successful business man, and coming from a country where there was nothing astounding about the presence of such animals,

Neuman installed a sobering influence into the debate. He believed that rather than having a destructive long-term effect on the environment, the cat phenomenon could be controlled. Kangaroo numbers were certainly declining, but he believed that, as in the United States, the introduction of wily hounds would one day enable the farmers to cut back the cat numbers, and hold them at a level where the bush established its own new line of ecological balance in the fauna. The cat numbers would be hunted down until they reached the stage where the animals confined themselves to the plentiful hunting grounds of the wild bush country. They would quickly learn to stay out of man's cultivated areas, any invasion of which could so easily be fatal.

'If you guys had dogs,' Neuman told the farmers, 'you wouldn't have no problems. You'll never wipe them out, but you can stop the big stock killings. You could control it to the point where you wouldn't be losing sheep like you are. You'd sure ease that up.'

In fact Neuman saw, in the cats, the potential of a new tourist boom for the State.

'Hell, them big money boys over in the east and in Perth would go crazy to have a weekend in the saddle, chasing them cats with the chance they might tree one and shoot it out. It could be as big as marlin fishing. When the Government finally announces it, I'd be closing down the stud in winter and bringing them boys down here for a bit of weekend hunting with my ole horses.' Neuman said.

🐾 🐾 🐾

On March 27, 1979, a public meeting was convened in Cordering's Moodiarrup Hall where, for the first time, all local people concerned about the cat mystery were given the opportunity to discuss it. Some of the farmers were becoming concerned that, despite their apparent interest, illustrated, for example by the visit of Bob Neuman, there was still a persistent scepticism evident among the authorities, and particularly in A.P.B. Charlie Sumner, for one, was incensed when the A.P.B. officers repeatedly criticised Jim Putland's claims. So, in the face of growing public unease about the whole matter, Sumner suggest to Dennis Earnshaw that a meeting be arranged. They hoped it would demonstrate the extent of community concern, though they were worried that because it was called at such short notice, only a handful of farmers would attend. The meeting was also seen as an opportunity to provide an independent assessment of the situation, so Sumner and Earnshaw invited Bob Neuman to attend because of his experience in the United States, and recent involvement in Cordering.

On the afternoon of the meeting Earnshaw was still receiving phone calls from people who had been informed the meeting was taking place, complaining they had not been given enough time to arrange to attend. Earnshaw hoped that at least twenty people would attend. In the end, 121 came, including Bob Neuman.

The meeting commenced at approximately 9.00 p.m., with the screening of an American film on cougars called *The Vanishing Prairie*, acquired by one of the locals. Bringing the meeting to attention, Sumner then gave a short summary of why it had been convened. He asked if anyone present objected to Dennis Earnshaw taking the chair, which he subsequently did.

Earnshaw then gave a summary of the efforts made by farmers over many years to either capture, shoot or explain the cat. He spoke of confusing allegations about a circus accident, and described in detail sightings made by himself or his brother. He alluded to encounters experienced by a number of other people, and pointed out the similarities in the various descriptions.

Bob Neuman was then introduced to the gathering and gave a long address, recounting his experiences in the United States, and pointing out his attitude to the Western Australian phenomenon.

Jim Putland then gave an account of his experience to the meeting, a significant talk which impressed everyone aware of his high standing in the community as a quality farmer, and a man of significant sobriety.

When the meeting was thrown open to general discussion a flood of questions were asked of Neuman. He agreed to the request that he help train the dogs. Half a dozen times he was asked by farmers if he believed mountain lions would attack man. He said firstly that from all he knew and had seen, he was sure a big feline predator was at work in the south west, and he was sure they were spreading over a large area of Western Australia.

' I couldn't guarantee that they don't kill people,' he told the meeting. 'Maybe if they're old and just plain hungry they might, but I never heard of one eating a man in the United States. Maybe a female would if she was protecting her kittens and cornered.'

The meeting then elected a working committee made up of seven farmers and businessmen from Collie. The committee would be chaired by Earnshaw and include Charlie Sumner, Jim Putland and Bob Crawford. Crawford, a local farmer had been concerned for many years about growing, unexplained losses of his stock. The committee also included Ian Milroy, a highly successful businessman, who owned and ran a gunsmith's business and sports goods store in Collie, and who also operated a wildlife sanctuary in the region. Two other local farmers, Colin Abbot and Henry Marsh, were also elected to the committee.

After the meeting, a letter was printed by the committee, to be sent out to all the state's M.P.'s and to the bosses of the A.P.B. and the Fisheries and Wildlife Department, expressing concern about the lack of official effort made by the authorities towards resolving the mystery. Attached was a document bearing the signatures of the 121 people at the meeting.

The letter read:

> *On Tuesday, the 27th March, a Public Meeting was held at the Moodiarrup Hall to co-ordinate efforts to capture at least one of the animals responsible for the killing of astronomical numbers of sheep, lambs and calves in the south west portion of this state.*
>
> *From this meeting a committee of seven farmers and businessmen was formed. It was also moved that a letter be sent to members of Parliament, officers of the A.P.B. and the Fisheries and Wildlife, to inform these people of the grave concern felt for the welfare of Australian wildlife and domestic stock.*

Guest speaker to the meeting was Mr Bob Neuman of Muchea, and former resident of Montana, U.S. Mr Neuman has had experience with the hunting and capture of cougars in the States. He is also quite familiar with their general habits, killing patterns and breeding cycles. From all the evidence presented to him, Mr Neuman is convinced that there are now indeed cougars running wild here in the south west.

Over the past 18 months many people have come forward giving eye-witness descriptions of these same big cats. In this same period, some 1000 sheep and lambs have been killed by the predators.

This committee finds it hard to comprehend the lack of concern shown by the authorities to this problem. It is quite evident that more concern and action is shown and taken over one sighting of one or two starlings, than there is to these big cats breeding here in the wild. Sightings by farmers at Arthur River and at Rosa Glen of female cougars with cubs at foot, prove that they are indeed breeding.

Evidence has been uncovered of a road accident involving a circus trailer that overturned near Bridgetown in 1961, allowing the escape of at least one pair of cougars and possibly two, into the bush. We also know that some people in both the Fisheries and Wildlife Department and the A.P.B. are aware of this accident.

One sighting of one cougar in the wild in this State should have been enough to have the responsible departments put on Red Alert, not waiting 18 years till we have the situation today of huge stock losses, and almost common sightings of both young and mature cougars in the bush. As a person in a responsible position in this State, we ask you now to call for this Red Alert with an all-out effort to rid this country of these imported cats now running wild.

The meeting was an important milestone. Prior to it, the farmers had been taking their concern to the authorities as individuals, and as such, their power was limited. But with the establishment of the Cougar Committee, the residents of what was an important agricultural region took on a very real political potency. This rallying of their forces would later become an important factor in the polarisation of opinions over the controversy. The meeting gave the farmers some heart that meaningful action would be taken to help them. That hope proved to be short-lived.

At about this time I discovered that, having been unsuccessful in his attempts to sell his picture to other newspapers, Barry Morris had taken it to the Government. Officials from the A.P.B. and the Department of Fisheries and Wildlife had inundated him with inquiries about it, and finally convinced him to hand it over so that reproductions could be made from it. Two blown-up colour copies of the slide were then placed in the file with roughly hand-scribbled and brief notes by an officer inside the Fisheries and Wildlife Department. This picture remained on file in the Department's Perth office, unexplained and virtually forgotten.

In late April, I decided it was time to write another story. It seemed that official action only ever coincided with the sudden publication of newspaper articles. For no other reason than to keep the pot brewing I analysed and drew together all the more recent developments, and filed the story which was published in *The Australian* on April 24.

It read:

> *Filed away in the bureaucratic bowels of the West Australian Department of Fisheries and Wildlife is a fascinating picture.*
>
> *It's a picture of what appears to be a big cat, a very large cat that one could easily describe as a mountain lion, jogging over the edge of a far-off horizon.*
>
> *The problem is the picture was taken in the Western Australian outback.*
>
> *Rubbish, you observe. No mountain lions exist in Australia. In fact there are no species of big cats anywhere in the bush.*

But are you sure?

Last year The Australian *revealed that a number of farmers in the south west of Western Australia claimed a large cat-like predator was killing increasing numbers of their stock and bush animals. The publication of* The Australian *story caused a storm in Perth.*

There's nothing new about stories of strange animals in the bush. The people of Western Australia in particular are pretty well oblivious to the wildlife wonders the State's 2.5 million square kilometres occasionally throw up.

Sightings of big cats have been reported periodically since the 1960s. But nothing apart from feral cats, wild dogs or mangy foxes have ever come to light.

Despite all the stories, Western Australians are, by and large, blase about the animals. Which is a shame because not one or two but literally scores of farmers are now quite seriously demanding that someone help them.

And they are unfortunately now in a savage Catch-22 situation. Senior people inside the State Government and its departments of Agriculture and Fisheries and Wildlife are now convinced that something strange is going on.

They concede in private that there is something in the ramblings of the cockies. But to admit it publicly is another question altogether. So they are waiting. And while they sit back and wait, the distressed farmers are now taking matters into their own hands.

Late last year two young Perth men took to the Government a picture of the animal they observed while travelling near Carnarvon, 980 kilometres north of Perth. The picture is now on file in the Wildlife department, but no one is saying what the animal is or even if the picture is genuine. The Agriculture Protection Board has been given other pictures of footprints and even plaster casts. Its officers are divided over what made the prints. Some insist big foxes or wild dogs but others - interestingly, some senior department men - concede there are major questions left unanswered about the conformation of the tracks.

Then there are the stock losses. One farmer in the Cordering region, 160 km south of Perth, last year lost 600 sheep, giving him a 30 percent lambing for the year. He is now forced to lock up every one of his stud sheep in sheds at night.

He is a former bush dogger, a retiring, almost shy man who insists he is being preyed upon by one or more cougars. Three times such animals have been seen on his property. The A.P.B. has been given dead lambs and other stock which farmers claim have been killed by the mysterious animal. And the Board has even taken hair from cougars at the Perth zoo to compare with hair sent in by the farmers. Officials claim no identification can be made between hair of different cat species.

Three weeks ago, when farmers from Cordering announced to their neighbours that the first public meeting would be held to discuss the problem, 120 people turned up. One after another they gave accounts of personal contact with animals they could only describe as American cougars.

The organisers were later inundated with inquiries from around the States, from farmers complaining that they had not been informed about the meeting or had been given insufficient notice. The meeting formed a committee which has, as the first step toward getting something done, written to every politician in Western Australia demanding that a full inquiry be set up.

Last year, The Australian *described actual sighting being reported by dozens of people. This year it appears the killing of stock has increased at times when farmers in different areas are lambing.*

To travel through the south-west as I have done repeatedly in recent months is to talk to people whose overwhelming first impression is relief that someone will listen to them and not scoff. Many have refused to discuss it for fear of ridicule.

There are two important factors to keep in mind. One is that the story is not the isolated ramblings of an individual or a small group seeking publicity.

The second is the people themselves. They are, almost without exception, ordinary farm folk, people living the hard but peaceful life of the bush: realists, but businessmen - some quite hard-headed - unaffected people who are overwhelmingly honest. Their stories are all the same.

An American, Mr Bob Neuman, who lived in Montana and hunted and captured cougars, attended the recent meeting. He outlined the cougar's killing patterns and breeding cycles based on his experience in the U.S. From evidence shown to him he is convinced that a large, cat-like animal is running wild in Western Australia.

Meanwhile the Cordering committee is circulating throughout Western Australia a questionnaire for people who have seen cougars in the wild. The response has been significant as in the constant similarity in people's observations.

The story concluded.

🐾 🐾 🐾

Gooding's claims about the footmarks had, for the moment, taken the impetus out of my inquiries. As well, the pressure of running the bureau was mounting and were demanding of my time. But always there was that dull ache of curiosity. Why, I kept asking myself, were so many of these people in the country fabricating this outrageous story?

Brian Pash had been speaking to farmers in the south west again, with a view to writing a story on current developments for *The Sunday Times*. He cornered me in the office one afternoon and mentioned he had received a phone call from Mr John Gilbertson, the manager of Perth's local Lion Park. Gilbertson was infuriated by the publicity the cat theory was getting, and had telephoned Pash to express his concern that such a preposterous suggestion was not being denied more forcefully by the authorities. He was prepared to say publicity that the matter was rubbish. He believed he was expert enough in the handling and characteristics of big cats to deny the theory categorically.

Neil Eliot had done photographic assignments for the papers at the Lion Park in the past, and was on excellent terms with Gilbertson, so the next day we went to talk to him and examine his criticisms.

The park sat on 40 hectares of land in the Perth suburb of Waneroo, and was owned by the Bullen Organisation. Gilbertson, with his extensive wildlife experience, had no compunction in totally discounting the farmers' claims immediately we began to talk.

'It's the biggest load of bullshit I've ever heard,' he said sternly, as he drove Eliot and myself in one of the park's safari trucks, through enormous steel gates into the parkland, just before dusk. It was common at this time of the day for the thirty-eight lions in the park to find their way into six big wooden cages distributed at various points around the sandy woodland.

It was in these cages that they rested for the night. Earlier Gilbertson had done a quick tour of the park, locking each cage to ensure our safety when he showed us around the park, which was surrounded by five-metre high steel fences. At one of the cages we dismounted from the yellow striped safari truck, and Gilbertson strapped a loaded revolver to his hip.

Inside the cage were a dozen huge lions, including one particularly unsettled male. He was agitated by our presence and followed Gilbertson's every movement, pacing to and fro, and treading between the other resting animals in the cage, as the park manager moved around outside.

Literally within a breath of the animals, Eliot and I were staggered by their size - long, thick, yellowing teeth protruding from steel jaws.

'He thinks I'm a threat to that lioness,' Gilbertson said, pointing into the cage as he walked around checking. The pride's dominant male continued to eye him threateningly. A bored looking female looked on, buried under a mass of bodies as swarms of buzzing flies descended on mounds of stinking dung in and around the cage.

'If he got out, there wouldn't be very much of us left,' Gilbertson added nonchalantly, between boisterous conversation with the lions. Eliot and I were both nervous about moving too far from the truck, and we were decidedly distracted while Gilbertson outlined his reservations about the mountain lion theory.

'I had to laugh when I read about those footprints,' he said. 'Have a look at my beasts' feet,' he added, poking into the cage with a long stick, much to the mounting chagrin of the big male, now coughing threatening rumblings from a massive throat. Despite his assurances that all the park's inhabitants were under lock and key, I beckoned Gilbertson back to the truck. Neil Eliot was sitting on the front seat, swathed in his cameras, when we arrived.

'Well, there you are - now you've seen them close up can you imagine one of them running around in the bush? It's just so ridiculous. Some of my beasts weigh up to 600 pounds, and these silly farmers are grumbling about a few stock being killed by a "mystery" animal. Look, if too many of my beasts got loose, there wouldn't be too much stock left anywhere . . .' Gilbertson said. 'Come over here and look at some of these footprints, and then tell me the little marks they're finding are lion prints. It's ridiculous.'

Having given our host a fair hearing, I could resist no longer.

'Mr Gilbertson, with all respect, I'd just like to point out a few of the facts,' I began. 'Number one - none of the people in the bush are talking about lions or tigers. They're talking about an animal they think resembles an American mountain lion. There has never been any suggestion that an African-style animal was loose.' Before he could interrupt, I continued: 'Given that, how much do you think a cougar weighs? Well, I'll tell you,' I said, 'the female weighs an average of 90 pounds, Mr Gilbertson, and many of them are less than that. And the males average around 140 pounds. Mr Gilberton, they don't weigh 600 pounds like your cats . . . We are talking about a completely different animal.'

The park manager was taken aback by my assertions. I politely tried to point out that he was so involved with his own animals he did not realise the debate concerned another, far smaller member of the cat family.

'I understand what you are saying about the size of your animals' footprints, but again, we are talking about an animal whose prints can be well under three and a half inches in width.'

Gilbertson looked hard at me, obviously unsteadied by my outburst, but still insistent. Somewhat more reservedly he said 'It's still a ridiculous suggestion.'

Despite his initial suspicions, however, Gilbertson, like so many of the others, became much more receptive when he began to hear the details of the farmers' claims. His curiosity began to rise. As we talked I was for some reason attracted to the hundreds of footprints scattered around in the sand, some immense reminders of the size and weight of the park lions. Some of the prints appeared to be 15 cm in width. Leaving Gilbertson and Eliot chatting, I weaved in and out of the clearer clusters of marks in the sand, looking for I knew not what. Something almost subliminal told me there was significance in the tracks. I was disturbed, but I couldn't work out why.

I wandered some distance from the truck and stooped down, searching the grassy sand mounds. With the sun rapidly disappearing on the western horizon, some of the deeper prints became more distinct because they cast their own internal shadows. In the approaching twilight they were clear black shadows cut in the sand granules. I bent down close to one sharp print. I stared hard into its grooves, increasingly irritated at not being able to identify their fascination for me. I could see the familiar feline shape of the toe pads and the vague triangular shape of the heel pad. And then it come to me.

The footprint did not have the three distinct nodes at the back of the rear pad. I quickly glanced at the other prints scattered around, and saw that none of them shared the characteristic either. Dozens of distinct prints confirmed it - not one boasted any marks in the sand that indicated the presence of the nodes on the pad of the animal that made it. Yet lions had the nodes as surely as any other member of the cat family. I was stunned. I realised that Des Gooding's key evidence was flawed.

A slightly bewildered John Gilbertson suggested an explanation in response to my pleas. He thought that although they all shared the node characteristic, members of the cat family were always stepping forward on the front edge of the back paw. Therefore the three rear nodes were often not making enough contact with the ground to mark it.

Controlling my excitement at the discovery, I helped him carry the argument ahead one more crucial phase. It was logical, then, that when such things as the conformation of footprints were being drawn for reference book diagram purpose, they were assumed to be the mirror image of the outline of a dead and captured animal's paw.

Could it be that the people who produced the diagram that Des Gooding was using as his starting point, drew it not from prints they had found in the wild, but from the apparent shape of an actual foot? This seemed a reasonable possibility, especially in the light of the reference books insistence that cougar foot prints were so rare in the wild.

I was astounded at the implications of the discovery.

At my Perth home later that night Dennis Earnshaw rang me. He informed me that the Agriculture Protection Board had asked local farmers to co-operate with a team of veterinary surgeons being sent from Perth to examine stock found dead on the properties. A vet and his assistant would hook in to the farmers' shortwave radios so they could be called to individual farms to examine carcasses before they were moved or deteriorated.

It appeared to me that the publicity had once again prompted the authorities into action. The vet would be based in the region for a few weeks, doing on-the-spot post-mortems, and eventually drawing up a comprehensive report for the A.P.B. As well, Earnshaw informed me, it was the Labor Party Opposition's intention, through the south-west M.P, David Evans, to raise the matter in State Parliament.

I informed Earnshaw I had stumbled on what I believed to be a major breakthrough in my investigations. He prodded me for details, but I explained the matter was confidential. I told him, however, that I could say it appeared I had contradicted a key part of the A.P.B.'s criticism of the cat claim.

'Beyond that, I can tell you nothing more till I've again talked to Gooding,' I said.

Then Earnshaw said: 'Oh, that must be the business about the node on the cat pads.'

'What?' I said.

He laughed. 'One of the A.P.B. local boys was here the other day and he told me all about their secret weapon, which they say shows there are only dogs doing all this.'

I shook my head. Not only was Gooding's key piece of information flawed, but it was also being dispensed by his officers, who were apparently less aware than he was of its crucial importance and confidentiality, to any interested party.

The next day I filed another story to *The Australian*, and subsequently it ran on page 3 under the headline 'Vets Join Hunt for Killer Big Cat' it read:

> *The West Australian Government will send out a veterinary team this week to examine carcasses of stock killed by a mystery predator in the south west of the State.*
>
> *A veterinary surgeon and his assistant will take up residence at Boyup Brook, a small town 270 km south of Perth, for a month to investigate the phenomenon.*

They will hook into farmers' shortwave network so they can be called to carry out immediate post-mortems on any stock found dead.

So concerned is the Agriculture Protection Board about growing stock losses and sightings of strange animals that extra A.P.B. officers have been assigned to follow up inquiries.

Next week the matter will be raised in an urgency motion in State Parliament.

The A.L.P. member for Warren, Mr David Evans, will call on the A.P.B. and the State Wildlife Department to launch an immediate full-scale inquiry.

Perth Zoo officials say farmers and travellers who claim to have observed a strange cat-like animal in the bush have been visiting the zoo regularly, demanding explanation.

One curator said: 'Once upon a time I scoffed, but I am now sure something is going on. It's so serious that now I believe there are mountain lions or a form of big cat in the area of the State.'

Last week it was revealed that the Wildlife Department has a picture of a strange animal allegedly taken by a traveller from a car in the bush near Carnarvon, north of Perth. There has been no official explanation of what kind of animal it might be.

Dozens of farmers insist that they have observed what appears to be a mountain lion preying on their stock and kangaroos.

Although the morning story was published, Des Gooding had not bothered to read *The Australian*. I arrived at his office fully expecting him to mention the story, but he made no attempt to. So I questioned him in detail about the visit of the vet, without referring to the article.

'They tell you everything,' he said, a little exasperated after confirming every detail. This yet again confirmed for me the absolute reliability of the information I was being given by the Cordering farmers. Gooding was decidedly wary when I asked him to precisely recount again the basis for his positive identification of cat footprints. I then outlined my visit to the lion park and the observations I had made there. I illustrated by reference to pictures Neil Eliot had taken. At the end of it I said to Gooding: 'Do you not now concede that your central argument about the identification of the footprints has just gone out the window?'

After a short pause he pensively replied: 'It would seem so.'

I further rubbed salt into the wound by pointing out that it had not been I who had informed the farmers of the "importance" of the rear nodes, but his own officers.

Largely for personal reasons, in May 1978 it became necessary for me to leave Western Australia. I did so with a real sadness, for the breakthrough in the mystery of the Cordering cougar had never come. I believed the story to be potentially of huge importance, but it had apparently dragged on into a part of the rural season when there was abundant native animals in the denser forest, and no need for the predator to emerge on to the farmland to feed. As well, the farmers themselves were increasingly pre-occupied with their work, and to some extent public interest had lapsed.

After so many months of inquiries I believed passionately that there was more to the farmers' stock loss problems than the authorities were willing to admit. While there was sympathy in some quarters, too many government officials were sceptical without examining the facts. Many were blinded by the extraordinary nature of the farmers' claims. More than a few of them were afraid of the story's implications.

At crucial times it seemed I had been doing the work that government agencies should have been doing. The Government's strategy seemed to be only to do and say enough to give the appearance of keeping an open mind, so that if an animal was shown to exist, it could be claimed that officialdom had long been sympathetic. The authorities were sitting on the fence, without really putting in the effort needed to analyse the details and face what was conceivable.

In any case, my enquiries, and the storm that had surrounded the publication of the stories in *The Australian*, had set in train official action at different times. We were not the first paper to print the stories. But in printing them, the other Perth papers were as much recording an eccentricity as investigating what could have been a serious phenomenon. My paper had entered the debate to examine the claims seriously, and our involvement provoked considerable community discussion.

Prompted in no small measure by *The Australian's* investigation, in 1978 and early 1979 the real story of the Cordering cougar began to emerge after I left Perth - a story of the courage and personal faith of a small troupe of unsophisticated country people in the face of significant community ridicule, and Government indifference and inaction.

🐾 🐾 🐾

Prints collected on the Earnshaw farm.

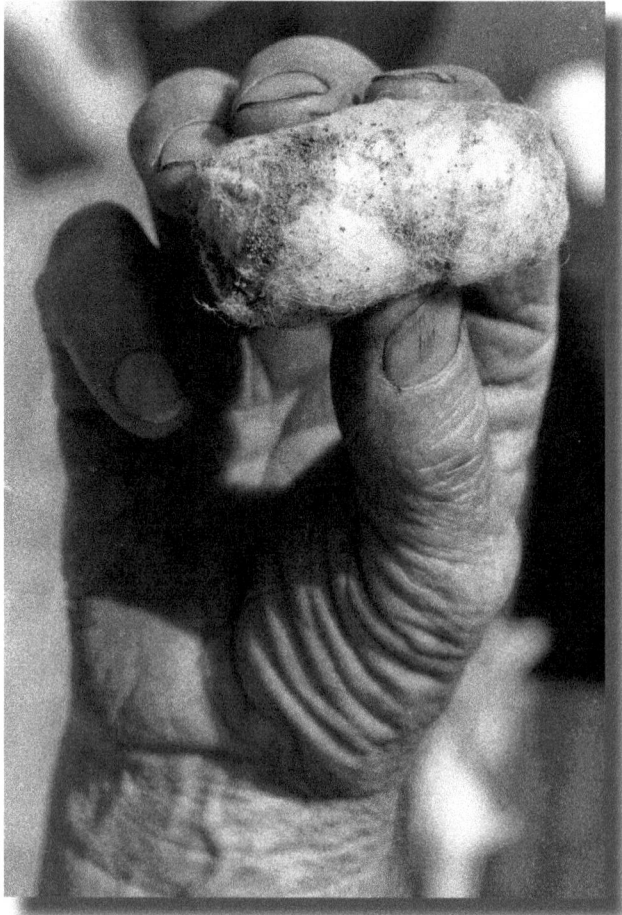

A cat-like scat with fur found on the farm.

Chapter Nine

THE INTRODUCTION OF ITS VET, Peter MacKenzie, and dogger, Alan McKenzie into the search for the Cordering cougar, was a major mistake by the Western Australian Government. Their involvement led directly to a total breakdown in relations between the farmers and the local authorities, and a bitter polarisation of opinions, at a time when both sides should have been working hand-in-hand to resolve an extraordinarily complex and mystifying problem.

Virtually from the moment he arrived, Alan McKenzie was deriding the farmer's claims. Major rows surfaced in the period he and Peter MacKenzie were examining the evidence. Both men made it clear that in their opinion the native fauna of the bush - in some cases wild pigs - were responsible for the tracks, killings and droppings. It was also later claimed throughout the region that various farmers themselves had fabricated some of the evidence. This led to a gradual breakdown in the farmers' confidence that the Western Australian Government was seriously examining their claims. For their part, the farmers began making allegations of cover-ups, and began calling for a Royal Commission to examine the question of mounting stock losses, and what they saw as the Government's puzzling failure to press on with meaningful efforts to resolve the matter.

The farmers' confidence in Dick Old also dissolved when, despite expressing private sympathy for them, it became clear that publicly he steadfastly defended the expertise of his Department. The farmers began to suspect that the authorities were attempting to play both sides against the middle. While some were privately ridiculing and attacking their claims, and even chastising them for speaking publicly and going to the press, publicly the authorities were maintaining they had an open mind on the matter and were sympathetic to the farmers' problems.

'What they seem to be doing at the moment is trying to shut us up, while intently making sure the public record shows they were concerned and involved all the way along - just in case we shoot a big cat one of these nights,' Dennis Earnshaw observed.

While there were obvious bureaucratic constraints on resources and what Government officials could do with them, the farmers saw the lack of action as nothing more than an attempt to sweep under the carpet a problem which they regarded as not only crucial to their livelihoods, but which was becoming increasingly a moral question. They were being called liars and fools, often very subtly, sometimes openly and publicly, so they took up the challenge to fight, and prove their claims to be not the ramblings of unsophisticated country yokels, but the accurate observations of professional, skilled farmers, in tune with their environment.

The two Agriculture Protection Board officers spend around two weeks in the Cordering district examining dead stock and talking to farmers. During that time relations between them and the farming community soured disturbingly. This happened for a variety of reasons.

Everything went smoothly for a few days, but once the farmers had time to scrutinise the activities of Alan McKenzie in particular, they became worried. The farmers had been told that Alan McKenzie was the Department's top dogger.

During the two weeks a number of serious incidents and allegations erupted. It was claimed in the district, at one stage, that Dennis Earnshaw and Jim Putland had stolen traps used by the A.P.B., charges the two farmers angrily denied.

A complaint was also lodged against Dennis Earnshaw over claims that he had in his possession a 'stolen' army rifle owned by another local resident, who had left it in Earnshaw's car after an all night hunting vigil. Another vigil was planned for the following evening and the two men agreed to leave the rifle and attached scope safely in the car for the day. The rifle was then seen by a number of people including Alan McKenzie who was observed to take down its serial number. Strict regulations cover the use of rifles but in the close, friendly, small-town environment of the bush much passes every day as common occurrence which technically borders on illegality. Earnshaw was tipped off that a complaint had been lodged with the police and the rifle was promptly returned. When ultimately no charges were laid Earnshaw confronted McKenzie to enquire what he knew of the complaint. The A.P.B. man initially denied involvement but was ordered off the property in an angry encounter which went to the verge of violence.

But it was primarily because no amount of reasoned explanation seemed to dent the A.P.B. men's scepticism that the farmers' concern grew.

'As far as I can see they have merely just come down here to squash the whole matter without listening to us,' Earnshaw told Sumner after his confrontation with Alan McKenzie.

One afternoon the dogger visited Charlie Sumner's farm.

'Look, let's get down to a few facts in all this crap about bloody cougars,' he said. 'We've looked at all your evidence and we're telling you it's pigs - you blokes have got to stop mucking around in the bush and causing trouble,' he said. 'Forget all this business about cougars - don't you realise all you farmers have been had? Earnshaw's got you blokes on a string - he's invented all this,' the government man said to Sumner.

On another occasion Alan McKenzie had visited Earnshaw and told him Sumner had admitted there were feral pigs in the bush around his farm.

'He's had pigs on his property since last January,' he told Earnshaw.

'Bullshit,' the farmer said, startled that his neighbour would say such a thing. That evening Earnshaw rang Sumner who exploded in anger when told what the dogger had said. In fact, he had admitted that on one occasion a wild pig had moved into the bush region near George

Wheeler's farm. Sumner had merely pointed out, as George Wheeler himself verified, that this one feral pig had been the only one in the area in years, and had come in and then left after a short period rooting at some tree stumps in a patch of muddy bush.

The farmers claimed that rather than being sympathetic and legitimately investigating their claims, the A.P.B.'s sole intention was to quash the idea, so much so that misleading statements were being made with the intention of confusing the issue, and dividing their resolve.

Some locals expressed concern about Alan McKenzie's statements. On one occasion he told Terry Hughes that he had picked up pig droppings on every farm in the area. Later, he was moving through the bush with Hughes when the two men came across animal faeces. McKenzie began picking it up.

'What are you going to do with that?' Hughes asked him.

McKenzie replied: 'I'm sending it to the Department - it's pig droppings.'

Hughes burst into laughter. 'Pig droppings, nothing,' he said, 'that's emu shit.'

The Cougar Committee had been planning to call a major public meeting to which Dick Old, Des Gooding and other Government officials would be invited. The meeting was organised, and as concern mounted about the A.P.B's approach Earnshaw and Sumner decided to question the A.P.B. bosses about the Board's approach. It would also be a good opportunity to question the vet and dogger publicly.

The Committee invited Old, his leading officials and key officials from the Department of Fisheries and Wildlife to the meeting, convened on May 23, 1979 at the Moodiarrup Hall.

In fact, Earnshaw rang Old and pointed out that such was the growing bitterness in the district, that unless he moved to appease the farmers' concern, there could be no guarantee that the meeting would be peaceful. 'Unless you do something, it could be a brawl,' he told the Minister.

Old agreed to attend a brief preliminary meeting with the Cougar Committee at the Earnshaw's farmhouse just prior to the public meeting to iron out the problems. He arrived for the talks with Des Gooding and the Director of the Agriculture Department, Mr Noel Fitzpatrick, who was also the chairman of the A.P.B.

The Committee explained details of the problems that had arisen, but Old was obviously angered, claiming the farmers were picking on his men. 'I'm not going to sit here and have my Department's men attacked,' he said. While the preliminary meeting was very tense, the farmers were insistent, and in the end, the Government officials conceded that Alan McKenzie be removed from work in the area. And Dick Old said he would make every effort possible to procure the services of a genuine expert in the activities of the big cat family.

This preliminary discussion had done very little to defuse the antagonism threatening to spill over at the larger meeting, later that evening. It began with a brief resume of events of recent months - the sending of the Committee's letters to all MPs and Department officials, Neuman's work in attempting to train dogs, and the work of Alan McKenzie and Peter MacKenzie. Accounts of various eye witness reports were also given to the meeting, and photographs of recently discovered mutilated stock were tabled.

Des Gooding then showed a collection of slides that his Department had produced from the United States on predatory animals in the wild. The slides included some depicting the behaviour and killing patterns of the cougar. Gooding's viewpoint was that the style of killings showed distinct dissimilarities to what was happening in Western Australia, an attitude, Earnshaw pointed out, not shared by people like Bob Neuman.

Dennis Earnshaw then showed a number of slides of footprints and mutilated stock bodies found in the district. One slide contained a large footprint which the farmers claimed was made by the predator. Gooding came to his feet and insisted it was a dog's footprint. When he pointed out what he claimed were toenail marks in the ground, he was howled down with derisive laughter by many of the one hundred people crowded into the hall.

Peter MacKenzie then delivered his report on post-mortem examinations he had carried out on fifteen animals since he had been in the area. 'He said that one animal, a wether which had supposedly been killed, had in fact died of the malady, water belly. To this farmers pointed out that he initially called on them to provide him with any, and all dead stock they found on the properties, regardless of whether they believed the stock was killed by the predator. Dennis Earnshaw insisted he knew the wether referred to, which he had handed to the vet, had died of natural causes. He pointed out that he had been merely following instructions.

MacKenzie told the meeting that all the dead lambs he had examined were mismothered and undernourished. To make this observation about some of the state's most respected rural producers, including farmers like Bob Jackson, whose stock had won innumerable awards at venues like the Royal Perth Show, did nothing to dissipate the growing antagonism. The claim that the stock was mistreated would become a corner-stone of the Government's criticism in coming months. It was virtually the last straw for the farmers.

MacKenzie also made the point that foxes were known to bite into the neck and skull of their victims, and that, along with eagles, they were Cordering's main predators. As well, MacKenzie observed that pigs 'could be responsible for the stock losses.

In a sarcastic aside during his address, he also said the way to pick a cat dropping was to hold two gold rings on a piece of cotton over it. If both turned in the same direction, it was obvious the scat was feline. Few of the farmers appreciated the humour.

It was during MacKenzie's report that the farmers' patience finally exploded. While he was speaking, one of the audience, an alcoholic leapt to his feet and, obviously drunk, launched into an angry and obscene attack on the Government.

'Oh, shut up, will you - what the fucking hell would you blokes know about us and our farms,' old Wal said.

For some minutes Earnshaw, as Chairman, attempted unsuccessfully to convince the interjector to desist. The rest of the evening's addresses by the Government men were punctuated by his outbursts.

Dick Old spoke, but only briefly, because he was yelled down by the rude interjector. He did, however, have time to say that there was evidence of strange predation in the area, but he was unable to provide any answers at this stage. Noel Fitzpatrick said his Department, like all other Government agencies involved, was anxious to see the problem resolved. Des Gooding said foxes were capable of killing lambs and that he did not believe cats were responsible for the stock losses. So disruptive did the interjector become, that it was suggested he might be removed forcibly from the meeting. However, when gestures towards this were made, the situation showed signs of becoming violent.

The meeting was closed by Earnshaw at 10.15 p.m. It had produced little more that a bitter stand-off. The rude and brutal interjections had offended many of those present. But for the Government officials, the interruptions had provided some brief relief, and a welcome, quick end to a meeting which they had attended under considerable pressure. And while the responsible farmers present had done all they could to quieten old Wal, and while he had chosen his words badly and spoken in bad taste, his sentiments were not that far out of tune with the overall feeling of the local people.

So concerned were they with what they saw as indifference and incompetence of the A.P.B. officials, that the Cordering farmers had decided, in virtual desperation, to seek other qualified help. They had decided that an alternative veterinarian opinion was necessary, so they took dead stock to a private veterinary surgeon for analysis.

The implications of the move was staggering. Peter Brighton, a gregarious, moustachioed veterinary surgeon, had run a successful practice in a big concrete-floored surgery in Bridgetown for over ten years. Before branching out privately, he had worked as a regional officer in the district with the Department of Agriculture. But, like so many young vets in the early 1970's, Brighten had realised there was a lucrative and much more stimulating living to be made in private practice in the south west. He had always felt hamstrung by the heavy-handed bureaucracy of the state's civil service.

When the farmers brought to him the first series of dead sheep and lambs in 1978, Brighton was amazed. He told them he had seen probably thousand of dead stock animals, both in his government work and his practice, yet he had never seen anything to match the injuries and wounds of this new batch of animals. Over the next two years the farmers, including Dennis Earnshaw and Charlie Sumner, brought to Brighton for examination up to 60 dead sheep, lambs, calves, and kangaroos.

The vet told Sumner and Earnshaw: 'The significant thing about all this dead stock and the autopsies I've done, is that a clear pattern of killing has emerged. If dogs were involved in the attacks they would go for a leg or a throat, the chest, and sometimes the back of the neck, but in these cases the style of attack is quite clearly a savage bite to the back of the neck. And the way the attacks have been executed shows that cats are involved - and sometimes very big cats.'

Brighton told the farmers that from the variation in the size of the injuries inflicted, he firmly believed that a family of cats of different sizes was involved.

'The wounds and lesions on the carcasses indicated a spinal attack, a bite across the back of the neck. The attacks are so vicious and efficient that they cause instant death, no matter what the size of the sheep or kangaroo.'

The vet told the farmers that the fatal attacks were easily distinguishable from secondary predation by foxes or eagles after death.

And he claimed that some of the bites on the neck and flanks of the dead sheep and kangaroos had revealed teeth marks to a depth of four inches.

"These are sharp, needle-like, puncturing bites, and I've never seen anything like it in all my years of practice. It can only indicate an attack from a feline animal - a cat and various members of a cat family up to a very large size.' The examinations indicated a deep fang penetration from a round, stiletto tooth, common to the cat family.

'On one of the sheep I autopsied the teeth punctured long ways through two vertebrae, and came out the other side. It was incredible, the most incredible bite marks I've ever seen. And the pattern remains the same on all the animals. I've examined, including a big kangaroo, which was obviously taken by a very large animal.

Sumner asked the vet to estimate the size of the predator. He said that from the way the killings were carried out, he would roughly estimate the body weight to vary from somewhere between 15 kilos through to 60 kilos. And he observed that it was impossible for any known feline animal in the Australian bush to attain that size.

'But as I say, the amazing thing about it is that the pattern of the kill is so repetitive - there is hardly any variation. Whatever it is, it hunts the stock down, stalks them and then hits them hard - its victims die instantly.'

Brighton claimed that the fact the attacks were nocturnal, that the animal was so practiced in concealment it could not be trapped and left little sign, which indicated again that it was a cat.

'If dogs have been doing this killing, some of them would have been shot, poisoned or even run over by motor cars.'

Brighton's examination revealed that the separation between fang puncture marks on skulls, necks, and in vertebrae, varied from 3 cm to 10 cm.

'They are really clever and they know the bush. It may not be a cougar like a lot of people are claiming - I can't say exactly what it is, but I can say it's definitely a big cat of some sort. There is the possibility that we may now have our own large native cat species, but if we do, the government officials are going to need to do a lot of work to find out exactly what and why,' Brighton told the farmers.

They also showed him the scats and various footprints they had gathered, and he microscopically examined material taken from the scat samples. There again, the cell structure of hairs from the scat seemed to indicate the hair came from a cat, and not a dog.

'Now either a bloody big dog has been eating feral cats, and the hair has come out in its scats, or there's a big cat out there that's swallowed some of its own hair, like any tabby does when it licks itself clean.'

After close examination of the photographs and casts of footprints Brighton told Sumner: 'If these are legitimate footprints, then the animal that made them can only be a big cat. Any competent pathologist would draw this conclusion from all this evidence that it's a cat, and there's a family of them operating.'

'There is enough evidence, quite apart from the sightings, and the possible, at times, emotive claims, that there is a big family of big cats killing stock and wildlife in the south west.'

During the May 23 Moodiarrup Hall meeting, Earnshaw had asked Peter MacKenzie his medical opinion of one kangaroo that the farmer had presented for examination. MacKenzie told the meeting that in his opinion, after having conducted an autopsy on it, the kangaroo had been killed by foxes.

Earnshaw rose to reply.

'Well, Peter,' he said, 'we've taken that kangaroo to an independent vet for analysis, and he's willing to prepare a report on it in writing. He believes that the 'roo was killed by a cat-type animal, with fang marks approximately 5 cm apart, and fang penetration into the rib cage of about 5 cm. He says that if the authorities want it, he is willing to provide a report on it.'

MacKenzie said the other vet must have examined a different animal, but Earnshaw, containing his anger, replied: 'Peter, I say to you, and I say in front of all these people, that it was one and the same animal. You say what you think about it, but this is what the other vet says. And don't forget, I know where that animal was found, and there weren't any signs of foxes around.'

Peter MacKenzie resumed his seat with clearly little support from the audience.

Within a few days of the meeting it had become the talk of the region. Many of the angry farmers at the Government's apparent indifference, and this prompted Dennis Earnshaw's Uncle Ron to compose a poem entitled *The Cordering Cougar Lament*:

We gathered one and all,
In the Old Moodi Hall
And listened to the A.P.B.
We sat on our stools and clapped like fools,
while the ladies made the tea,
Old Wal objected
for he was neglected
And struth it was plain to see,
They pulled the wool
with a load of bull,
and Wall saying worlds like b . . .
Said give us a chance
let's have a dance,
Come on Dick and have it with me.
He's drunk as a skunk
said Goodie to Mac,
Let's be off and down to the Local.
There ain't no cougar cats,
only hogs and rats,
from Collie Burn to Bokal.
Mac looking slick said don't tell Dick,
Good said listen Mac, old matie,
best thing to do, let's make a brew
using our good old 10.80.
Like knights of old, counting their gold,
they told the feral cat story.
They smiled and smiled
while bulldust piled,
and revelled in their glory.
Let's have a try, dog skulls they'll buy,
round the bush and up at the farm.
A few little flies will fool these guys,
and it can do us no great harm.

It was said with a rasp
and the old hand clasp,
we have got to stop this menace.
The thing to do is to tighten the screw
we'll take it out on Dennis.
It's always a delight said our skite,
the prospect seems delightful.
I'm telling you he's hard to screw
his sense of humour frightful.
Come on boys, put away your toys
let's go to the top and see.
Do your bit and teeth do grit
and forget the A.P.B.
So to get it done they'll go for the gun,
and phantom magnetic bullet.
With fairy gold rings hanging on strings
they'll find the scat and smell it.
So farmers all, don't be sold,
for he is a 'Thommo'.
Don't get bowled, do as you're told,
quit rocking the jolly old boat.

While the second Moodiarrup Hall meeting had resulted in the culmination of the farmers antagonism toward the Government's efforts, within days of it the A.P.B. had acted.

🐾 🐾 🐾

Koenig the German Shepherd was brought in to track the cats seen on the Earnshaw property.

Chapter Ten

DES GOODING HAD LONG HAD A PRIVATE INTEREST in the showing and training of dogs. He had many friends and acquaintances involved in training, breeding and showing a variety of dog breeds. One such man was Rick Richardson who, with his wife, played a major role in the promotion of the German Shepherd breed throughout Western Australia. Both members of the German Shepherd Breeders' Association, they trained people in the care, breeding and tuition of their animals. Their love of the controversial German Shepherds bordered on a passion. Richardson was so committed to the breed that he was strongly critical of the public image that had grown up around the dog - painting it as a fierce and dangerous animal, capable of killing.

At their comfortable Balcatta home in Perth, the Richardsons had put together one of the most comprehensive libraries in Australia, covering not only the German Shepherd breed, but also such things as the psychology of the dog and up-to-date innovations in training techniques.

Koenig would, without doubt, have been one of the most extraordinary dogs in Western Australia - a tribute to the Richardsons' commitment to modern training styles. A seven-year-old sterilised male, Koenig was big - larger than the average fully grown Shepherd. He was, in fact, too big to be shown, but with care and love he had been trained to a high degree or proficiency as a line tracker - a dog that tracks by ground-scent, rather than by air-borne scent.

The Richardsons did not believe Koenig to be exceptionally intelligent - they attributed his astounding development to their own novel training methods. While discipline played a role, severe chastisement was discouraged, and the dog was developed from a very early age with a greater degree of patience and insight into its potential than many other breeders employed. The result was that Koenig had become a dog of great talent. He had appeared on television programmes, where his ability to count, among other things, amazed audiences. The Richardsons could not explain the dog's apparent ability to solve simple arithmetical problems, barking out the answers.

He had been used by the State Emergency Services and police in tracking lost humans and animals, and had been extraordinarily successful. He was, quite simply, a remarkable dog.

Des Gooding of course knew of Koenig's talents. He approached the Richardsons, enquiring as to whether the dog could be used to track the mysterious predator in the south west. Richardson initially said he was unsure how successful the dog would be in such an unlikely exercise, especially when the very existence of the "predator" was in doubt, but he was determined that with enough preparation, Koenig could be trained to track anything that left a scent.

A bundle of rags was placed in the cougar cage at the Perth Zoo, until the rags were substantially impregnated with cougar scent. And then an amazing experiment was conducted.

Gnangara, a lakeside tourist and recreation area about 30 kilometres north of Perth, is surrounded by some of the most scenically beautiful pine-forest country in Australia. It was here that Koenig's first cougar track was laid. On pushbike, Rick Richardson drove a winding course through the pine forests, flicking the cougar-scented cloth through the scrub on the end of a long stick. He drew a track of scent on the ground, but occasionally tossed the rags into bushes and up against trees, on a fast and free-wheeling jaunt through the area. He tried to touch ground as little as possible himself, minimising the chance that Koenig would recognise and pursue his master's familiar scent.

Then Koenig was given the taste and smell of the scented cloth and placed in his tracking harness. Richardson took up the dog's six metre leather lead, and gave him the disciplined instruction that told him to track. The dog then followed the scent precisely over the track that had been laid for him. In fact he successfully followed the track repeatedly in following experimental exercises, including one in which he was put on the scent over four hours after it was laid.

Richardson told Des Gooding that if either of the Perth Zoo animals escaped, Koenig would not have any problem in tracking them. But the dog's owner could not be sure he would respond to the scent of another individual member of the cat family.

The plan was that once successfully introduced to the scented cloth, Koenig would be held on standby until a sighting was made in the south west. The Richardsons would be called in as quickly as possible, and a search set up if the dog showed signs of detecting scent in the bush.

It was not long before another sighting was reported.

The Earnshaw brothers drove out to the spot where the sighting had been made, on the western perimeter of Bob Crawford's property. They believed they detected scuff marks on the road where an animal had crossed, heading north. The prints were not distinct in the dark, but they marked the spot on the side of the road clearly, intending to return at first light.

Dennis Earnshaw rang Gooding, and later that morning the A.P.B. officer and Rick Richardson arrived with Koenig, and another, younger German Shepherd, a female called Cherie, still in the early stages of training in the art of scent-tracking. The bitch's owner, Klaus Braun, and his wife attended the dog, and at around 8.30 a.m. Earnshaw and Terry Hughes showed the new arrivals the marks in the gravel. By now Charlie Sumner and Bob Crawford had also arrived.

Des Gooding began by outlining to the farmers the training that had gone into preparing Koenig for the chase. He explained that in nine test trials, the dog had appeared able to track cougar scent successfully.

He insisted, however, that if the dog did not respond, then the farmers had to accept that there was no animal marauding the bush. Dennis Earnshaw interrupted by pointing out that they had never seen the dog working, and could not be sure of its competence. The suggestion that the dog's efforts would somehow determine the argument once and for all, was totally unacceptable to the farmers. But they held high expectations that Koenig would add a new dimension to the debate.

Richardson then explained that the dog would need a short time to search out and establish the scented trail if, in fact, there was one. He warned the farmers that, because Koenig would presumably be pursuing a different individual scent to the zoo animals, he would need a period of adjustment - again, *if* there was a trail to be picked up.

After sweeping through the bush on the northern side of the road, Koenig busily sought out a scent, his nose hard to the ground, his tail beating in an enthusiastic frenzy. The dog then began to concentrate on one small section of bush and was becoming more and more agitated. Observing his dog's movements from a distance, Richardson announced he appeared to have picked up a scent. On his order, Koenig came to heel, and Richardson strapped on the dog's tracking harness, and gave the order freeing him to move off on the scent.

Within minutes, Koenig was lunging through the bush, due north from the roadside, dragging a somewhat surprised Rick Richardson behind him. The search party then split into two groups - behind Richardson and his wife followed Dennis Earnshaw, Des Gooding and two or three other armed farmers.

The Richardsons were sure the dog was now tracking. It moved excitedly through the brush, searching out the microscopic indicators that its prey had passed through the area.

The farmers excitedly asked the Richardsons whether they believe the dog was tracking a cat, but Rick cautiously observed it was far too early to make any assumptions.

'If only we could read his mind,' Dennis Earnshaw said of the dog.

After Koenig had drawn the party a short distance into the bush, Richardson called for a temporary halt to allow the tailenders, now stretched out behind, to catch up. It was clear that Richardson himself was cautiously attempting to disguise his own growing excitement about the dog's frantic response. Pressed by Earnshaw, he now conceded the dog was definitely on a significant scent.

On a number of occasions in the first hour, the hunt was halted to allow the party to regroup and rest, and also to give Koenig a short, sharp reminder with the bundle of scented cloth. The hunt moved initially due north, but then began to swing in a westward direction, into heavy jarrah country, on State Government land bordering Bob Crawford's property. The unlikely caravan of hunters breathlessly pursued the dog, which fought the end of its leather lead, stopping occasionally to swing in small arcs left and right, his nose running over the ground's surface as he constantly re-established direction. When the dog began to weave into a south westerly direction, it was becoming clear that an enormous circle of pursuit was unfolding.

On a number of occasions Koenig stopped and ran to the base of large jarrahs. Richardson was perplexed by the dog's action. The Shepherd leapt up, his big front paws high on the tree trunk, sniffing it and peering into high boughs. Then he dropped to the ground, enthusiastically circling until he had re-discovered the scent. Koenig's interest in the trees was baffling Richardson.

The dog was attuned to a rigid discipline while working, which left no room for distraction such as seemingly unnecessary excursions up trees. Richardson told Gooding that he believed the dog's interest in the trees was significant. The farmers wasted no time in pointing out that this seemed to fit the pattern of behaviour they observed in the predator, which included the marking of certain trees across a large area of timber country.

The dog's course had moved over hundreds of groupings of kangaroo footprints. In the early stages Dennis Earnshaw suspected the dog was pursuing an individual 'roo. But when Koenig stumbled over what appeared to be a clear, large feline footprint it was obvious to Richardson that they were definitely not chasing a kangaroo, but a large-bodied animal. After roughly an hour the dog led them to a large fallen tree, with a flaking bark branch pointing parallel to the ground, some metres in the air. He indicated to his handler that he wanted to follow the track over the bough, but Richardson pulled him up to inspect the area before going any further. On the branch he found a clear, recent scratch mark, which had splintered a piece of the shredding bark. And then on the ground, beyond the tree, Richardson found a big footprint.

When the party had examined the track, the farmers insisted that it was, by the standards of the bush, an unusually large, readable footmark. Richardson in particular was impressed by its size, although Des Gooding insisted it was too unclear to be identifiable even as a footprint.

'I can't read too much into that,' he said contemptuously.

Despite the A.P.B. officer's scepticism, Richardson, searching a small radius of bush, said he believed the animal they were chasing could have leapt on the tree bough, scuffing it, before it vaulted to the ground, one of its front feet biting deeply into the soil. And the dog handler claimed, despite Gooding's continued reticence, that the animal would have to have been of substantial body weight to scar the bark in such a manner.

Richardson closely examined the footprint and compared it with Koenig's paw. The mark that Gooding claimed could not be identified was significantly larger than the print left by the outsized dog.

'That print is larger than Koenig's and he's a big dog,' Richardson mused, his puzzlement deepening as the morning wore on.

A short time later the farmers claimed to have come across three separate scuff marks in the dust, again left by the predator. Although they conceded to Gooding that the marks were too indistinct to even determine whether a dog or cat had made them, the farmers asked Richardson to measure the distance in the apparent gait of the animal responsible, and then do a comparison with that of Koenig. After taking some measurements, the farmers believed the scuff marks were spaced quite evenly at 55 cm intervals. Koenig's gait measured 60 cm.

'I would reckon that the animal we are chasing would be around 110 cm in body length,' Earnshaw told the still unmoved Gooding. The A.P.B. man continued to refuse to be drowned out in detailed hypothesising over the scuff marks. He was insistent that the lack of clarity made the measurement exercise, and attempts to identify the marks, futile.

Koenig was still quite excited on the line, but the long and winding run through dense, inhospitable terrain was beginning to take its toll on the dog's human companions. Richardson and his wife took turns on the lead as their dog plunged confidently on. The locating of the footprints was, by now, confirmation for the farmers that the dog was tracking the animal they believed they were seeking. Earnshaw again asked Richardson directly, during one rest spell, what he believed Koenig was tracking. Richardson said he could not be sure, but it was definite from the dog's behaviour that they were getting close to its prey. Despite Richardson's growing exuberance, Gooding's major criticism was that it was impossible to come to definite conclusions about markings in the hard forest coffee-rock. After a frantic march that had now extended over an estimated 15 kilometres, everyone, including Gooding, was tiring. Koenig was now moving in a southerly direction, and Richardson again rested the dog to allow Gooding time to catch up. Arriving at a small clearing, panting heavily, Gooding restated his belief that it was impossible to find reliable tracks in the area, and he proposed that the search be called off. So, despite the continuing keenness of the dog, and the farmers' insistence that they were tracking a cougar, the hunt was terminated. The group of men made their way through the bush in a southerly direction until they reached the bitumen of the Collie road. Then they headed up the road to where they had left the rest of the original party, including Klaus Braun and his dog, at the parked cars.

Cherie had also been put into the search for a scent by the roadside, once Koenig had moved off into the forest. Charlie Sumner and Bob Crawford watched the bitch meander, apparently aimlessly, seeking a scent on the ground. The dog's handlers had pointed out that she was a younger, less skilled tracker than the big male, so Sumner and Crawford walked some distance down the Collie road examining the sandy wash at its edges for any sign of tracks. To make matters worse, Klaus Braun was totally unfamiliar with the Australian bush, and he had no way of knowing which tracks were significant. Cherie, baited with the cougar-scented cloth, steadily grew more restless, and from her zigzagging movements it was obvious that she was in some confusion. Sumner and Crawford suggested that Braun test the dog on some fresh kangaroo and fox tracks they found on a railway line embankment on the opposite side of the road to where Koenig's pursuers had disappeared. Walked on to the kangaroo and fox tracks, Cheri would not respond to either, encouraging Braun that she, like Koenig, had a fair idea of exactly what scent she was seeking.

After the initial period of confusion, the bitch suddenly began to pull to the end of her lead, and Braun announced she seemed to have picked up an important scent. Cherie then moved determinedly away from the road towards denser bush. Some 100 metres into the timber line, she led Braun past the three-day-old remains of a kangaroo. It had obviously been attacked by secondary predators which left only parts of leg bones and pieces of intestines and paunch contents. The dog was only momentarily distracted by the corpse and persistently strode on, growing in confidence in yet another arcing procession. After about two kilometres she was leading her handler directly back to the road where Sumner and Crawford were waiting. Klaus Braun decided to call a halt to the search - the bitch was weary, and Braun admitted that he was confused by the terrain. He did mention, however, that the dog had also crossed a large dropping on the track which he had noticed was partially covered by leaves and grass.

Sumner and Crawford took instructions from Braun, and wandered into the bush themselves, where minutes later they located the piece of faeces about 18 cm long. Sumner and Crawford agreed it bore all the characteristics of a large feline dropping. Sumner placed it in a plastic bag and took it back to the parked cars further up the main road, where both groups of hunters shortly met up. Sumner handed the plastic bag to Des Gooding, and the consensus among the farmers was that the faeces was fresh, probably deposited during the previous night. When Richardson brought Koenig back to the cars the dog drank liberally from a container of water, and slumped down in the back of his handler's stationwagon, exhausted by the search which had lasted well over two hours.

Des Gooding remained non-committal on the events of that morning. Earnshaw, Sumner, Crawford and the others were well pleased with the hunt, but Gooding quietly insisted that no significant conclusions could be drawn from it all.

As the group stood around drinking coffee and tea from thermos flasks, Earnshaw turned to Richardson.

'What do you think the dog was chasing Rick?' Earnshaw asked directly.

Richardson replied: 'I've got no idea what it was. All I can say though is that Koenig was interested in a fairly large animal. It wasn't a fox, and it certainly wasn't a dog.'

The handler then mentioned that during the search he had detected in some parts of the bush a quite pungent ammonia smell, which reminded him of cat's urine.

'Koenig tracked an animal for all that distance and I reckon it was a very large animal - I can't tell you what it was, but all the signs indicate it would have been cat-like,' Richardson said. He agreed with Sumner that it would have to be a very large animal to travel the distance they had covered in one night. The old farmer was adamant that a feral cat would never have travelled over such a circuitous distance.

'I'm afraid it would have to be a pretty big animal to leave the imprint we found on that log,' Richardson said.

The following week Dennis Earnshaw and a friend, Geoff Martin, a butcher and semi-professional 'roo hunter from Carnamah in the State's northern wheat-belt, who was holidaying at the Earnshaw farmhouse, went out at midnight to hunt with spotlights and the starscope. On the darkened road the spotlight detected a pair of bright eyes in the brush. Martin took aim with his .308 calibre rifle, using a conventional binocular scope, while Earnshaw held the spotlight. The shooter could just detect the outline of a large animal sitting in the light on the edge of a timber line. In a moment of breathlessness Martin whispered to Earnshaw: 'It's just sitting there . . . will I fire?'

'Yes,' Earnshaw said tensely.

The .308 exploded and the men lost sight of the shadowy animal in a billowing cloud of smoke.

'That's it,' Martin yelled, as Earnshaw flashed the spotlight along the treeline, trying to detect movement as the smoke dissipated into the clear night sky. For Dennis Earnshaw those few moments were ones of chest-wrenching apprehension. He knew his friend to be, reputedly, one of the best shots in Western Australia, and a man who took fierce pride in his near fail-safe aim.

Martin was virtually beserk, screaming about how he had to have hit the animal, but Earnshaw reached for the starscope, still sitting atop his own .243 on the back seat of the stationwagon. Through it, the men suddenly saw the dark silhouette of a big animal, its body clearly contrasted with the scope's hazy yellow world. The animal walked along the tree line, and then sat down, seemingly ignorant of its human observers. Martin whispered that he saw it stand up and grip a tree with its front feet, scratching down on it, before dropping to the ground and again walking into the scrub and disappearing.

'What do you see?' Earnshaw asked.

'A cat - a big cat, just sitting there. It's just swung its tail around its back legs while it sits. It looks like it is a brandy colour, but I think I've totally missed it. Why though? It was a leaning shot and it was just sitting there . . . I've bloody well missed it!' he howled.

After the animal had disappeared without giving Martin time for a second shot, Earnshaw said he believed it could have been wounded. 'And that means it probably won't go far before it dies,' he said.

The farmer drove the wagon up to the tree line. The animal had disappeared into what was virtually a small island of bush, separated from the denser and larger forest area by a track cut through so that vehicles could move around in the area. It occurred to Earnshaw that if the animal had gone into the bush injured, seeking cover, it could only come out by crossing the track into the forest country or by moving out on the other three perimeters, all open cultivated farm land. The two men then began patrolling the cleared track that split the bush, gambling that the animal would remain within its confines, panicked by its injury, and their noise and lights.

Earnshaw radioed his wife at the farmhouse with instructions to contact Des Gooding in Perth and request that Koenig be brought down.

232

He also told her to call in other members of the Cougar Committee to help search early in the morning. While Henny put the instructions into effect, Earnshaw and Martin continued to patrol the track all night, driving back and forth along its winding path. Henny rang Gooding around 1.00 a.m. He rang her back an hour later to say that he'd be at the farm by daylight. In the meantime he had contacted Rick Richardson at home, but the dog handler said it was impossible for him to go south because he was needed at work the following day by his employer, the Stirling Shire Council.

Gooding drove to Cordering and at his arrival, just after sunrise, the farmers expressed disappointment that Koenig had not been rushed down. As neighbours gathered in the paddock, Earnshaw, Martin and Charlie Sumner were searching in the morning light for tracks. Initially it was difficult, but as the light strengthened they gradually pieced together what had happened, and finally they stumbled onto the spot where the animal had apparently sat and moved around. There, running for about 3 metres through the sand was the heavy trench where Martin's bullet had hit the ground. Later the farmers co-operated to peg out the estimated flight of the shot from the truck had stood to where the earth was grazed. The farmers believed they could detect scratch marks where the animal had sprung away from the bursting bullet. In the end they reluctantly came to the conclusion that Martin had missed, the shot coming into the animal a metre above the ground, but passing between its front legs and chest as it sat up. In a million to one chance, the bullet had missed, perhaps by inches, the heavy-bodied chest region, which would have been immediately fatal, or the chunky front legs, which would have certainly crippled, and probably eventually killed the animal. The specially prepared 180 grain bullet had travelled approximately 185 metres, but had not broken up when it hit the ground, a certain indication that the target was missed.

'He's gotten away from us again - you missed him by inches, Geoff,' Earnshaw said to the bitterly disappointed butcher.

After conferring with Gooding, the farmers decided to make a sweeping search through the bush, much of its trees and scrub bulldozed to the ground some weeks earlier, preliminary to clearing for cultivation.

Two long drives through the bush by lines of the farmers proved unproductive. By 10.00 a.m. they gathered again at the eastern edge of the bush. Frustration was beginning to surface.

The farmers asked Gooding again why Koenig had not been brought to Cordering when Dick Old had given personal assurances, following the dog's first visit to the area, that he would be available on request. Dennis Earnshaw was becoming angry, and told Gooding he would contact Dick Old to complain. That prompted the A.P.B. officer to concede he would make another attempt immediately to get the dog brought down that day.

At Dennis Earnshaw's farmhouse Gooding rang the Director of the Agricultural Department, Noel Fitzpatrick. Then Dick Old personally contacted the Stirling Council, and around lunchtime Richardson received urgent instructions that he was to take the dog to Cordering with all speed.

By 2:30 p.m. the dog and its handler were at the search scene.

It was now a hot and dry day, an extremely difficult time for scent tracking because most of the night and morning moisture had evaporated. At first Koenig veered away in the opposite direction from where Martin said he saw the animal disappear. Very quickly the dog came across the remains of a dead lamb which the farmers claimed had the now familiar killing characteristics, despite Gooding's insistence it had been attacked by foxes. Koenig was brought back to where Martin said he saw the cat clawing the tree, but it was clear the dog was struggling to find scent. Once he tracked towards and then through a flock of sheep. The farmers considered for a moment he was confusedly pursuing one of them, but when he charged through, oblivious to their startled bleatings, they realised again he was pursuing another scent. After two hours in which he circled from the paddocks, in and out of the bulldozed bush, Koenig had lost his way and was too exhausted and confused to continue.

'If only the damn animal had been brought down here last night when the scent was hot, instead of over twelve hours late,' Charlie Sumner complained. One of the more positive aspects of the hunt was that the dog had tracked to yet another large piece of faeces which the farmers believed was left by a large feline, and which Des Gooding examined closely.

The party chatted briefly with Richardson after the hunt was over, and he agreed again that his dog had been tracking something that was fairly large in the body. The handler also showed the others a magnum of champagne his wife had given him before he left Perth. It significantly underlined, not only the handler's confidence that the farmers were pursuing a significant animal, but also the optimism that given optimum conditions, Koenig would have given them something to celebrate that day.

Des Gooding, however, remained, as always, unconvinced. He was exhausted after being awakened at 1.00 a.m. and forced to rush two hundred and fifty kilometres into a hectic search through the bush in high temperatures. But in the A.P.B. man's scepticism lay another watershed in the steadily mounting antagonism between the Cordering farmers and the authorities.

As far as the cockies were concerned, the dog should have been on the scene within hours of Martin's shot. Unschooled in the not so subtle intricacies of bureaucratic red tape, they were unable to see the enormous difficulties under which Des Gooding was working.

The A.P.B. may not have been impressed with the significance of Koenig's exploits in the Cordering area. The farmers in the region, however, claimed that it was a further example of the authorities' indifference and refusal to acknowledge what they saw as continued growth in a landslide of circumstantial evidence. Koenig's involvement became the talk of the region, and became the subject of pub chat everywhere from Bunbury to Esperance.

By now more people than ever throughout the southwest were beginning to accept the cougar theory as fact rather than fiction. There were further sporadic stock killings east of Cordering which prompted renewed talk among the farmers about the possibility of the predator representing a threat to the bush's human inhabitants. This talk prompted

Bunbury businessman and well-known identity on the south coast, Jack Patterson, to compose the second poem on the phenomenon which he called simply *The Cordering Cat*:

The Cordering Cougar has struck once again
Marauding young cattle and sheep.
The Farmer's fatigue, is shared by his men,
As nightly their vigil they keep.

There's a whisp of a cloud in a star studded sky,
The moon slowly peeps over the hill.
The Easterly breeze gives a last mournful sigh
Then suddenly everything's still.

On a large rock outcrop the Predator waits,
Patiently licking her paws,
Then slowly she rises, and slinks to a tree,
and commences to sharpen her claws.

With sheer feline grace she climbs out of the rocks,
then slowly she creeps down the hill
To a paddock below, where her quarry awaits,
As she swiftly moves in for the kill.

Her yellow stained teeth are now covered in blood,
The flock herd together in vain
Until several dead sheep lie there in the mud,
She strikes out again and again.

The lust to kill over, her hunger well slaked,
She silently moves to her Den,
And there she will hide, midst the rocks and the trees,
Till she's ready to kill, once again.

Some people may laugh at the Cordering Cat,
Some say it's a pussy gone wild,
But would they still laugh, if the Cougar's next prey,
was maybe, an innocent child.

Let's give serious thought to the Cordering Cat
Before too much blood has been spilled,
No matter what species the animal is,
It has to be captured or killed.

🐾 🐾 🐾

Just a portion of the lambs killed on the Earnshaw property - all dispatched and eaten in the same manner.

Chapter Eleven

EARLY IN 1979 THE CORDERING FARMERS realised they needed to correlate the plethora of reported sightings coming in. They decided to put together a questionnaire to be dispatched to anyone they had reason to believe had made a legitimate sighting. Ian Milroy compiled a twelve-section questionnaire in which he hoped to extract as much key information as possible from respondents, without leading them to concoct observations. The aim was to piece together patterns of behaviour and areas of activity in the south west.

Within months a reasonable sample of completed forms had been returned to the Committee. Often respondents requested that their observations be kept confidential. Later in the year the Committee decided to halt this information-gathering exercise. The farmers believed they had accumulated enough information up to that date, in the returned questionnaires, to throw light on what appeared to be a state-wide problem. They also stopped distributing questionnaires because, as the year wore on, the cat controversy continued to generate considerable interest throughout rural Western Australia. They wanted to keep the questionnaires confidential to eradicate any element of community hysteria. They realised they could not afford to have such a valuable weapon as the questionnaire exercise complicated by over-exposure. There were obvious cases where over-zealous respondents had mistaken natural phenomena for the much-talked about cat. The farmers sought to minimise the chances of this problem undermining the authority of the growing nucleus of meaningful sightings.

The questionnaires came in from areas through the south west. But they were also returned from areas as far north as Carnarvon and Exmouth; from Latham, just north-east of Perth; and from Denmark, west of Albany.

Milroy's questionnaire requested information on the locality of the sighting, the type of country involved, the time of day, the general appearance of the animal - its colour, size and distance from the respondent, as well as how many times it was seen. It also asked whether the animal appeared dog-like, cat-like or of another form. And it asked the respondents to indicate what they frankly thought it was, and which method they believed would best effect a capture.

The answers related to sightings made in all types of country - cleared farmland, spinifex scrub, bracken paddocks and undulating or rocky terrain. Sightings occurred at all times of the day and at different periods going back quite a few years. Ninety-nine percent of the respondents claimed the animal was cat-like, adding observations to emphasise the point such as 'cat-like - very definitely,' or 'but it didn't look like any house cat.'

In every instance, the animal was described as being one of two distinct colour types - black, often described as 'blue-black', 'shiny black,' or 'black, like a crow.' But many were described as being tawny, brandy, or shades of brown and were often compared to shades of kangaroo colouring. The two quite distinct colour observations were consistently either black or a shade of brown.

The respondents revealed chillingly similar observations about the animal they observed. Many simply remarked that it was about the same height as a Labrador, Alsatian or (Border) Collie. But a surprising thirty per cent of respondents nominated one height specifically for the animal - they all estimated it to be 'two foot six inches' high.

Asked to comment on its most outstanding feature, thirty percent remarked about its tail. They described it as a surprisingly long, curly tail, 'of equal thickness from beginning to end, no point, nor bushy,' or a 'long tube-like tail.' Overwhelmingly though, the most significant feature of the animal for many respondents related to how it moved and how quickly, and in what manner it made its departure. For example, typical observations ran like this:

> *It was very solid and fluffy and its tail hung down and was very thick. I had a cattle dog and a Corgi with me and they just stood there and looked at it. They didn't bark or make any attempt to go towards it. I only saw it the once. When it turned to go its feet didn't seem to touch the ground - it went away like a cat with a flowing gait . . .*

> *The manner of running, like the family cat runs . . .*

> *An enormous cat-like animal - round head, graceful movements, long body, long neck, tail like a cat, slight curved and end of tail about half way the height of animal*

> *Big bounds when running - different to dog . . .*

> *A little bigger than my border collie dog. Tail as long as body - it had slender legs and long tube like tail. It looked like a large cat of the sort you see in zoos - a lioness or tiger - definitely not a house cat . . .*

One respondent described the outstanding feature thus:

> *The fact that it wasn't perturbed by our presence or a barking dog. It seemed familiar with the place.*

Another respondent observed:

> *It had a long rolling way of walking exactly the same as a cat. It had absolutely nothing dog like about it - cat's head, etc. The growling and rumbling it made definitely ruled out any other animal except cats.*

Another respondent said the outstanding feature was its:

> *Slinking, cat-like movements.*

Others said:

> *While watching the animal walk, he stopped and sat on his haunches, adjusted his front legs to suit his stance. This is not similar to any Australian animal I've seen. I believe it to be an American Puma.*

> *Its quickness . . .*

> *The size of it in relation to normal cats. My dogs would not track it.*

> *Eyes very bright . . . (8.00 p.m. sighting near Denmark.)*

> *Pointed ears and long tail . . .*

> *Length of stride and speed . . .*

> *Tabby-grey with orange type colouration which may have been due to late afternoon sun or light coloured fur. A definite cat, about the size of a golden labrador dog. Speed and agility, especially as it easily cleared a four foot barbed wire fence, and then ran off and leaped up and over a pile of jarrah trees which had been felled and stacked to an approximate height of 20 ft.*

Other respondents saw the outstanding feature as:

> *Unconcerned with my vehicle - long tail, long legs . . .*

> *The eyes and its very heavy, powerful build and the way it rolled as it walked . . .*

> *The immediate speed it demonstrated upon seeing me and the way in which it ran, stretching out like a horse . . .*

> *Sleek way animal ran as if pursued, body moved as if all one . . .*

> *Length of body and tail, large luminous eyes . . .*

> *Strong front legs and slinking walk - no apparent fear of passing traffic . . .* (This sighting occurred two kilometres

north of Arthur River Roadhouse in a paddock adjacent to
the Albany Highway)

. . .

Relations between the farmers and the A.P.B. were further under
strain when the Cougar Committee learned that Alan McKenzie had
given a local farmer a young feral pig that had been trapped in the Wilga
area, south of Collie. The Committee members were stunned. The whole
basis of the authorities' rejection of their claims had been the suggestion
that feral pigs were running wild in the area, and responsible for the
killings. The Cordering farmers, of course, flatly denied the pig claim.
But when they heard a rumour that McKenzie himself introduced a feral
pig into the area even they were struck with disbelief. The Department
of Agriculture runs regular publicity campaigns in pig-free areas of the
State, urging people to take every precaution lest they be introduced. The
transfer of feral pigs into pig-free areas has always been illegal.

Dennis Earnshaw and Charlie Sumner were so stunned by the
suggestion that McKenzie, the Government's investigator, and the man
who claimed wild pigs were the predator, had actually brought a feral pig
in, that they decided to formally ask the Agriculture Protection Board to
explain. On July 31, 1979, Dennis Earnshaw wrote to Des Gooding:

> It has been brought to the attention that Alan McKenzie
> of your Department is working in the Wilga area catching
> Feral Pigs. It now has been reported to me that Mr
> McKenzie left a live feral pig caught in the Wilga area
> on the property of T & E Chapman of North Dinninup.
> As we do not have Feral Pigs in this area we request the
> matter be investigated. If such a pig is found we demand
> that it be destroyed.

On August 22, 1979, Gooding wrote the following letter to Earnshaw:

> I regret the delay in replying to your letter of July 31 regarding
> a feral pig which was left on the property of T & E Chapmen,
> North Dinninup.

Subsequent to receiving your letter I did arrange for an inspector from the A.P.B. to visit Chapman's property and they showed him the remains of a pig which they said was the one given to them by McKenzie and which had been slaughtered prior to the arrival of our inspector. I have taken the matter (sic) of leaving the pig with Alan McKenzie and I am confident action such as this will not be repeated in the future.

The timing, as well as contents of Gooding's letter was significant. It was interesting that an A.P.B. inspector had visited the farm in question, to find the pig already slaughtered. In his letter, Gooding made no mention of why the pig was slaughtered, or why McKenzie had seen fit to introduce it to the area, to a farmer known to be highly sceptical about the cat theory propounded by many of his neighbours. Was the pig merely donated for a baked Sunday lunch? Could McKenzie not see that it prejudiced the validity of his own claim about pigs killing stock? And if it was, in the end, a harmless gesture, why did Des Gooding 'take the matter' up with the dogger? The Cougar Committee was told at the May 23 preliminary meeting in Dennis Earnshaw's lounge room that McKenzie would be withdrawn from the Cordering enquiry and area. Why was it then that up to two months later it appeared he had been back, depositing a feral pig on a local farm?

Another festering issue of contention which exacerbated the rift, was the A.P.B.'s assessment of the tree markings. Right up until the end of 1979, the A.P.B.'s counter-claims about the markings strongly disaffected the farmers. For them it was another case of presenting what they believed to be tangible observations about their environment, which were disregarded by officialdom.

But it went further.

Allegations began to surface that the farmers had manufactured the tree markings. A.P.B. officers who examined some trees reported that the marks did not penetrate the bark deeply enough, or in long enough cuts for a large feline animal. Yet I, and other media representatives saw, over a period of time, markings of different lengths which bit hard and deeply into the trees. In fact, as were sometimes revealed to be cut through into underlying layers. There can be no doubt that some of the markings were certainly long, and often quite deep into the bark.

The A.P.B. men took exception to the width of some scratches. Late in the year, Dick Old said officially that the width of a cougar front foot, especially when climbing a tree 'probably' would be in excess of 9 cm. His suggestion that the markings were sometimes too small to be a big cat-like animal was, however, strenuously rejected by Bob Neuman and later by other important experts. Experienced bushmen expressed amazement at some of the markings. Known tree climbers, such as possums, made distinctive, often superficial marks high up the trunks of trees. A.P.B. officers said the marks being pointed out by the farmers were also made by possums. But a possum, for example, marks the bark in two distinct sets as it hugs the tree, its legs stretched some 35 cm apart. Significantly, its marks cut the tree at about a 45-degree angle to the horizontal, leaving quite superficial scratches, about 2.5 cm long.

But the farmers were pointing to something new. The scratches in question were etched in at different angles, but often virtually vertical. And there was usually one distinct type of tree marked. The farmers claimed the cat animal invariably chose leaning trees, angled off the vertical with upper boughs parallel to the ground and stationed within sight of open clearings - a handy tree-top lookout. On some of these trees the farmers found hollowed-out upper limbs. From one of these, small hair samples were found by a Cordering farmer, and sent to Don Hart, the A.P.B. Research Technician who had previously been sent to Cordering at various times to examine evidence. Dennis Earnshaw sent the hair sample off, but did not tell the A.P.B. that it had been found inside the hollowed out trunk of a tree. Later Earnshaw rang Des Gooding to inquire about the hair sample, and the A.P.B. man told him it had been identified as cat hair. Earnshaw told him it had been found inside one of the marked trees. The next day Don Hart arrived again in the area to take away further samples.

Relations between the two sides in the controversy were already at breaking point when a piece of correspondence from Dick Old fell into their hands later in 1979. Up until then the farmers had only heard dull murmurs about allegations that they, themselves, had marked the trees. But in a letter to another state M.P., Mr Old said:

> *We have the report of another officer in which he draws attention to the fact that scratch marks shown to him appeared to have been artificially made since one of the claw marks deviated in a Y shape half way down the scratch.*

To suggest to the farmers that they had marked the trees to prop up their claim left them speechless with anger.

But it was when they obtained a copy of the official departmental report on the cougar enquiries that the final straw was reached. Old had come under pressure from even some Government backbenchers to explain what his Department was doing about the Cordering claims. He received correspondence from at least one Government M.L.A. suggesting inquires would be aided by closer co-operation between the Department and the Cougar Committee. The farmers' tactics of lobbing State M.P.'s was paying off.

Old told the backbenchers that his Department and the A.P.B. had been doing 'a lot of work' on the matter. And he sent at least one a copy of an undated summary prepared by his officers which was eventually leaked to the Cougar Committee. The report was ostensibly a summary of the Government's efforts to investigate the Cordering mystery up until that time.

Titled *Report on A.P.B. and Department of Agriculture involvement in the Cougar Investigation* it began with the words:

> *The following is a resume of the involvement of Agriculture Protection Board and Department of Agriculture in investigations and possible future control of American Mountain Lions (cougars) in Western Australia.*

It was significant that while the authorities had constantly rejected the farmers claims, this report referred to 'possible future control.'

The report went on:

At the time the first serious reports were received about a year ago, a dogger was dispatched to the area to carry out investigations and any control operations that were necessary. Baits and traps laid, and it became obvious that our dogger was not welcome in the area. At the time of the recent reports he was again sent to the area, again carried out baiting and was again criticised by the local people.

The farmers were concerned by this. They insisted that in the initial stages of the dogger's involvement in early 1978 they had extended courtesies to him, including the offer of laundry facilities and the use of a television, while he was working in the area. He returned to Cordering again later, at a time when communication between the farmers and the authorities was rapidly breaking down. The farmers also became concerned when, without warning them, the dogger laid poison baits on Crown Land immediately adjacent to their properties, and in one case less than 400 metres from a farm house. It was always the custom when baiting an area, for the locals to be informed so that they could ensure none of their farm animals ventured into the area.

The report continued:

Both district officer and regional officer staff have been involved in endeavouring to find out information regarding the cause of the reported losses. The district officer initiated a system of asking selected people to report all losses of sheep and lambs to him; however, he subsequently suffered a heart attack and his programme has now been taken over by the regional officer and has been expanded. No pattern which we consider significant has yet emerged which could indicate the presence of an animal such as the cougar. A research technician has already made two visits to the area during the past year to spend time with the farmers and to participate in some of their hunting and searching operations. He has not seen anything yet which would lead him to believe that there is an unusual predator in the area.

The research technician referred to was Don Hart. It was significant that Hart had accumulated various pictures of tracks found near the Earnshaw properties in 1978. On the back of these he jotted down his own observations. And on four photos he referred to the apparent confirmation of five toe marks - a feature referred to as strikingly unusual by the farmers and, according to them, indicative of a feline footprint. In fact, on one photo, Hart wrote "Front track of ? note fifth toe marked by match.' On July 12, 1978, Don Hart apparently thought that feature of the tracks significant enough to make special mention of it. Yet according to the department account of his finding, it had not been quite significant enough to prompt him to give the farmers' claims more credence:

The report continues:

An officer of the Board's executive has also visited the area on six separate occasions, has discussed the problem with the farmers concerned, and has brought sample material to Perth for examination. He has also offered to provide any back up facilities which the farmers in the area thought could be useful.

One of the developing complaints voiced by the farmers related to the inadequate feedback they had received about the various samples - faeces, hair and dead stock. They complained that they never received any detailed laboratory or test information. For example, from six separate samples handed to Don Hart at the end of July 1978, only the most cursory descriptions were sent back to the farmers. One hair sample was identified as cat hair, one as human hair, one as fox hair and another as horse hair. But from the two scat samples, mouse hair was identified as well as feathers and seeds. The lack of more detailed data than the simple reference 'cat hair' or 'mouse hair' or 'feathers and seeds' worried the farmers. They also made the point that because a mouse hair and samples of feathers and seeds were found inside scat samples the possibility could not be ruled out that the scat was dropped by a feline predator. What they wanted to know was detailed scientific information about the scat sample itself, not just brief references to a few items found in it. And in fact after July 1978, the Agriculture Protection Board never even produced written acknowledgement of the receipt of samples, let alone an explanation relating to tests done on them.

The Department report went on:

When the information first came to hand, footprints were obtained from the cougars in the South Perth Zoo, in an effort to compare these with local prints found in the area. So far no conclusive evidence has been obtained that the local prints were made by cougars or other large, cat-like animals. It is possible, using microscopic techniques, to determine from which animals hairs have come, but in the case of cougars it is impossible to differentiate these from domestic cats. However, many samples have been taken from the field and have been examined to see whether there is some possibility of positive diagnoses by this method. To date no success has been achieved.

Only Dennis Earnshaw, of all the farmers, was ever shown the Perth Zoo footprint casts. It could have expedited matters considerably had the casts been made available to the farmers for comparison purposes. And why was it that the zoo casts were not produced at the Moodiarrup Hall meeting to refute the farmers' casts?

The report said:

Faeces samples (scats) have been collected and examined wherever possible, but the size of these would indicate that they were not made by an animal of the size of a cougar, although I have heard there is a photograph in existence of one scat which could be of cougar size. This is as yet unconfirmed.

Yet Dick Old, A.P.B. and Fisheries and Wildlife officers were all shown at different times either photographs or actual faeces which the farmers claimed were cat-like, in sizes ranging up to 30 cm in length. Slides were shown to Old and the Moodiarrup Hall meeting, and Don Hart took away numerous samples from the region. Des Gooding saw the scats uncovered during Koenig's hunt, and took one back to Perth in a plastic bag for analysis. Yet the farmers never received any detailed reports on these samples.

The report read:

When the problem first became important in 1978 the Agriculture Protection Board was instrumental in locating Mr Bob Neuman, an American who spent many years hunting cougars in Montana, U.S.A. He was taken to the area to discuss the likelihood of cougars being present with some of the farmers, and subsequently the A.P.B. paid the expenses for him and his horses to make a return trip to the search area.

It was interesting that the report failed to make mention of Bob Neuman's findings. He had observed to Earnshaw after his second visit to the area: 'Man, you sure got cougars'. To this day, he believes there is some kind of large cat species proliferating in large stretches of the Western Australian bush. Yet the Agriculture Department report made no mention of this. The authorities were at pains to point out that they financed Neuman's involvement. In fact, the A.P.B. paid for his petrol. Yet, if Neuman was taken to Cordering as some kind of expert, were he and his opinions later denounced purely because he found he agreed with what the farmers were saying?

But Bob Neuman was only one of a number of overseas visitors to examine the evidence. As well as the Americans Estin Jones and Casey Collins, yet another stud farm operator, Lymon Tenney, also from the U.S.A., later visited Cordering and basically agreed with Neuman's findings. Two Perth residents, formerly from India, and one a leading Police officer in the Indian provinces, also visited Dennis Earnshaw. Once again they insisted that a big cat was involved, though, from their knowledge of wildlife in India, they said the signs indicated that the Western Australian animal was not as big as a lion or tiger. And then at the end of 1979, perhaps the most explosive observations of all were made on the Western Australian phenomenon by an acknowledged, expert in the behaviours of cougars in the Canadian wilds. More of that later.

The report went on:

At the same time arrangements were made to purchase extensive audio visual slide-tape series on the cougar from the Texas University. This series was only in the course of preparation when the initial request was made, but was completed approximately two months ago. Two sets of the series have been obtained and have been shown to a recent public meeting in the district. This series has proved invaluable in identification, particularly in determining the cause of death in the livestock.

The farmers claimed the series only confirmed the consistency of killing patterns in Western Australia, such as the covering of carcasses on occasions, and the neck attack style.

It has been reported that circus accidents occurred in the southwest in 1961 or 1962, and from one of these up to four cougars escaped. We have subsequently checked all the circus arrivals and departures into and from Western Australia from 1958 to 1974 and during this time only one cougar came in as part of a circus. This was brought in by the Moscow State Circus in 1968 and was subsequently checked on leaving the State. It can be safely said that this reputed accident as a source of possible cougars in the southwest has now been eliminated,

the report said.

Of course, when I first made my inquiries of Dick Tomlinson, the A.P.B. Executive Director told me there were no records covering the movement of circuses prior to 1965. Des Gooding later said they had been discovered in a little-used filing cabinet. But, what then of the possibility of some circus accident prior to 1958?

> *Another rumour is that American warships, particularly submarines, often carried cougar cubs as mascots or illegal pets when they left America. The story goes on to say by the time the ships arrived in Western Australia the cubs had grown to the extent that they were causing embarrassment and were subsequently either released or swapped for joey kangaroos. Contact has been made with the Acting American Consul who has obtained information from the American naval historian that these facts cannot be substantiated. Also in this area the Customs Department, under Section 59 of the Customs Act, requires the masters of all naval vessels entering Western Australia to complete a form detailing all livestock carried on the ship. The Collector of Customs in Western Australia has now advised these records are no longer available,*

the report said.

It went on:

> *Several carcasses have been brought back from Perth on different occasions and submitted to the Animal Health laboratories for post mortem examination. These have all been lamb carcasses which have been reputedly killed by the unidentified predator. From none of these lambs has it been possible to positively diagnose death from cougar attack. It is very difficult with the sample material provided to make such positive diagnoses some time after the animal has died.*

But Peter Brighton has no real problems making definite observations about the mutilated stock brought to him. Certainly, Brighton could not say a 'cougar' was definitely involved. But what he did say was that a large family of large felines was. With all the resources at its disposal, why was it that the Government was not able to come up with 'positive diagnoses'? And would it not have been a matter of common courtesy for the farmers providing the dead stock to be informed in detail of the results, whatever their form?

The report continued:

As from May 8 an experienced veterinary officer was stationed in the area for three weeks and available seven days a week to examine carcasses of livestock which had reputedly been killed by the mysterious predator. This officer was provided with assistance by the Agriculture Protection Board. His investigations were unable to turn up any evidence from any of the carcasses examined to indicate the presence of a large cat-like predator. Greatest losses were occurring on properties where farm management was low, where insufficient hand feeding was taking place, and vaccinations were not regularly administered.

The farmers, some of whom were among the most successful in the south west, angrily denied the allegation of farm mismanagement. Many were providing their sheep with higher than the recommended hand feeding ration. To suggest that they were guilty of bad management and poor stock feeding and vaccination programmes, infuriated them. But all this was quite apart from the fact that they were pointing to a pattern of attack being suffered by their stock. How could feeding and lack of vaccinations - even had they existed, been responsible for fang marks up to 10 cm in depth, and the consistent feline pattern of mutilation identified by Peter Brighton?

The report said:

Most of the lambs presented for post mortem examination showed typical fox damage, whilst in many cases the intestines had been removed. This is not usual in the case of cougars, but does occur regularly when pigs are involved.

*There are numerous foxes, dogs, eagles and wild pigs present
in the area.*

The farmers never denied that foxes killed small lambs and quite
often came in to eat from carcasses in secondary predation. What they
were pointing out was that even with the involvement of existing animals
there was still this consistent and unexplained activity of an animal they
had never recognised before. To suggest, for example, that a fox could
attempt to kill a frisky six-week-old lamb which could offer considerable
resistance, when there were ample supplies of smaller, more vulnerable
new-born lambs available in the fields, verged on the ridiculous. Why was
it that so many farmers talked about this new style of attack which had
only grown up in recent years when foxes had been present for decades.
And how could a fox cleanly kill and then eat out a 70 kilogram wether?
Even had any army of foxes attempted such an assault, fleece and piece
of the unfortunate sheep would be spread everywhere, consistent with a
dog-style attack.

George Wheeler insisted he had trapped the last wild dog seen in
the area years before. He had never found evidence of wild dogs or dingoes
involved in this new predation. In any event, had dogs been involved,
stock would have been torn to pieces in wounding attacks. Wheeler
constantly pointed to the cleanness of the attack, from rib cages stripped
bare, to lack of internal organs and wool scattered around the carcass.
Furthermore, if dogs were responsible, why was it that A.P.B. officers
came up with no bodies after months of intensive tracking in the area.
As Wheeler pointed out, there had just never been any evidence of dog
activity on the scale necessary to decimate the farmers' flocks. An eagle
would have great difficulty in breaking the neck of a fully grown sheep,
and the farmers claimed the only feral pig known in the area for years
had been brought in by Alan McKenzie, the A.P.B.'s key troubleshooter.

In an incredible reference, the Department report then went on to
observe:

*The veterinary investigation failed to turn up any evidence
of predation by a large cat-like animal. Alternatively, if an*

unknown predator is present, it is not having any substantial effect upon the livestock in the area.

In the seasons between 1977 and 1979, the area covered by the farms of the Cougar Committee members lost upward of 2000 sheep and lambs through unexplained predation. To the men suffering this significant financial loss, the report's denouncement of their claims was bad enough, but the statement that the predator was 'not having a substantial effect upon the livestock in the area', was unconscionable.

The report went on:

Recently the A.P.B. made arrangements with the owners of German Shepherd trained tracking dogs to travel to the area whenever a positive sighting has been made by a "reliable" person. To date two such visits have been made, but no success has been obtained in finding any evidence to support the reported sighting.

Apparently the officers responsible for compiling the report had neglected to ask Rick Richardson and his wife what they thought their dog was chasing, as Koenig charged eagerly through the Cordering bush on two occasions.

The report claimed:

The Board itself, and the staff of the A.P.B. have kept an open mind as to whether cougars do exist in the area and have to date responded to all requests for assistance. The Board's executive has offered to do anything that the local farmers considered would be of assistance but has been told that all that is required is to provide technical back up facilities for examination of such things as prints, hairs, scats, carcasses, etc. This has been done whenever requested.

Why was it, then, that the farmers were so concerned about the lack of technical feedback that they were forced to seek what could have been quite costly, private veterinary advice.

The report continued:

In discussion with the people concerned in the area it was agreed that there was little point in the Protection Board sending teams of men to the area to search for cougars when there were already several hundred farmers in the areas from which reports have emanated, all of whom would know their own properties much better than any visiting A.P.B. officers, and would be better able to search for cougars.

This was an astonishing reference. If all the farmers knew their own properties and area 'much better than any visiting A.P.B. officers', why was it then that such little credence was put in their claims that eventually communication between them and the Government completely collapsed? At one and the same time the farmers could be relied upon to know their environments and yet their claims were rejected outright because they were guilty of farm mismanagement.

The report then went on to say:

It is important to note that there is very substantial involvement by the press and television in this problem. On nearly all occasions, information first appears in the media before being relayed to the Agriculture Protection Board. Two recent examples of this are the meeting which was held on March 27 to which the Agriculture Protection Board was not invited to send a representative, and secondly the reported sightings of female cougars with cubs at foot in both the Arthur River and Rosa Glen areas.

But of course, as my involvement had shown, it was largely through the media's interest at various states that the Government was prompted into virtual action.

The Department report concluded by saying that requests for assistance by the farmers had been met by

. . . the provision of staff, technical back up, new information,

verification of possible sources of cougars, post mortem examinations, tracking dogs and offers of further assistance.

Whilst there had been many reported sightings, all the work to date has failed to turn up evidence to support them, or to confirm the presence of a large cat-like predator.

While the controversy wore on through the middle of 1979, David Evans, the Labour M.L.A. for Warren, began making plans to raise it in the Spring Session of State Parliament.

At the beginning of August, the A.P.B. said publicly that after two years of investigation, it had found no evidence to prove that cougars existed in Western Australia. In yet another curiously worded statement on the matter, the Board Chairman, Noel Fitzpatrick, was quoted publicly as saying:

Cordering cougars may not exist. If they do they are not significantly affecting livestock.

Fitzpatrick again repeated, in comments printed in *The West Australian*, that abnormally high stock losses 'appeared to be associated with management problems such as low feeding levels and failure to vaccinate.' Description by farmers of the damaged animals were consistent with fox, eagle and wild dogs attacks, he said. In many cases intestines and paunch were eaten. This was common where wild pigs were involved, but overseas reports indicated that cougars did not eat the intestines and paunch. Mr Fitzpatrick said his doggers had found evidence of foxes, wild dogs and wild pigs at Cordering.

🐾 🐾 🐾

A homemade sign tells the story no one wanted to believe.

Chapter Twelve

ON WEDNESDAY, AUGUST 22, 1979, DAVID EVANS rose as the Member for Warren in the Western Australia Legislative Assembly to move a motion on the question of mysterious animals in the South West. Evans moved:

That in the opinion of this House the Government should take immediate action to have the Agriculture Protection Board and the Department of Fisheries and Wildlife investigate reports of the existence of large cat-like animals in the south west of Western Australia which are reputed to have killed significant numbers of sheep and wildlife; to report on and make recommendations to the House regarding their findings.

The motion set in train the first ever full Parliamentary debate on the subject, lasting for nearly two hours. Evans began to make public a detailed breakdown of everything that had happened in the Cordering district over the past year. He said:

Twelve months ago when I first had my attention drawn to a series of attacks in the lower south-west I would have been too sceptical to bring this motion forward in this manner tonight. Since that time and as a result of the accumulated material that has been shown to me over the course of the last 12 months, I believe there are such a number of unexplained points that it is more than time some action was taken in this regard - more action than has been taken up to the present moment.

I shall draw members' attention to a number of points which up to this stage are unexplained, having regard for the fact that in Australia we have an increasing problem; a problem which was introduced many years ago, probably by well-meaning settlers. I refer to foxes, rabbits, and quite a variety of noxious weeds.

The House should give consideration to a number of these aspects, such as the following: visual sightings which have been recorded; the extent of killing; the number; the area over which they have extended; the manner in which the killing occurred; the manner in which the carcasses have been eaten; the ineffectiveness of trappings and poisoning; the tracks that have been found; the hair that has been presented; the reports of strange cries of large animals at night; the presence of animal faeces - or scats - of a cat-like nature; the size of the strides ;and the reaction of other animals to predators of this kind. This information has been gathered by people who have had some experience in this field, including four Americans, a private veterinarian, and the operator of the dogs on a recent chase.

I know the A.P.B. has published a report which has been available through you, Mr Acting Speaker, and there are several points in regard to this report that should be aired; but first I shall deal with some of the points to which I have already referred.

I have copies of sheets that were circulated to anyone who had had an experience with any strange animal in the lower south-west. I have over 30 reports to which I can now refer. The detail required in these sheets included such things as the place, the date, the time, the size, the colour, the locality, the description, and the evaluation or estimate of what the particular creature was in the eyes of the viewer.

It is interesting to note the areas involved which can be gleaned from these reports. They include areas such as Northcliffe, going back as far as 1963; Pemberton in 1996; Wellington Dam; South Easter Latham; North Borden: Capercup; Harris River; Collie; Donnybrook; Grimwade; Palgarup; Duranillin; North Dinninup; Cordering - three reports; Donnybrook; Witchcliffe; Bokal; Denmark; Arthur River; and South Collie. That will give an indication of the extent of the area over which such animals have been seen.

I will not give the full details of the reports of sightings. By way of illustration, I shall mention three of the reports and refer to the salient points in each. In the first case I wish to mention, the animal was sighted 12 mile south-east of Latham. The name of the farmer is shown on the report. The animal was sighted in an open paddock of scrub and the general appearance of it was 'light brown with tail half curled up, large pad approximately two inches in diameter.' The pad mark was estimated. As far as the size of the animal is concerned, the report says 'twice as large as the biggest domestic cat I have ever seen." The report goes on, "In your opinion was the animal dog-like, cat-like, or otherwise?' The answer to that question was 'definitely cat-like'. The most outstanding feature mentioned in the report was 'the tail position, pad size left in the sand.'

Mr Nanovich, a Liberal Party backbencher, then interrupted to ask? 'How did it meow?'

David Evans continued:

The further question is asked in the report: 'What distance were you from the animal?' And the answer is 'approximately 50 yards.'

Then the Premier of Western Australia, Sir Charles Court, interjected, 'I did not think you would be conned so easily.'

Mr Evans continued:

Bearing in mind one must have proper regard for the time of the sighting, the appearance of the animal, the light at the time and everything else involved, I suggest the Premier should not treat this as a laughing matter. He should discuss it with some of the people who signed the reports of sightings before he ridicules them.

Some people to whom I shall refer later are quite adamant about the matter. They have lived in farming areas all their lives and have had wide experience with foxes, dogs and feral cats. They would not be inclined to make an error of this nature.

If members disregard half the 30 reports I have mentioned, they must agree that the matter still requires explanations. I do not believe members opposite should laugh at the matter out of hand.

Perhaps the Premier would like to talk to such farmers as Mr Putland who saw one of these animals at a distance of 20 metres in good clear torchlight. Mr Putland is regarded in the district as being completely reliable; therefore, the consensus is, if Mr Putland saw something, something was there.

The same situation applies with a man like George Wheeler who, although over 65 years of age, has, over the last 40 years, been called upon by his neighbours to trap dogs which appear in the area. He has lost hundreds of his own lambs and he has been unable to trap the animal responsible for the killings. He caught a fleeting glimpse of something, but he was not prepared to try to identify it. It is certain that a man of his experience would have trapped a dog, fox, or feral cat. This is the sort of situation which should be explained.

Before scorning the reports which I am quite happy to table, members should look at the matter seriously. I have received further reports, and one relates to the Scott River area where my brother-in -law, in whom I have absolute confidence, was camping. He was awakened by a very loud screech. He said the cows brought their calves close to the hut. He considered it to be a terrifying experience. He heard the screech again about half a mile away. He has never heard that type of sound before or since.

Another farmer whose veracity and integrity cannot be doubted in Ross Muir of Manjimup. A couple of his lambs were killed. Their heads were crushed and a dog is not cable of doing that. All the farmers in the area are aware that a dog could not get his teeth through the skull of a full-grown lamb. This actually occurred. This man lost a pet kangaroo at the same time also.

These people are prepared to stand by their reports of sightings.

Therefore, I am not prepared to regard the matter with the same levity as the Premier displays. In excess of 1000 sheep and lambs have been killed in the area from the Wellington Dam south, including Cordering. The number of sheep lost in the area has been assessed at over 1000. It is interesting to note that some of the losses have seen as high as 400 out of 1000 in one particular area. Foxes do not kill like that. Every farmer in the area who has had the experience with sheep grazing knows that is the case.

I should like to point out that some of the animals were killed outright. One farmer lost three fully-grown wethers which were partially eaten. The rib cages of the sheep were chewed from the back bone, apparently with ease. A dog or fox would not be capable of doing that.

Mr Grewar, the Liberal Member of Esperance said:

A dingo would do that.

But David Evans continued:

Had a dingo killed these sheep it is certain it would have been trapped. I must point out also that dingoes are not prevalent in that area and the method of killing, by attacking at the back of the neck, is not the manner in which dogs or dingoes kill.

I have a report by a private veterinarian who considers the lambs taken to him were not killed by dogs, foxes or feral cats. He has signed the document and points out also that the mouth pattern of the animal which killed the lambs would not correspond with that of a dog, fox or feral cat. However, he considers the animal which killed the lambs to be of the cat family.

The veterinarian measured the incision of the fangs and he estimated it was an inch to an inch and a half deep. He also saw fang marks which went through the skull of one of the animals. No dog, dingo, or fox would do that. He said the strength of the jaw of the animal which killed the lambs was considerable and the method of killing was biting at the back of the neck. The vertebrae of the lambs were fractured and he referred to the teeth marks and the mouth pattern. This is the report of a private veterinarian.

I asked this man whether he would allow me to quote his report as being his professional opinion and he said he was quite agreeable.

Mr. Grewar then asked:

Were there any tracks seen at all?

Mr Evans replied:

Some tracks have been seen. Some casts have been made, but I am not prepared to claim what they are. They have been given to me as being casts of tracks, and I have them here. The A.P.B. has suggested they are not the tracks of cats. However, the A.P.B.'s opinion differs from the opinions I have received from other sources and to which I shall refer. The number of tracks have not been considerable, but these casts have been taken. I could indicate the difference between a dog, cat, and fox; but most members would be aware of it. Whether or not these are distinguished enough to make a firm identification I am not sure, but I am certain I could not do it. The matter in which carcasses have been eaten is in itself rather unusual.

In the main, the animals are eaten from the shoulder back towards the loin or from the hock upward, and in the case of small lambs and kangaroos only the feet are maimed. The suggestion has been that it could have been wild pigs, but no wild pig would eat in that manner. Foxes certainly do not either. The manner of eating is an unusual sort of operation and so perhaps someone such as the Premier could offer an explanation. The eating pattern is not consistent with those that are already known.

I refer to the cries and screeches that have been heard by one person. Others, especially in the Dinninup area, are quite firm in their statements that the noises they have heard are nothing like those of a dog, fox, wild boar, or feral cat, because they know these sounds. These people are quite sincere in their statements and their bone fides without question are beyond reproach.

Mr Bert Crane, a National Country Party member asked:

Have they tape-recorded it?

Mr Evans replied:

Not to my knowledge. That would be quite interesting.

Specimens of faeces have been found - scats, as they are know in the trade - and a number have been collected and forwarded to the Museum, the Department of Fisheries and Wildlife, and the A.P.B. Acknowledgement has not been received from all these organisations.

As a matter of fact, only a couple of the half-dozen have been received or acknowledged. Traces of hair have been found in some of these scats but there is some conjecture here as to the identification of the particular cat family because there are many different types.

I do not know whether the scientific apparatus in Western Australia is sufficient to identify this but it seems that it is not beyond the realms of science to make some conclusive determination. Whether or not this has been prosecuted in the fullest manner, again, I do not know.

With respect to the trapping of animals, I refer to the situation where George Wheeler - I cite him because he is a man of many years' bush background - last year lost some 700 lambs to this animal. He has trapped over a period of months and even though he is a dogger of great renown - he is the person to whom the district refers when a dog has come into the area - he has been unable to trap the animal. In his opinion if it had been a dog he would have caught it.

In 1978 the farmers of the area were concerned that a great deal had not been done to rectify the problem. A meeting was called and a committee set up - it is known as the Cordering Cougar Committee - in Moodiarrup. I was unable to attend but understand that the signatures for the petition were obtained without any great effort.

Mr Old, the Katanning Minister for Agriculture asked,

What date was that meeting?

Mr Evan replied,

It was a meeting early this year, I think it was the one the Minister attended.

I attended the same meeting as Wally. You should have been at that one! Mr Old said.

Mr Evans continued,

This was the second meeting. A circular letter dated the 5th April - which I believe members of this House received - was sent out indicating the response to the meeting held on the 27th March. It stated that over a period of 18 months some 1800 lambs and sheep had been lost. Of course the frustration of the farmers involved had increased quite considerably. Regrettable there has been friction and a resultant deterioration of public relations between the A.P.B. and the Committee. The deterioration has developed to such an extent that the Committee has virtually refused to have anything to do with the A.P.B., which is a most unfortunate situation.

I can appreciate the reasons for the Committee's dissatisfaction, but believe it most regrettable that the body which is making formal and official attempts to overcome this problem is not involved fully.

A report on the A.P.B and the Department of Agriculture involvement in the cougar investigation was made, and I would like to quote a number of points. The first is as follows: At the time the first serious reports were received, about a year ago, a dogger was dispatched to the area to carry out investigations and any control operations that were necessary. Baits and traps were laid and it became obvious that our dogger was not welcome in the area.

That statement is significant and it is unfortunate that the Committee did not believe that this was so. In the first instance, the farmers offered the dogger the use of a washing machine; they offered to put his caravan under shelter; they supplied him with a television set, and they accommodated him in the community. So to say the dogger was not welcome in the area is not factual. This has probably caused the further deterioration in the relationship between the APB and the committee.

A technician visited the area on several occasions but did not see anything to lead him to believe there was an unusual predator in the area. He took photographs of footprints with five padmarks found in the sand. This was considered unusual. He also examined a tree that the Committee felt was marked by the scratchings of a cat and he took samples of hair found nearby which were subsequently identified as cat hair.

The technician offered to provide back-up facilities which the farmers in the area felt could be useful.

An American who has had experience with the large cat families in the United States indicated that the tree was one which would be used by a she-cat and kittens. The casts of the footprints shown to the same American, although rejected by the A.P.B., could well have been those of a large cat.

Photographs of the cat's track actually had been sent to the Museum. The Museum admitted they were cat's tracks but doubted their authenticity.

The A.P.B. brought the American into the area and he told the officers of the A.P.B. that he considered the tracks could well have been those of a cougar. He offered to train dogs, having had experience in that regard in the United States. He subsequently brought in two other Americans from Montana. They were even more experienced than Mr Neuman and they seemed to be of the same opinion; that is, that it could well be that these animals did exist.

Of the scats sent to the A.P.B., at least four or five have not been identified to this time. There has not been an official department report on them. In this regard, the report refers to the droppings of cats.

The A.P.B. purchased a pair of image intensifying binoculars to help in the search for the animals. The binoculars cost several thousand dollars, but on arrival they were found to be faulty and were returned to the manufacturers in the United Kingdom. I understand similar binoculars were used in the research into rabbit control. They were never offered for use in the search for cougars. The A.P.B. did assist in the purchase of a night sight. This present incident was instrumental in that piece of apparatus coming to Western Australia. Subsequently, it has been used with an appropriate rifle.

When the problem first became obvious in 1978, the A.P.B. was instrumental in locating Mr Bob Neuman, an American who had spend many years hunting cougars in Montana, in the United States of America. He was taken to the area and discussed the likelihood of cougars being present there. Subsequently the A.P.B. paid his expenses to return, with horses, to examine the area. The report does not state that Mr Neuman told the A.P.B. he considered there were cats in the area. There is additional information by way of supportive material and films, and that reference is perfectly correct. That is some of the work done by the A.P.B.

I would like to allude to the comment that from the 8th May this year two officers have been in the area. From that date an officer was provided with assistance from the A.P.B. As a result of his investigations he was unable to turn up any evidence to indicate the presence of cat-like creatures.

The report stated that the greatest losses occurred when farm management was low, where there was insufficient hand-feeding, and where vaccinations were not regularly administered.

This is an unfortunate statement because the area included some of the best managed properties in the southwest. I have with me a letter which is worth reading to the House. It is open, and it is signed, and when I mention the name of the person who wrote the letter I do not think anyone will question its authenticity or the capability of the farmer. The letter reads:

To whom it may concern.

Dear Sir,

We have had strange killings of lambs with broken necks and crushed heads and large wide teeth marks. Only a few have had chest eaten and all the rest killed with broken necks. Early lambing ewes had to be shedded as killings were occurring 150 yards from the homestead. Our first killing was six years ago and thought it to be foxes but have poisoned dozens and killings still continue. Muled and tailed lambs up to 8 weeks old have been killed. That would be most unusual for a fox, as farmers would know.

The letter continues:

Within 3 days, 2 different men have sighted a strange type of animal in same area in car, headlights have picked up bright eyes never sighted before. They described the animal the size of a large dog, cat-like with a long tail.

That letter is signed by Bob Jackson. The Jacksons have turned out some of the finest animals and their husbandry is beyond questions.

The report goes on to say that no-one can claim these killings are as a consequence of poor management; that does not add up. The report also states that most of the lambs presented for post-mortem examination showed typical fox damage. This is not entirely correct on the experience of veterinary investigations. A veterinarian in private practice, who examined a number of lambs, gave the professional opinion that the damage was not caused by foxes. The report states that whilst in many cases the intestines had been removed, that is not usual in the case of cougars. It does occur regularly when pigs are involved. It states that there are numerous foxes, dogs, eagles, and wild pigs present in the area.

We are not dealing with babes in the woods; we are dealing with farmers who have spend their lives on their properties. They know their farms, they know their stock, and they know the bush. They do not know the actions of the creatures mentioned here.

Eagles will do strange things, but they are easily identified. There is no question when a pig attacks a carcass. It is a messy eater and readily identifiable.

The report states that veterinary investigations failed to turn up any evidence of predation by a large, cat-like animal. I can simply refer again to the veterinarian who has made a professional judgement, and who is prepared to be quoted. The report continues and states that, alternative, if an unknown predator is present is not having any substantial effect on the livestock in the area. If the demise of well over 1000 animals, during the last couple of years, is not have an effect on livestock I would like to know to what extent the impact must be felt. That is the position.

It seems to follow a pattern with lambs and larger sheep and also small kangaroos. The joeys seem to be the most seriously predated.

On the question of tracking dogs, it is to the credit of the A.P.B that two dogs were made available and taken down when sightings were made. Originally the A.P.B. made arrangements with the owners of trained German Shepherd tracking dogs to travel to the area whenever a positive sighting was made by a 'reliable' person. To date, two such visits have been made but no success has been obtained in finding evidence to support the reported sightings. However, one particularly large and outstanding German Shepherd followed a scent through rugged country for eight to ten miles and the owner, Mr Richardson, considered he had definitely been following a cat. I think there were nine previous trial runs in which then animal had reacted in much the same manner. Mr Richardson is the President of the German Shepherd Association and I think he would be quite reliable. The dog was following the track from 8.30 to 11.30 a.m.

before it was called off because A.P.B. officers had another commitment in Perth.

Mr Davis, the leader of the Opposition asked,

Lunch?

Mr Evans replied,

No, they had a legitimate reason to return to Perth.

Mr Jamison, the Labor Party member for Welshpool added,

Someone lost a bird from his aviary and they had to come back.

Mr Evans continued,

Mr Richardson is an experienced dog handler and he considered the dog was following a cat scent, for which the animal has been trained.

I am perturbed about the deterioration of public relations and the subsequent abrasiveness, to the extent that the committee will not have anything to do with the A.P.B. The farmers became frustrated when the previous dogger laid baits when a spate of killings was reported in July, 1978. In October or thereabouts the dogger returned for one and a half days and then left the district. He returned this year saying he had poisoned two dogs, and he produced the skulls. For some time he would not tell the farmers in the area where the remains were, but when he told them the location of the carcasses of the dogs, five experienced people who knew the area went to the exact spot indicated and could not find them. They claim that had the dogger poisoned two dogs which were causing damage he would have been racing around showing them in the district, not coming back four months later and saying, 'I got these when I was here last October'. The questioning of that story is understandable and no doubt it accounted for the attitude those committee members expressed. It was felt the problem was not being treated seriously and was being approached in a rather cavalier manner.

The Chairman of the Agriculture Protection Board virtually repeated in the Press the statement which was released to the Member of Bunbury and to which I have referred. I indicated there was a number of disparities in it. There was the question of the dogger who was sent into the area of the 8th March. It appears he was not a qualified tracker in any way. His experience in that Field was rather limited but his experience in public relations and handling people was even more deficient. Because of his method of interrogation and some of the stories he spread around the area, the Committee finally decided it would have nothing further to do with the A.P.B.

That is a fair summary of the points which have been made. There were indications over a period of at least two years before the matter began to be raised seriously. It can be said on the part of the Committee, that the actual sightings can be discounted and may be open to distortion, but reliable bush people have made sighting at distances of up to 10 yards. Perhaps half of them could be discounted but the remaining half of those reports should have been investigated thoroughly. All those people should have been approached and their reports should have been followed up in a scientific and professional manner to decide what weight could be placed on them.

I make the point that the matter has not been handled in a scientific, professional manner. The absence of tracks is an element of weakness, but if it is a large cat the tracks probably would not be easily found. I have done a little reading on the North American mountain lion, which appears to be a very secretive and elusive animal. An American, Mr Neuman, in many years of hunting them has never seen one in the wild. It is not until they are shot that it is known for certain what they are.

The number of carcasses brought in for inspection during the period the veterinarian was in the area - only 15 - does not reconcile with the number of killings in 1978. But once again there was a further escalation of killing in Boscoville and subsequently in Chowerup. The number of lambs is open to question. Some lambs die, and foxes, being scavengers, take them. A number of lambs could have been weak or diseased. That cannot be discounted. It is a factor which must be taken into account in relation to the attitude of the Committee.

The Committee did not acknowledge the assistance it obtained in being given the use of the nightscope. That is a matter which should have been applauded, not hidden. At the same time, the job the A.P.B. has done over the years is regarded with the highest esteem.

I must report some facts here so that we have the picture full and clear. The result of the examination of the scats and the interpretation placed on it indicated that no acknowledgement was received in most cases. I point out too that the record of the sightings was not analysed in a true professional manner. An approach was not made to those people who were prepared to come forward to say that they had actually experienced a sighting, or some other unusual circumstances , and I quote the case of Mr Jackson in this regard. He has had experiences for six years, but he was prepared to say something about it only when a committee was established and the matter became more generally known.

I point out too that the officer of the Agriculture Protection Board who was sent down to handle the matter as from the 8th May was not well chosen at all. I will not go into detail on that point unless I am called on to do so.

It was claimed also that two dogs had been poisoned, and the particular operator was reluctant to show where the further remains were. I feel that a more scientific approach to the problem is warranted. If no further steps are taken, the problem could continue for some considerable time, and it could reach such proportions that it will be difficult ever to overcome it. If animals do exist and they breed, the farmers will have to learn to live with a continual problem. In the case of an animal which can adapt itself to the climate change from the Arctic Circle to Arizona, and which has access to the amount of food that the Australian sheep flock represents, the potential danger is enormous.

The matter is of some urgency, and the levity of the Premier did him no credit. Up to the present time the investigation has not been adequate. The Agriculture Protection Board took some good initiatives. Dogs were made available, Mr Bob Neuman - an American with some authority was called in, and a nightscope was procured.

However, there is room for a more detailed, a more scientific, and a more thorough approach to the problem. For this reason I believe that the

Agriculture Protection Board and the Department of Fisheries and Wildlife must go further. They should secure the services of a CSIRO scientist.

Many matters are still unexplained, and the stakes are high. It is all very well to say that it will be all right, but, if it is not, the rural producers of this State will pay dearly for many years. For that reason I commend my motion to the House,

Mr Evans concluded.

Mr Old then rose to reply:

I have listened with great interest to the Member for Warren. He told a story I have heard many times before,

he said.

Mr. Evens interrupted,

You have been in the area a couple of times I believe.

Old replied,

It is a story with which I am not unfamiliar, and one which certainly has been of some concern to many people in the area described by the Member for Warren.

I would like to point out that there has been no lack of cooperation or activity on the part of the Agriculture Protection Board. I have been involved in this particular exercise for the past eighteen months or so, even since Mr Earnshaw first telephoned and suggested that there was something a little different from the usual predator in the area, and that he wanted some assistance.

The first assistance he was given was help to obtain a night telescope from America and he claimed he could not obtain one here. I would like to point out also that the Agriculture Protection Board at that time decided to invest in a pair of night binoculars, and I emphasise the phrase 'at that time'. I understand that these are produced only in England at a cost of approximately $8000 a pair. Although the binoculars were ordered, delivery was not possible because the various armed forces on the Continent had placed orders for the whole of the very limited production of these binoculars.

However, we were fortunate enough - although the word 'fortunate' should be quoted - to secure a pair of these binoculars. On arrival they were found to be faulty. They were never used at Cape Naturaliste or anywhere else.

The specific primary purpose of the acquisition of these binoculars was to assist the people in the area referred to by the Member for Warren. After the exercise in the Cordering-Bowelling area, the binoculars were to be used for the observation of rabbits in the Cape Naturaliste area.

I admit that before this problem was brought to our attention there had been thoughts of purchasing such binoculars. They are necessary to observe the experimental work being carried out in the Cape Naturaliste area, work which is known to quite a few members.

To say they were never offered to assist in locating this unusual predator in the Cordering area is quite erroneous. I would like that to be understood by all members of the House.

Mr Davis, Leader of the Opposition, asked,

What area is that?

Mr Old replied,

The Cordering area is the one experiencing problems at this stage, but as the Member for Warren pointed out, reports have been received from various areas throughout the State. In fact, sightings have been reported, not only in the areas enumerated by the Member for Warren, but also as far afield as Carnarvon and Ravensthorpe. So the reports are nothing new; it just happens that they are now coming in from this particular area.

I would like to let Members know of some of the action taken by the Agriculture Protection Board, and I impress upon the House that there has been no lack of co-operation or action on the part of employees of that board. I resent the implication that the employees of the board have not done their job properly.

Before I eventually sit down, I want to give members some idea of what has been happening. When this matter was first reported to the

Agriculture Protection Board, through me, a dogger was sent to the area immediately, and the zone control officer worked there constantly until he was transferred to Perth for health reasons. From memory the dogger worked in the Cordering area for some two months, and in the first instance he was well received. However, when he failed to produce the goods and he suggested some dog activity was occurring in the area, he was not well received. He trapped some foxes, and he was of the firm opinion that dogs were causing the problem.

The problem flared up again this year at lambing time. It is not only in that area that lambs are being lost. I am sure the Member of Warren would be well aware that it has been a lean season right throughout the region; and that applies not only to the Cordering-Darkan-Bowelling area, but also to the Kojonup-Katanning area. Some heavy losses have occurred, especially by the farmers who lamb early. Much of the loss has been caused by mismothering, because insufficient feed is available for the ewes.

However, I am not discounting the fact that some of the losses may be due to predation. We decided after consultation to send a veterinarian into the area for three weeks - as a minimum term to study the situation. We also sent a technician experienced in dogging and predation. To me it is quite a bold statement to say that a private veterinarian is now able positively to identify that the predation is not caused by foxes or dogs, because the departmental veterinarian from Narrogin whom we sent to the area is very experienced and well respected.

Mr Pete Jones, the Minister for Education, Cultural Affairs and Recreation, interrupted,

I'll say he is.

Mr Old continued,

That has been substantiated by my colleague on the left, who happens to have a farm in the area from which that veterinarian came. In fact, the veterinarian was reluctant to leave Narrogin because of the amount of work he had there. He received co-operation at first, and lambs were delivered to him. He concluded that most of the lambs were predated post-mortem and had met their death either through mismothering or lack of nutrition. Certainly some had been predated prior to death, but he found no evidence to indicate there was any animal apart from normal predators in the area. He came to the conclusion after studying marks on the animals and the way in which they were killed.

I make the point that like the Member for Warren I am not convinced there is not something unusual in the area. I have visited the area on two occasions in the lambing season during the last two years. In the first place I met Mr Earnshaw and a couple of neighbours. In the second instance I attended a meeting at Moodiarrup. That meeting had been very well documented by a wildlife officer in Manjimup who could probably give us a report of the outcome of it.

When I visited the area I took with me the Chairman of the Agriculture Protection Board, plus officers of the board. We met Mr Gooding, who was acting officially in his job; and we met the committee at Mr Earnshaw's house and spent two or three hours there. Not only did the department supply a veterinarian and a technician on a full-time basis for a period, but also a senior officer of the Agriculture Protection Board was assigned to the task, and he was regularly in and out of the area whenever an alleged sighting or some unusual predation occurred.

Was the dogger previously with the Department of Fisheries and Wildlife?

Mr Evans asked.

Mr Old replied,

No, he was Mr Gooding. The Department of Fisheries and Wildlife has taken part in this exercise too, but I am referring to the A.P.B. because it happens to be the subject of the motion.

Mr Evan then asked,

I am talking about the dogger you sent in there. What were his qualifications? Was he previously with the Department of Fisheries and Wildlife?

Mr Old replied,

I understand he was.

Mr Evans asked,

Do you know his background?

I know he is experienced, according to the Chairman of the Agriculture Protection Board. The Member for Warren probably knows otherwise,

Mr Old replied.

I suggest you check that.

Mr Evans said.

Mr Old continued,

I will, certainly, I am a little tired of the scurrilous remarks made in this House about the officers of my department and, in particular, tonight, about the officers of the Agriculture Protection Board. However, I will look into that matter.

I want to make a few points regarding what has been done. We provided the technical backup facilities to investigate the various problems, despite allegations by the Member for Warren that this area was not done. It is my understanding - and I am no more a scientist than the Member for Warren - that the hairs of a cougar are unidentifiable from those of a cat. So even the A.P.B., despite its technological advancements, was not able to tell the difference. It could identify the hairs as being from member of the cat family, but that was it.

The officers of the A.P.B. obtained written information from the United States. We went to the trouble also of obtaining some audio-visual material which was presented to the meeting at Moodiarrup. Incidentally, I do not think the Member for Warren was at that meeting.

Mr Evans said,

I think my apology was recorded.

Mr Old added,

I merely said the Member was not there; therefore he did not see the audio-visual material which was taken to Moodiarrup specifically for the utilisation of the Committee so the people at the meeting could see and hear about the problem.

It has been established from the information we have received from America and also from the audio-visual material that a cougar after killing will take only the lungs, liver and heart. The predation in the area invariably involves removal of the whole of the viscera. I am informed by the experts that is not indicative of the work of a cougar.

Mr Bob Neuman was located by the A.P.B. and sent into the area as an alleged expert on mountain lions or cougars. He and his horses were transported there at the expense of the A.P.B.; and he spend some time in the area. Incidentally, I have since had communication with another expert from the United States; I do not know how expert he is, but he tells me he is the supreme expert and that Mr Neuman is no good.

Modest to a fault!

Mr Davis interrupted

Mr Old continued,

Absolutely. We could go on and on and send experts down there every week.

We have been trying to assist these people, and we have in no way denigrated their efforts or ridiculed their allegations. I find it incredible that the Committee in its wisdom decided to have nothing more to do with the Agriculture Protection Board after the chairman issued what I considered to be a reasoned and well-balanced Press release. He suggested in his Press release that there was no evidence of a cougar in the area, but he said also there was certainly predation there. I find the Committees decision incredible, because the A.P.B. stands ready to assist the people in the area. If the people want any research work done or any post-mortems carried out on animals that have been predated, the A.P.B. is ready and willing to assist them.

Nobody can say the A.P.B. has not co-operated; if anyone says co-operation has not been forthcoming, the only alternative would be to be down there 24 hours a day.

In fact, the officer who virtually has been put in charge of the operation asked the Committee what help is required. My understanding is that the Committee said it would not be necessary to provide a permanent presence because the local people knew their own farms better than any incoming A.P.B. man could know them; they would call upon him and the A.P.B. if and when necessary. That is the way the exercise has been conducted.

Allegations have been made that there was a circus accident somewhere in the Donnybrook area in 1961 or 1962 and, as a result of the accident, some cougars escaped into the bush. Somebody even telephoned me from Collie and told me the name of the circus - I think it was a small rodeo and circus. Two men in Collie 'well remembered' going down to let the cougars go. I got the A.P.B. to go down there and investigate these allegations. They interviewed the person who was supposed to be concerned and he said, 'that is pure baloney'. As it transpired, a certain gentleman who attended the meeting at Moodiarrup and made some very unkind thrusts at me was the same gentleman who allegedly put these stories around.

It was established that the only animals owned by that circus - if one could call it a circus - were a few horses and a couple of camels. I am quite sure that none of these animals or their descendants are causing the problems being experienced in this area.

Mr Blaikie, Liberal member for Vasse, said,

Perhaps if we cross a horse with a camel we finish up with a cougar.

Mr Old continued,

The A.P.B. has thoroughly investigated the possibility that an animal may have escaped from a circus. It has been established that between 1958 and 1974, only one cougar came into Western Australia, and that was with the Moscow Circus; they valued it too highly to let it go.

Mr Burke, Labor member for Balcatta interjected,

A communist cougar!

Mr Old said,

It was a red cougar; probably it was under the ALP bed every night while it was here.

Mr Jamieson added,

Under Commonwealth regulations, all exotic animals entering Australia with circuses are checked into and out of the State, and I assure members that that particular cougar left the State.

Allegations have also been made that during the war, members of the United States Navy had cougars as pets on board their vessels. I must say if I were going to have a pet on a warship or submarine, it would not be a cougar.

It would be a blonde,

Mr Des O'Neill, the Chief Secretary, said.

Mr Old continued,

Yes, and if I could not get one of those, it would be a pussycat; but certainly, it would not be a cougar.

Mr Jamieson added,

That might be less dangerous than a blonde!

Mr Old said,

At my age, that is probably quite true. We have checked out this allegation with the Department of the Navy.

Mr Old replied,

They have no knowledge of any cougars being on ships. I have been assured by the Acting American Consul that the American naval historian has no records to substantiate these allegations. I do not know where these stories have come from.

The investigation has been fairly thorough.

Mr O'Neil remarked.

Mr Old replied,

Yes, I have also seen the cast of the tracks in the possession of the Member for Warren. Quite frankly, I would not know if they were made by a cougar or a dog. However, the audio-visual material we received from America displayed the paws of cougars, and they did not resemble the cast shown to me by the Member for Warren.

The A.P.B. has also taken casts of the tracks of cougars at the South Perth Zoo, and has found no resemblance to the member for Warren's cast.

Mr B.T. Burke, Labour Member for Balcatta, asked,

Are there any cougars at the zoo?

Mr Old replied,

Yes.

Mr Burke asked,

Are they all present?

I can assure the honourable member they are checked each night and morning.

Mr Old said,

The Member for Warren quoted Mr Neuman as saying there were cats in the area; that probably is quite right. In fact, there are wild cats everywhere, so there are likely to be many cats in this region. However, that is not to say there are cougars in the area.

I do not take a hard line on this issue and say there are no strange animals causing problems in this region. I accept the veracity of the people who claim to have seen these animals; some of these people are known personally to me and I would not doubt they have seen something unusual.

It has become quite a thing down there for the local Press and the local experts to criticise the A.P.B. because it has not managed to locate one of these animals. However, nor have the local people managed to locate one, and they are there all the time. People have sat up all night and claim to have seen these animals. At one stage, a person claimed to have shot one. At that time, I made personal representation to the Stirling City Council to allow the tracker to go down there with his trained Alsation dogs; he has been to the area twice.

However, to say the A.P.B. officer had to leave because he had an appointment is not correct, unless my information is sadly wrong. I was told by the officer in charge of the operation—whose veracity I do not doubt—that the dogs simply lost the scent. Apparently they were quite excited for a while, but then they gave up the ghost; the dogs could not go on tracking if there was nothing to track.

I have an open mind and will continue to have an open mind on all events that have been taking place in this region. However, by his own admission the Member for Warren no longer has an open mind on this matter. I quote from the Western Herald—*such as it is—as follows:*

Descriptions by farmers of the damaged animals were consistent with fox, eagle and wild-dog tracks.

However, Mr Evans said earlier this year that he believed dogs or foxes were not responsible for the attacks.

He had previously kept an 'open mind' but has been persuaded otherwise and wanted to have the matter decided once and for all.

In other words, the Member for Warren by his own admission no longer has an open mind and therefore has put forward what I consider to be a biased case. Therefore I reject the motion.

In conclusion I do not believe officers of the A.P.B. can be in any way criticised for the efforts they have put into this operation. They stand ready to continue their efforts to find this predator,

Mr Old said.

The debate adjourned, on motion by Mr Brian Burke, Labour Member for Balcatta, shortly before 10.00pm.

At the beginning of January 1980, the Agriculture Protection Board's Annual Report for the year to June 1979 was released by the W.A. Government. The brief report outlined the various activities of the Board over the period under selected headings. And under the title *Cougars* the report said:

Considerable effort by the Board staff was devoted to reports of unidentified animals in the Cordering area which local farmers claimed were killing stock. Experienced doggers camped in the area for many weeks: a research technician and Board executive staff visited the area several times: hair and faeces samples were examined: overseas information was obtained on the type of damage done by cougars: trained tracker dogs were taken to the area: historical records were searched for evidence of circus escapes. No evidence could be obtained from any of this work that cougars or other unidentified animals were present. Stock losses in the area were attributable to other causes, such as predation by wild dogs, feral cats or feral pigs, or malnutrition or environmental stress.

🐾 🐾 🐾

A felid print framed by 12 gauge shotgun cartridges - what made those tracks?

Chapter Thirteen

EVER SINCE THE EARLY DAYS OF SETTLEMENT, rural Australia has been alive with folklore about legendary animals creeping unseen through the bush. The nation even developed its own version of the Himalayan Abominable Snowman, an ape-like, hairy creature called the Yowie. Sydney naturalist Rex Gilroy collected a wealth of information about the Yowie, claiming it was sighted in the Blue Mountains, the Jamieson Valley, near Orange and Canberra and as far north as Queensland. He claimed the animal stood 180 centimetres tall, covered with an orange tinged hair—a real throwback to an age when it formed a link between modern man and his prehistoric origins.

The nation's bush mysteries, though, have often been only as colourful and imaginative as the outrageous characters propounding them. There's been the Minto Monster, the Nullabor Numph, the Emmville Panther, the Tantanoola Tiger.

Obviously frauds have been perpetrated. The Nullabor Numph would probably be the most famous case—a publicity gimmick thought up by some live-wire as a means of promoting the outback town of Eucla. The story went that a scantily-clad girl was being seen dashing about on the Nullabor living in the wilds among the kangaroos. The controversy caused a major storm, even exciting keen interest overseas until it was learned that a photograph of her allegedly among a herd of 'roos was a fake. And of course there was the university student gimmick with the Nannup Tiger in W.A.

In virtually every state of the Commonwealth over the past two hundred years there have emerged strange stories of a wiry dog like creature with a bulbous head, kangaroo-type tail and heavy stripes across its back. Automatically, speculation has arisen that the Tasmanian tiger, the near-legendary Thylacine, was still alive. Rumours about this species, believed to have become extinct on the Australian mainland 40,000 years ago, have excited scientific postulation over the years. The last animal died in a Tasmanian zoo in 1933, ironically just after it had dawned on the authorities that it was in danger of extinction. To this day there are people in Tasmania who are sure the animal still lives in the bush. There are even those who believe it is running loose in W.A.

While most of these stories about mystery animals come to nothing, even the most sceptical scientist concedes there are vacuums in our knowledge about the fauna of the bush. Harry Butler, who privately derided the suggestion that there was a large feline in the Western Australian bush, still conceded that more and more new sub-species of animals come to light every year. In many ways we are still only scratching the surface of our knowledge about the bush's inhabitants. For example, in 1976 the W.A. Fisheries and Wildlife Department proudly announced that one of Australia's rarest mammals, the Ningaui, a soft, red-tinged, mouse-like animal had been found in the Gibson Desert. A distant cousin of the Tasmanian tiger, the discovery of the Ningaui was a major scientific breakthrough. Likewise in 1979 another rare animal, the marsupial mole, was found for the first time in W.A.'s Great Sandy Desert. Scientists have long agreed that little is known of the mammals, birds and reptiles inhabiting some of the remote areas of the Australian Continent.

The Western Australian Government said publicly that there was no reason to believe that escaped or released big cats could have made their way onto the mainland from passing naval vessels. But what about the case of the Tantanoola Tiger—not a ghost-like phantom but a snarling, flesh and blood killer introduced onto the continent, a part of which it then terrorised? The Tantanoola region of South Australia was alive with claims that a savage new beast was ravaging flocks of sheep in the late 1890's. It was said at the time that there was 'a great deal of gossip but no real evidence' that such an animal existed. Or at least, that was until one Tom Donovan stumbled upon it one afternoon in 1895, took aim with his trusty Winchester Rifle and shot it dead. The Tantanoola Tiger measured 155 centimetres from its snout to tail tip, was 82 centimetres high and 58 centimetres around the collar.

Today the stuffed remains of the Tiger take pride of place in the foyer of the Tantanoola hotel. Hundreds of tourists a year stop off to marvel at how an Assyrian wolf apparently escaped off a ship wreck on the coastline of the Great Australian Bight some years before its death. It had managed to assimilate to a successful predatory existence in the Australian bush. If nothing else the Tantanoola Tiger created the type of precedent the W.A. Government rejected.

What then are we to make of the mystery of the Cordering Cougar?

There can be no doubt that the farmers of Cordering were responsible, to a limited extent, for the failure of the Western Australian Government to provide them with more assistance. In some respects they were over-sensitive when aspects of their 'evidence' was criticised. While it is true some government officers sought from the start to gag debate on, or stifle investigations into, the farmers' claims, the Cordering people themselves were simply not versed in the intricacies of preparing a scientifically irrefutable case to substantiate their insistence that something was very wrong. Their point was that they knew and understood their environment and had been warning a disinterested government about it for a considerable period. They saw it as the authorities' job to do something about it.

On the other hand the upper echelons of the A.P.B. advised the state government through Dick Old that there was simply not enough scientific evidence. For every claim put forward by the farmers, the more sceptical senior A.P.B. men could find a counter argument. The A.P.B. claimed it was not being provided with enough samples. But the Cordering peoples' antagonism was so sharpened by the ridicule that they had very little patience with what they saw as the blind incompetence and inability to read the signs displayed by some A.P.B. men in the field. When the farmers broke off all communication with Des Gooding and his men in 1979, they were making a big mistake. Nothing could be achieved by shutting down channels of communication.

Several incidents reflect interestingly on the way the farmers' lack of sophistication hamstrung the changes of a resolution in the controversy.

At the second Moodiarrup Hall meeting Des Gooding had attested that a footprint found by a Collie resident had been made by a dog, much to the boisterous annoyance of the gathering. Neil Dowey, a young man living in the coal town, had been confronted by a large, greyish animal on a bush track outside Collie one dark night. While he had been unable to make out its form before it disappeared in the bush, it had still come close enough for Dowey to realise it was a very large animal. He had no light with him and his normally aggressive Doberman bitch had been strangely reserved for some moments on the darkened track. On returning to his automobile, Dowey found big black blotches all over his car—including one on the roof. They appeared to be the muddied footprints of an animal.

And in the morning he dropped two twelve gauge shotgun cartridges in the mud for size reference along one quite distinct, large footprint which he photographed. The footprint dwarfed the rifle shells and Dowey was staggered by its size.

Elsewhere on the track he could see the quite clear footmarks of his own bitch. One of her prints had in fact marked the ground within inches of the strange print he photographed. He placed one shotgun shell vertically and another horizontally around the unexplained mark which was substantially larger than the dog's print.

Dowey then sent the slide transparency to the Western Australian Museum for analysis. He merely inquired whether the Museum could determine what had made the mark. But he failed to give any detailed explanation about the background to the discovery of it, or his own observations about it.

Darrell Kitchener, the Curator of the Mammals Survey Division at the Museum returned the slide to Dowey with the following brief note:

Thank you for your photograph of unusual footprints. These prints are most like cats [my emphasis], *however, the position of the prints and their impression on the ground leads us to doubt their validity. Could you send us more information and/or photographs?'*

Dowey had, of course, failed to point out that it was his belief that the smaller scuff mark in the upper part of the photograph had been made on the muddy track by his own dog. He was only interested in finding out what made the substantially bigger and clearer print bounded by the shot gun shells.

Kitchener observed 'these prints are most like cats, however the position . . . and their impression on the ground leads us to doubt their validity.' Did the words 'position of the prints' indicate the Museum assumed both marks had been made by the stride of the one animal? After receipt of the letter, Dowey believed the Museum had assumed his claim was that one animal had made both marks.

And what did Kitchener mean by 'leads us to doubt their validity . . . ? Dowey became angry to think the Museum could have been suggesting the footprint was a fake. Once again, as in the case of the tree markings, the authorities seemed to be casting doubt on the credibility of what the Cordering lobby claimed were key pieces of evidence.

In yet another attempt to establish some type of independent scientific analysis of their 'evidence', some of the farmers began sending samples of faeces and fur to a leading Perth pathologist early in 1979. Again, hopelessly inadequate explanatory information accompanied the samples. Pieces of faeces and fur were distributed to various academics at the University of Western Australia by the pathologist. Only one major test was done, in the end, on one 'ball' of fur about 2.5 cm in length.

Only one test was done, basically because the university people were not told exactly what they were testing for. The fur ball examination was instructive in this. There was nothing uncommon about fur balls excreted from the digestive systems of various bush and farm animals. Lab tests were run on this particular fur bar and after considerable analysis and reference to hair slides, the technicians announced the ball contained sheep's wool. It was this kind of finding which undermined some of the farmers' claims. The point was that the farmers themselves knew all along that the ball was sheep's wool. What they had failed to inform the technician was that it had been found as a section in a 17.5 cm long scat, which they believed exuded other significant feline characteristics.

Informed of this much later, the Perth pathologist, himself a keen amateur farmer, expressed concern. 'Why didn't they tell us that when they sent it up?' he groaned.

Late one evening in November 1978, a Kojonup farmer, Steve Bellotti, left his farmhouse to investigate his sheep dog's persistent, near hysterical barking at a back shed. Once outside, Bellotti could detect another noise echoing from the darkened scrub over the dog's crazed howling. It sounded like the noise of cats fighting—but it was much louder. It was eerie—Bellotti and his wife Maxine had heard nothing like it in years in the bush and suddenly it ended with a choking, cough-like noise. Bellotti realised cows in a nearby paddock were panicked and nervously milling around in a group.

In his truck the farmer drove to his back sheds and into a paddock beyond. He unlatched a gate and as the truck rumbled into the field, its lights detected two large bright embers, obviously the reflection from a pair of eyes. There sitting in the paddock Bellotti saw a cat-like animal roughly the size of a farm dog. It was sitting upright, unperturbed, seeming to observe both the farmhouse and Bellotti's activities.

'That's the strangest bloody thing I have ever seen,' he whispered to himself, amazed.

Bellotti drove back to the farmhouse and telephoned two of his friends who lived nearby. Within minutes he and the two friends, accompanied by their wives, were in the back paddock searching.

Incredibly, they all then saw the animal, not thirty metres away—again seated, but this time on a small ridge of rocks. One of Bellotti's mates took aim with a shotgun and fired. The shot hit the animal directly and its impact tossed it backwards and away from the rocks, rolling end over end, its long tail pirouetting in the air. Then it charged away into the dark at fantastic speed and was lost to sight.

The farmers were frantic. They searched the entire farm area but the animal was gone. In bewildered and animated conversation they agreed it had definitely been a cat-like animal, the size of a dog, with short legs, a thick body and very short neck. Its head was definitely feline with small rounded ears. Bellotti observed that so bright were its eyes shining in the headlights that it was difficult to make out exactly what its facial features resembled.

'And the sound it makes is blood curdling,' he added.

The farmers were in no doubt that the gun blast had hit the animal. But it was obvious that the shot was not heavy enough to have killed or stopped it. The pellets would have stung and wounded the animal but were simply not powerful enough to impede its escape.

The following day Bellotti, a jovial and paunchy farmer of Italian extraction, informed the local A.P.B. officer Graham Blacklock about the incident. Blacklock, a gangly softly spoken South African, had worked for the A.P.B. at Kojonup for two years. He listened incredulously as Bellotti explained in detail what had happened. Despite his initial scepticism, over the following days Blacklock sought out and questioned the other individuals who had made the sighting with Bellotti.

'In the first place I thought it was rubbish but now I've got to believe something happened because of the similarity in the different accounts,' he later told Bellotti. Thus Graham Blacklock's fascination with the phenomenon was sparked. It so intrigued him that in the following months he investigated in detail every conceivable reported sighting of strange animals in the bush around Konjonup. While quite often he could explain accounts brought to him as genuine cases of mistaken identity, he became fascinated by a number of inexplicable incidents involving alleged large felines.

Some time after the first incident, Blacklock was with Steve Bellotti visiting the farm of Bellotti's brother. Emerging from the farmhouse that evening the three men heard a loud noise far off in the bush.

'That's it', Steve Bellotti said, as the noise suddenly tapered off. Blacklock only heard one short cry but he believed it sounded like the noise made by a screech owl. Despite that, he agreed with the Bellottis to go out around the farm that night to do some spotlighting.

Later in a distant paddock Blacklock suddenly detected the distinct and bright eyes of an animal low down in the scrub. When the light pitchforked directly onto the eyes they disappeared, inexplicably, without a trace. Blacklock was initially amazed that such bright eyes could disappear so quickly, so totally. While the men drove around the scrub where the eyes had first appeared to meet up with another spotlighting vehicle, their light suddenly detected the eyes again. This time the animal was in a crop paddock and the truck gave chase. But within seconds the animal had apparently dashed to a group of rocks and disappeared through it and into denser bush.

The incident mesmerised Blacklock - so much so that he intensified his inquiries and began to come to a few conclusions about what was happening in the bush. He believed it was distinctly possible that a large foreign predator was loose and responsible for stock killings in the Kojonup area.

'While I couldn't make out the animal's body when I saw the eyes, I would think from its behaviour that it could be around the size of a large dog,' Blacklock said. He was struck by both the size and the prominence of the eyes, and the fact that they just seemed to evaporate the first time and then again the second time after the animal had plainly covered a huge amount of ground in a short space of time. Blacklock observed that this fleeting anonymity just did not tally with the behaviour of indigenous bush animals.

The A.P.B. man examined some of the dead stock around Kojonup. He saw, for example, a year-old wether with its back leg bones snapped in half in the attack which killed it. 'Whatever did this had very powerful jaws,' he said. 'It's clear that this animal is not a fox because a fox couldn't kill like this. I've never seen any sign of feral pigs in the district, and it's unlikely that it would be wild dogs,' he said.

Blacklock's gradual introduction to the mystery was of crucial importance for a number of reasons. Prior to his migration to Australia in the 1970s, he had had considerable experience with the wildlife in his native Africa. His family was involved in the hunting and conservation of jungle animals including the big cats. In fact, while he chose to live and work in W.A., he had been regularly offered other employment positions with circus organisations and wildlife bodies like Sydney's Taronga Park Zoo because of his detailed knowledge and experience of the big cats.

Graham Blacklock came to believe that a large unexplained predator was on the rampage in W.A., and that it displayed a number of curious, apparently feline traits. But more importantly than that, he followed up his work by filing reports to his immediate superior, the Regional A.P.B. Officer based Katanning on all the incidents in which he was involved. He filed reports on stock losses and his own sighting, and included some detailed observations about possible explanations. In one report in the A.P.B.'s hands he even hypothesised about the possibility that Australia could have its own native large cat animal which was now emerging from the forests into cultivated land because of the pressure of clearage and its own population explosion.

When the Cordering farmers heard of Blacklock's work, Dennis Earnshaw visited him one evening at his Kojonup home. Earnshaw believed he could have at last found a man with the experience and expertise the authorities needed at the forefront of their inquiries.

Earnshaw then wrote to the A.P.B. asking why it was that a man of Blacklock's knowledge had not been given broader responsibility in the inquiries. The farmer suggested that Blacklock be given greater responsibility and be temporarily released from his daily duties to visit other areas of the south west to examine problems being experienced there.

In April 1980, Earnshaw wrote the following letter to Des Gooding:

> *In my capacity as Chairman of the Cordering Cougar Committee I would like to enquire as to whether you are aware that the Agriculture Protection Board employs Mr Graham Blacklock as a District Officer in the Kojonup area?*
>
> *Are you also aware that Mr Blacklock has had extensive experience of the hunting and conservation of animals in the wilds of his country, South Africa? He is particularly expert in the habits and features of the big cat family.*
>
> *In keeping with the public assurances issued to this Committee by the W.A. Minister for Agriculture, Mr Dick Old, that your department stands ready and willing to afford us every assistance in the continuing investigations of our heavy stock losses, we would make a number of requests in relation to Mr Blacklock.*
>
> *If as appears likely, you are unacquainted with his background, this Committee formally requests you bring him to the centre of A.P.B. investigations of the cat predator*

problem. We suggest that provision be made to allow him to be temporarily relieved of his daily duties so that he could travel throughout the south west in an attempt to meaningfully co-ordinate for the first time A.P.B.'s enquiries.

It is clear to us that your investigations suffer from the lack of co-ordinated approach as well as lack of expertise in the habits of big cat animals.

Mr Blacklock's involvement would be doubly important because he has been investigating in detail and reporting to his Regional Officer in Katanning all incidents in his area. Mr Blacklock claims he saw the eyes of an animal one night which he could not recognise. He now believes an unidentified animal is running wild in the bush.

Surely his already extensive experience, as well as involvement in the W.A. phenomenon, equip him well to be given a more significant role in enquiries which currently suffer from the scepticism and incompetence displayed by many of your men in the field.

Furthermore, given that Mr Blacklock has filed reports to his Regional Officer, we formally request the A.P.B. make available to this Committee copies of them and any subsequent reports he files,

the letter concluded.

There can be no doubt that the A.P.B. bosses in Perth cast doubt over the veracity of the cat claim despite significant concern among some of the Board's District Officers - the men paid to know what was happening in their regions - that something was amiss.

But there were others. District Officers knew a problem existed for quite a few years before it became the subject of parliamentary debate. For example, the District Officer for the West Arthur Shire, Gordon Burton, filed a report in October 1977 to his Regional chief.

It read:

. . . I investigated reports of a sheep-killing animal in the Cordering and McAlinden areas of this Shire. Analysis of the

findings is difficult as confirmation of what is responsible is impossible to obtain.

It is apparent that more than one animal is responsible and I think it possible that more than one species in involved as tracks around killed sheep indicate the presence of both canines and felines.

Senior Officer R. Strang and Regional Officer P. Ripper visited the area this month and saw colour slides and casts of footprints purporting to be that of the animal involved in the stock losses.

It is estimated that a total of three hundred head of stock, mainly lambs, have been killed since lambing started in May of this year,

Burton's report concluded.

To this day Burton is puzzled about the Cordering Cougar. Too many things have happened in his District that can't be explained. Why is it that after 'considerable effort' by the A.P.B., its 1979 annual report said no evidence could be found of unidentified animals being present, when as far back as October 1977 Gordon Burton was filing reports referring to the presence of unexplained feline tracks around the sites of stock kills. The A.P.B. claimed publicly in that curious wording that 'if there is an animal such as a Cougar operating in these areas, it is not having any economic effect upon the livestock'. Yet as far back as October 1977, Burton reported to his department that in the early months of that lambing season up to three hundred stock animals, mainly lambs, were lost on farms in his district.

One of the key aspects of the mystery was the question of the extent of its geographical spread. In early 1980 farmers in Wagin began expressing concern about their own stock losses. Locals were invited to specially convened public meetings and the Cordering farmers travelled the fifty kilometres to attend as guest speakers. Led by Dennis Earnshaw, they questioned the Wagin people about the apparent growing activity in their area and outlined their own experiences and observations about the Cordering situation.

It was clear from early on that the cat phenomenon was not something limited to as small a geographical area as Cordering. The label 'the Cordering Cougar' was a short cut by which the media introduced the debate to public attention. It was a convenient means of identifying a phenomenon that extended however, over a far greater range - even as far north as the state's Red Centre. After all, Barry Morris's key photograph was taken just outside Carnarvon, 1000 kilometres north of Perth.

In early 1980, Greg Power, the A.P.B. District Officer in Wagin became very concerned about the apparent sudden appearance of an unidentified animal in his region. He, too, filed reports on stock losses and alleged sightings to his superiors. He believed one of his reports had been given verbatim to Dick Old. His reports were based initially on interviews with ten Wagin residents, most of whom claimed to have seen an animal with 'a distinctive tail'.

Either the predator made its presence felt first or was identified first in the Cordering district. Sporadic sightings occurred virtually everywhere in the south west of Western Australia. But it was the Cordering people who believed they recognised patterns of behaviour and the re-occurring presence of individual animals first. It was the Cordering people who organised first, who saw the need to lobby the Government and set out to co-ordinate their own enquiries first. As other communities such as nearby Wagin and Kojonup became aware of the animals presence, it was the Cordering farmers they turned to for help and advice.

Soon after Earnshaw and Charlie Sumner addressed the first Wagin meeting - a gathering of thirty concerned local farmers, some of whom spoke for the first time publicly about their own recent sightings - Dennis Earnshaw met Greg Power. The A.P.B. man agreed it appeared a marauding animal was killing stock. He ruled out foxes. In two years he had seen no sign of feral pigs in the Wagin area. He didn't believe dingoes were responsible and he doubted the presence of wild dogs.

Many of the district officers grew concerned at what they saw as intrusion from above in their inquiries. Instructions came down from Perth that all inquiries on the matter would be handled by Perth. The district men had regular meetings where they often discussed the incidence of sightings and stock deaths. Some became bitter that they were getting little feedback from their superiors in Perth on how, and in what form, they should proceed with their investigations. They were obviously hamstrung because publicly their bosses were saying the farmers' claims were false, when they themselves believed something was going on. Officers like Greg Power and Gordon Burton were placed in the difficult position of maintaining effective working links with the farmers when the farmers only had them to blame for the public pronouncements made in Perth. On one hand, district officers agreed something was wrong. On the other they had to suffer in silence the antagonism of the farmers they were paid to service and represent, because of the public A.P.B. rejection of the cat theory.

In early 1980, Des Gooding visited the United States on a fact-finding mission on behalf of the State Government. One of the reasons for the trip was to gather information about the habits of the coyote because so little was known about Australia's own wild dog, the dingo, which shared many characteristics with the American animal. The coyote research, it was hoped, would be invaluable in dealing with the dingo, but Gooding took time while in the United States to research the cougar first hand. He talked to American wildlife bosses about the features pointed to by the farmers in Australia.

As far as he was concerned, everything Gooding learned about the cougar, and all he saw, confirmed the information given to him by officers such as Alan McKenzie.

When he first took charge of the Cordering investigation, Des Gooding was genuinely fascinated by it and thrilled at the potential it offered him, professionally, if a wild animal was found to exist. Yet, based on his own observations from visits to Cordering and based on the reports he had read, as well as the opinions of sceptical A.P.B. district officers, by early 1980 Gooding was convinced there was no evidence proving the existence of a large, feline predator.

He disregarded the farmers' claims as unscientific, totally unsubstantiated and at times, near-hysterical. The opinions of people like Bob Neuman, Rick Richardson and Peter Brighton were disregarded. Presumably, so were the reports of concerned district A.P.B. officers like Graham Blacklock, Gordon Burton and Greg Power.

The Government's position totally relied on the premise that if an individual had never seen such an animal it could not exist. The farmers were told that though they might protest, a scientifically unanswerable case could not be made until a body of the alleged animal was presented to the Government.

The ostensible vital claim made by the farmers that the predator appeared to be damaging the bush fauna was totally disregarded by the authorities. But they claimed the population of joey-kangaroos had declined markedly in some areas of the south west. They also insisted that possum numbers appeared, also, to be in decline. In early 1980 the W.A. Government, itself, announced that a six month survey in the south west had revealed a 'sharp' decline in the population of numbats, commonly known as banded ant-eaters - the animal emblem of the state. Only a handful of previously widespread animals were found to be living throughout the south west in the survey. All the biologists who conducted the survey could suggest was that destruction of the native habitat by land clearing and a succession of drought years could have reduced their numbers. Yet the annual report of the W.A. Wildlife Authority in 1978 also made interesting observations about the number of rock wallabies in at least one area of the state. A survey was taken of high rock areas in the wheat-belt district of Kellerberrin, west of Perth.

> *Each outcrop has been surveyed and mapped for wallaby population,*

the report said.

> *To date wallabies have been recorded at 10 sites, but many of the sights carry, at most, only 2 to 3 animals. Moreover, there are numerous sites that seem to be suitable habitats for wallabies, but no sightings have been made, nor have fresh scats been found. Only one juvenile rock wallaby has been observed. Information on Departmental files indicates that rock wallabies were more numerous in the past and a similar picture emerges when local residents are interviewed. In certain areas where rock wallabies were once frequently observed, repeated surveys have failed to sight an animal. At this state, it is too early to explain the causes of the population decline,*

The report said.

It went on to suggest that further research be conducted to determine whether foxes or other known predators were responsible. When Des Gooding was alerted to this reference and asked whether it could be related to the feline theory, he was insistent that no such conclusions could be drawn. And while it was obviously difficult to make valid assumptions, the Cordering farmers leapt into the attack by hypothesising about the possibility that the feline predator could be playing a major role in changing the population density of species of animals, whose dwindling numbers were gradually being observed by various government authorities.

In January 1979 Dennis Earnshaw received a letter in the mail from a former Western Australian woman, Lyn Hancock, who was living in Canada but on a holiday visit to Perth to see her family and friend. She introduced herself in a letter as having long been interested in the press publicity given to the Cordering mystery over recent years. With her fiancé she lived in Summerfield, a farming community in British Columbia, the backwoods of which were known to be inhabited by cougars. In fact, she was compiling a thesis at the Simon Fraser University where she was studying in Burnaby, near Vancouver, on the cougar animal itself. Miss Hancock asked Earnshaw if he would meet her when she visited the Cordering region during her holiday. He happily acceded.

Lyn Hancock then became a crucial cornerstone in efforts to unravel the perplexing enigma of the Cordering cougar. In late January 1980, she drove from Perth into the south west. A friendly, affable girl, she had hand reared the two female cougars in British Columbia later donated to the Perth Zoo. In discussions with Earnshaw she confirmed that there was a major vacuum in the documentation of knowledge of the mountain lion in the America wilds. She told him that the cougar was one of the most misunderstood and inscrutable animals on earth.

Her thesis would, for the first time, attempt to compile a sophisticated and complete data bank on the cougar's biology and habits. So little research work had been done on the animal prior to the 1970's that very little scientific data had been accumulated, and the work that was done mainly seemed to involve head count surveys in various parts of Canada and the United States. Miss Hancock told Earnshaw that she was also attempting to document within the thesis a breakdown of all previously known information on the animal, and the mass of misconceptions that and grown up over the years. At the time she visited the Cordering district, Lyn Hancock was, without doubt, at the forefront of international scientific research on the cougar.

She spent two days in the district travelling around farms and talking to many of the local residents. The farmers produced the evidence they claimed indicated a large, cat-like creature was at work, and significantly , she was also shown the controversial claw-marked trees that some government officials had claimed were man-made to prop up the theory. Miss Hancock said the tree scratchings could indicate the presence of a big cat animal. She said they could indicate a female animal was marking the trees as a territorial gesture. The female would often leave kittens in the vicinity of various trees when she went off on hunting expeditions.

At the end of her stay Miss Hancock returned to Canada with hair samples, the skulls of kangaroos bearing splintered crackmarks on the forehead, and pictures of dead stock and wildlife. She also took detailed outlines of killings and firsthand encounters from people like Jim Putland.

On her return to Canada the scientific and wildlife fraternity there expressed great interest in the Western Australian situation. One individual enthralled by Miss Hancock's findings was Dan Lay, British Columbia's most experienced and most respected trapper-hunter. Lay had worked for years with Canadian wildlife authorities and was acknowledged as something of an expert on the cougar. After seeing the pictorial evidence and Lyn Hancock's recounting of the farmers' accounts of sightings, and details of stock losses and the style of the kill, Lay claimed the total weight of evidence bore the trade marks of the animal he knew as a cougar. He did express some reservations about some of the less clear track marks, but he enthusiastically asked Lyn Hancock about his chances of visiting Australia. He explained that based on what he had seen and heard from her, he would be very anxious to visit Western Australia to organise hunting expeditions.

One aspect of the mystery Lyn discussed with wildlife authorities in Canada was the question of eyes sighted at night. She was told that, as a rule, there was very little difference between the eyes of animals shining in bright light at night in the Canadian wilds, with one exception - the cougar. Because of the size of the animal's eyeballs they shone bigger with more brightness and sharpness.

Even before she took the evidence back to Canada, Lyn Hancock told the farmers she believed there was some kind of large feline animal in the Western Australian bush. All the work she later did on it in British Columbia merely confirmed what many people on farms in the south west claimed they knew as fact. And after she processed much of the data and talked to experts in Canada, she was adamant.

'There can be no doubt,' she said. 'If all the evidence I saw in Western Australia - the style of killings, the markings and the tracks were found in Canada, I would have no hesitation in saying that one animal was responsible for it - a cougar.'

There were a number of complications in the mystery for Hancock. She was puzzled by some of the footprints - their size and conformation were, at times, out of character with the cougar. But the crucial evidence for her was the style of killing.

'Apart from the obvious credibility of the people in the south west there are two positive factors in all this,' she said. 'One is the description of the animal coming in - if it was happening in Canada or the United States there would be no other animal it could be, but a cougar. And then, there are the kills - I showed the pictures to animal control officers and they said it looked like a cougar kill. Again, if it was in the United States they would say one animal was responsible.'

Hancock claimed it was not unusual for many aspects of behavioural patterns to be blurred with the cougar. For example, the animal would react differently in different parts of the United States. She claimed it as only as recently as 1976 that researchers realised that different types of cougars did not necessarily behave in the same way in key features in different habitats of the Americas.

And crucially, against the background of the sightings of the dark animal in W.A., Hancock revealed that speculation was growing about the existence of a jet-black cougar variety in remote areas of the United States. Such speculation had long been scotched, but Hancock said modern research into the animal was piecing together evidence which indicated such an animal was alive.

Lyn Hancock was not surprised that the Agriculture Protection Board had expressed doubts about its ability to differentiate between different samples of hair. She said that hair analysis and identification was a complex, newly-developed area of research.

When she returned to Canada she sent to the F.B.I. in Washington, D.C., a hair sample for analysis. It had been taken from a tree in Western Australia on which the Cordering farms claimed the feline had climbed.

The F.B.I. analysis could conceivably have been the breakthrough the farmers needed to add weight to their case. Hancock herself procured and sent a sample of the United States' cougar hair to the F.B.I. laboratory in the J. Edgar Hoover Building, to help in testing the W.A. sample.

But, unfortunately, the hair sample was found to be eighteen months old, and too badly damaged by weathering to be identifiable.

Two aspects of the feline predator puzzle were used by the A.P.B. to undermine the farmers' claims. One was the question of footprints. There is no doubt that footprints of foxes and dogs were put forward by the farmers to substantiate their case, in some instances. This was a crucial overlap, where in their enthusiasm and frustration, some farmers were mistakenly ascribing to natural phenomena the characteristics of the animal they believed was there.

There were certainly a number of inexplicable footprints found. But there were few of them. Darrel Kichener said Dowey's footprint was 'most like cats' but he went on to doubt its 'validity'. A.P.B. officers like Gordon Burton observed that there were feline footprints around the kill sites. There were, it must be said, a few of them though.

The farmers were understandably confused by the footprints. Why should they not be? Kitchener claimed the Dowey print was 'most like cats' but Des Gooding was adamant at the Moodiarrup Hall meeting that it was made by a dog. If the 'experts' were confused why was it not conceivable that the people most directly wrestling with the problem were not confused as well?

And, of course, research into the habits of the big cats indicated there was nothing unusual about the absence of clear signs. It was often said that the only time the cougar hunters in the Americas could find clear signs was when they were tracking through snow. The animal's sign, otherwise, was 'invisible'.

The second key area of contention was the apparent appetite of the W.A. predator for the intestines of its prey. By all accounts, while it relishes the internal organs, the cougar will not eat the intestines. The A.P.B. leapt upon this as a clear inconsistency.

However, it is clear that the cougar will remove and bury the intestines. And in any event, the farmers of the south west of W.A. were never saying categorically, at any stage, that they were prey to a cougar. They claimed the animal they witnessed in their paddocks resembled what they believe a cougar to look like. They were, likewise, not willing to say categorically that the animal was an introduced cougar or an indigenous cat with its own personal habits and characteristic. What they were saying, and continue to say, is that an animal is causing a problem of such import and dimension that its identification should be a major priority for the W.A. Government.

A labyrinthine web of questions remain to be answered about what is happening in the Western Australian countryside. There has been too much bitterness, too much rancour, too much narrow-minded ridicule, and not enough action.

The debate has centered on several crucial arguing points. Central to them has been the simple question: given that large felines are at work, how did they get there and when?

From the jarrah forests of Cordering to the leather upholstery of Perth's Parliament, discussion has touched on allegations of a circus accident in the early 1960s and the clear growth in the marauders activities in the years since then. But the question of timing, like everything else in the mystery is not simple or straightforward. For a time the farmers heatedly argued about the possibility of a circus accident in the early '60's. The Government said it was not possible for any animal to have escaped in this period.

If a valid hearing is to be given to the reasoned judgement of men like Jim Putland and Bob Crawford, then what is to be made of the experiences of Cliff Munyard? Now a senior engineer with the West Australian Small Business Advisory Service, he was travelling at dusk towards Albany, several kilometres beyond Broomehill in the south west. He noticed at the extreme range of his headlights an animal which he first took to be a large dog standing on the side of the road.

'Not knowing whether the 'dog', as it then thought, would attempt to cross the road in front of me, I slowed down to some 15 mph, and then stopped as the animal moved. I discovered to my amazement that the 'dog' was beyond doubt of the cat family. It appeared to be identical with a mountain lion in form, and was of a sandy brown colour.

'When the animal moved I thought it was going to take off into the bushes near the roadside. However, this was not the case and it loped along for some fifty feet or more while fully illuminated by the kerbside headlight.

'It then turned away from the road and disappeared from view. Before it disappeared, however, the animal turned its head towards the car, and with its ears laid back and squarish mouth opened, apparently snarled at the car.

'I was used to the bush before this episode and had come into contact with dingoes and a variety of breeds of dogs, including cross-bred (some of which had become wild), together with foxes and some fairly large bush bred cats. I can state with certainty that the animal I saw was none of these.

'It is worth mentioning at this point that I was impressed enough by the beast to be glad that I was inside the car.

'When in Mt Barker the next day, I mentioned that I had sighted the animal and was told by several people that various reports had been made of sightings of a similar animal in adjacent farming areas. Later again in Tambellup I was told of sighting in local areas.

'May I say finally that I was only a matter of two or three yards from the animal before it began to lope along in front of the car, and its head was approximately level with the top of the car mud guard.

'In late winter of that year, while negotiating some sticky patches of road on a wild and stormy night, along the back road from the Lake Grace area to Kulin, I had to add petrol to the car tank from a drum that I carried in the boot. I chose the nearest firm part of the road quite near to a large clump of bushes which afforded some shelter, and proceeded to syphon petrol from the drum to the car tank.

'While juggling with the drum and syphon hose, and holding a torch also, I was startled by a half-seen movement in the nearby bushes. Some animal gave not a bark, yelp or snarl, but rather a throaty scream, and this was followed by more movement in the clump of bushes - this was quite distinct from the movement of the outer bushes by the wind.

'Not unnaturally, I think, under the circumstances, I decided to cease the refilling, returned the drum to the boot and entered the car. I manoeuvred the car until I could shine my headlights into the bushes, whereupon a fairly large animal broke out of the bush and made off - I did not get a good look at the animal on that occasion, but I did note that it moved much more like a cat than a dog,' Munyard said.

As surely as veracity is ascribed to many of the other alleged sightings, so must it, in fairness and in logic, be given to the engineer's account of what he bluntly swears he saw.

The problem is, Cliff Munyard's sighting occurred in 1949.

And what of the case of Trevor Rowe? Now a successful Perth business man with an importing company, Rowe spent a holiday as a fourteen-year-old schoolboy on his uncle's farm south-east of Latham, 270 kilometres from Perth. His uncle. Mr R.E. Rowe was a devout member of the Church of Christ, and a respected property owner in the Latham region.

At 6.30 a.m. one morning during his fortnight's holiday at the house, he went to check on a group of rabbit traps he had laid in the bush the previous day. The young lad brought up in the back streets of Fremantle was bewitched by the wonders of the bush. He had been shown how to use the traps by his cousins, and was thrilled at the prospect of catching some rabbits. Short of the brushline at a property fence he saw a huge cat-like animal.

'I stopped dead when I saw this almighty big cat - I was really petrified. I'd seen cougars in the movies and all I can say is that's what this was. I was so terrified I will never forget it as long as I live.

'The cat was maybe 60 metres away, and was light brown with a long tail which sort of curled up behind it. The tail had a round 'C' shape at the end, at one stage.

'I got off my pushbike and watched it lope along for about half a minute. It went along for about 40 metres and then went into the bush where I had laid the traps. It terrified me so much I got straight back on the bike and to this day I have never been in there looking for traps.

'Back at the house I told everybody including my uncle, and although he is a very religious man, he intimated that I was a liar. I remember that I didn't argue back with him because he was an adult, but I was very annoyed within myself that nobody would believe me. They sort of said that I was a city kid with a vivid imagination.'

Trevor Rowe clearly remembers the date of the confrontation because as a High School student he had recently been given a new pair of shoes of which he was proud, and the holidays were the first he had spent on the farm.

It was January, 1950!

🐾 🐾 🐾

If you liked
Savage Shadow,
then you'll love
Australian Big Cats: An Unnatural History of Panthers.

www.australianbigcats.com.au

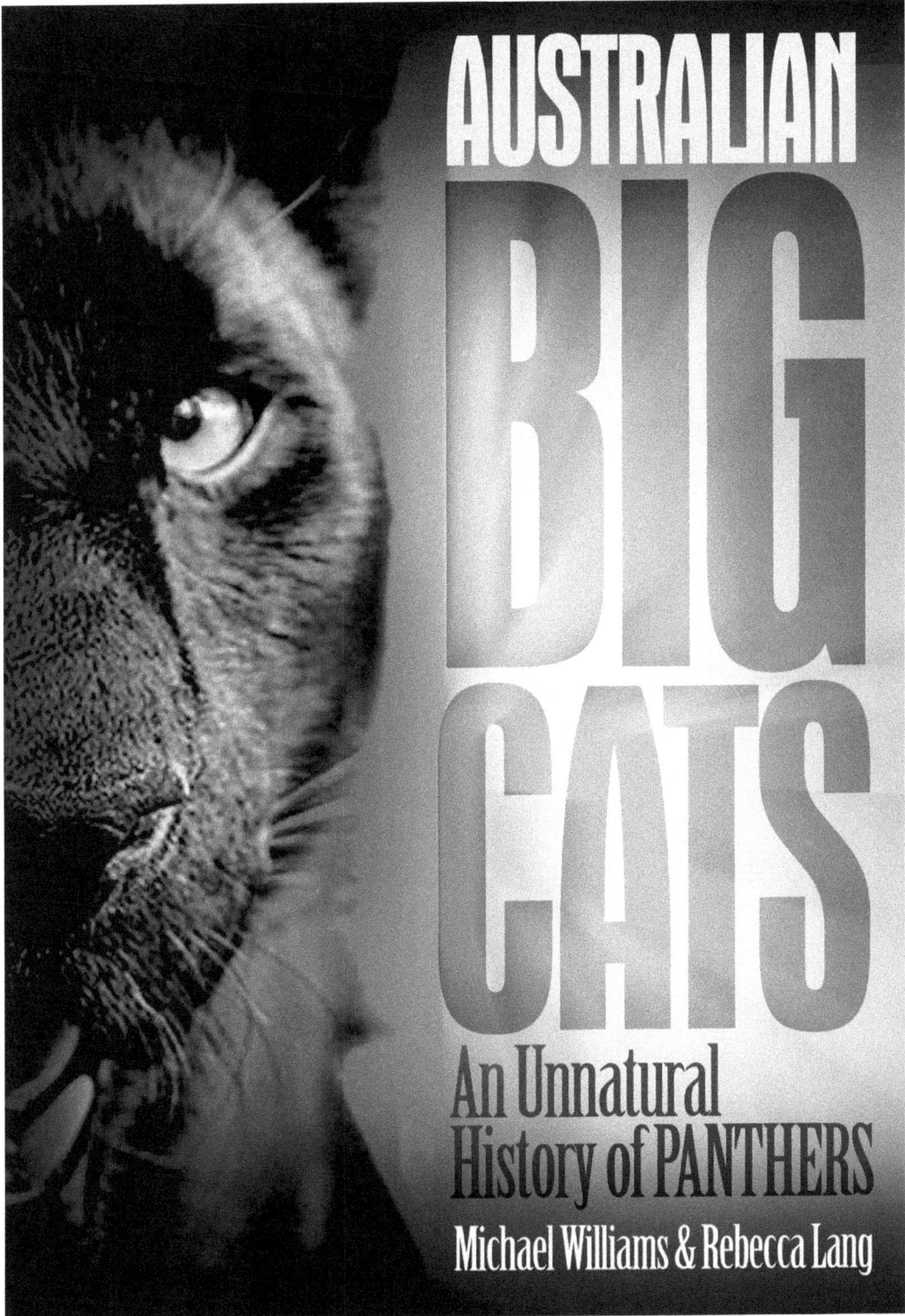

AUSTRALIAN BIG CATS

An Unnatural History of PANTHERS

Michael Williams & Rebecca Lang

www.ingramcontent.com/pod-product-compliance
Lightning Source LLC
Chambersburg PA
CBHW080230270326

41926CB00020B/4198